Taras Kuzio

# Ukraine – Crimea – Russia

# Triangle of Conflict

# SOVIET AND POST-SOVIET POLITICS AND SOCIETY

ISSN 1614-3515

Recent volumes

39    *Михаил Лукьянов*
      Российский консерватизм и реформа, 1907-1914
      С предисловием Марка Д. Стейнберга
      ISBN 3-89821-503-2

40    *Nicola Melloni*
      Market Without Economy
      The 1998 Russian Financial Crisis
      With a foreword by Eiji Furukawa
      ISBN 3-89821-407-9

41    *Dmitrij Chmelnizki*
      Die Architektur Stalins
      Bd. 1: Studien zu Ideologie und Stil
      Bd. 2: Bilddokumentation
      Mit einem Vorwort von Bruno Flierl
      ISBN 3-89821-515-6

42    *Katja Yafimava*
      Post-Soviet Russian-Belarussian Relationships
      The Role of Gas Transit Pipelines
      With a foreword by Jonathan P. Stern
      ISBN 3-89821-655-1

43    *Boris Chavkin*
      Verflechtungen der deutschen und russischen Zeitgeschichte
      Aufsätze und Archivfunde zu den Beziehungen Deutschlands und der Sowjetunion von 1917 bis 1991
      Ediert von Markus Edlinger sowie mit einem Vorwort versehen von Leonid Luks
      ISBN 3-89821-756-6

44    *Anastasija Grynenko in Zusammenarbeit mit Claudia Dathe*
      Die Terminologie des Gerichtswesens der Ukraine und Deutschlands im Vergleich
      Eine übersetzungswissenschaftliche Analyse juristischer Fachbegriffe im Deutschen, Ukrainischen und
      Russischen
      Mit einem Vorwort von Ulrich Hartmann
      ISBN 3-89821-691-8

45    *Anton Burkov*
      The Impact of the European Convention on Human Rights on Russian Law
      Legislation and Application in 1996-2006
      With a foreword by Françoise Hampson
      ISBN 978-3-89821-639-5

46    *Stina Torjesen, Indra Overland (Eds.)*
      International Election Observers in Post-Soviet Azerbaijan
      Geopolitical Pawns or Agents of Change?
      ISBN 978-3-89821-743-9

Taras Kuzio

# UKRAINE – CRIMEA – RUSSIA

# Triangle of Conflict

*ibidem*-Verlag
Stuttgart

**Bibliografische Information der Deutschen Nationalbibliothek**
Die Deutsche Nationalbibliothek verzeichnet diese Publikation in der
Deutschen Nationalbibliografie; detaillierte bibliografische Daten sind im
Internet über http://dnb.d-nb.de abrufbar.

**Bibliographic information published by the Deutsche Nationalbibliothek**
Die Deutsche Nationalbibliothek lists this publication in the Deutsche Nationalbibliografie;
detailed bibliographic data are available in the Internet at http://dnb.d-nb.de.

*Frontcover Pictures*:
1.  Tatars rally on 60th anniversary of 1944 deportation,
2.  Ukrainian Cossack,
3.  Russian Black Sea Fleet badge.

Source: www.artukraine.com © 2004-2006.


*Technical Assistance*: Olena Sivuda.


∞

Gedruckt auf alterungsbeständigem, säurefreien Papier
Printed on acid-free paper

ISSN: 1614-3515

ISBN-10: 3-89821-761-2
ISBN-13: 978-3-89821-761-3

© *ibidem*-Verlag
Stuttgart 2007

Printed in Germany

*To George Wolodymyr Danyliw*

# Contents

*Acknowledgements*                                                    11

*Abbreviations*                                                       12

*List of Tables*                                                      13


Introduction                                                         15


1    Borders: Theory and Practice                                    19

   ▪ Empires, Minorities and Borders                                 20

   ▪ Borders as National Symbols                                     23

   ▪ Potential Territorial and Border Disputes                       30

   ▪ Separatism and Public Attitudes to Borders                      32

   ▪ Conclusions                                                     36


2    Regionalism and Separatism in Ukraine                           39

   ▪ Regionalism                                                     40

       - Is Regionalism a Threat to Ukraine's Borders?              40

       - Centre-Periphery Relations                                  44

   ▪ The Donbas                                                      58

       - Regional Clans                                              61

   ▪ Conclusions                                                     65

3    Russia-Ukraine: The Border Issue                          67

   ▪ Ukrainian Insecurity                                      67

   ▪ Territorial Conflict with Russia                          70

        - Territorial Claims                                   76

        - Tuzla                                                79

   ▪ Ukrainian Responses                                       81

   ▪ Russia Recognises Ukraine's Border                        83

   ▪ Border Demarcation with Ukraine                           85

   ▪ Russia Steps Up Influence in Ukraine                      89

   ▪ Conclusions                                               92


4    Ukraine-Crimea-Russia: Triangle of Conflict               95

   ▪ The Impact of History                                     95

   ▪ Tatar State and Russian Empire                            99

   ▪ The Russian Revolution and Ukrainian Drive to
     Independence                                             100

   ▪ Soviet Rule                                              102

   ▪ Transfer to Soviet Ukraine                               103

   ▪ Tatars Return to the Crimea                              105

   ▪ Russia and Ukraine: Dispute Over Crimea                  110

   ▪ Crimean Conundrum                                        115

   ▪ Conclusions                                              118


5    Ukrainian Policies to the Crimea in the 1990s            121

   ▪ Oblast to Autonomous Republic                            122

   ▪ Ukrainian Policies towards the Crimea                    128

   ▪ Bagrov and the Crimean 'Party of Power'                  140

- Organised Crime and Corruption                                      145
- Conclusions                                                         148


6    Elections and Constitution Making in the Crimea, 1994-2002    151
- 1994 Crimean and Ukrainian Presidential Elections              151
- 1994 Ukrainian Parliamentary Elections                        157
- Rise and Fall of Meshkov                                       160
- Marginalisation of Russian Separatism, 1995-1998              162
    - Centrists Re-gain Control of Crimean
      Supreme Soviet                                            162
    - Political Parties                                         165
- Crimean Constitution Making                                    168
    - The 'Separatist' Constitution                             168
    - Grach's Crimean Constitution                              169
- Elections Since 1998                                           176
- Conclusions                                                    183


7    Crimea and Security Forces                                       185
- Ukraine Takes Control and Builds Security Forces
  in the Crimea                                                  186
    - Internal Troops                                           187
    - Border Troops                                             187
    - National Guard                                            188
- Military Pressure on the Crimea                                189
    - Subversion                                                192
    - Paramilitaries                                            194
    - Reluctance to Use Force                                   197

- Tug of War over the Crimean Security Forces        198
  - Trans-Dniestr and the Crimea        202
- Conflict over the Black Sea Fleet        204
  - 1992-1993        206
  - 1994        209
  - Kravchuk, Kuchma and the Crimea        211
  - 1995-1997: Towards and Agreement        219
- Conclusions        221


*Bibliography on Nation Building and Inter-Ethnic Relations in Ukraine and the Crimea*        223

National Integration        223

National Identity        227

National Integration, National Identity and
Foreign Policy        229

Regionalism and Separatism        232

Inter-Ethnic Relations and Nationality Policies        238

National Minorities        240

   Russians        240

   Tatars        241

Foreign Policy        243

   Domestic Sources of Security Policy        243

   Russian-Ukrainian Relations        244

# Acknowledgements

The author gratefully acknowledges the grant received from the Wolodymyr George Danyliw Foundation in 2003 that entirely made the research and writing of this book possible during the author's two year Resident Fellowship at the Centre for Russian and East European Studies, University of Toronto. The Wolodymyr George Danyliw Foundation (http://www.danyliw foundation.org/) was created in 2002 as a charitable organization in memory of Mr. Danyliw as a memorial tribute to a man who devoted most of his life to Ukrainian studies and the Ukrainian community as philanthropist, patriot, lawyer and businessman. The Foundation's mandate is to encourage research, teaching and the study of contemporary Ukraine and Ukrainian issues.

# Abbreviations

GUUAM   Georgia, Ukraine, Uzbekistan, Azerbaijan, Moldova (regional group)

SBU   *Sluzhba bespeky Ukrayiny* (Security Service of Ukraine)

MVS   *Ministerstvo vnutrishnikh sprav* (Ministry of Interior)

ISD   *Industrialnyi soyuz Donbasu* (Industrial Union of Donbas)

KNDS   *Kongres natsional-demokratychnykh syl* (Congress of National Democratic Forces)

ZYU   *Za Yedynu Ukrayinu* (For a United Ukraine [bloc])

SDPUo   *Sotsial-demokratychna partiya Ukrayiny (ob"yednana)* (Social Democratic Party of Ukraine [united]) headed by Viktor Medvedchuk

NDP   *Narodna demokratychna partiya* (People's Democratic Party) headed by Valeriy Pustovoitenko

MRBR   *Mizhregional'nyi blok reform (*Inter-Regional Bloc of Reforms) headed by Vladimir Grynev

KPU   *Komunistychna partiya Ukrayiny* (Communist Party of Ukraine) headed Petr Symonenko)

SPU   *Sotsialistychna partiya Ukrayiny* (Socialist Party of Ukraine) headed by Oleksandr Moroz

PEVK   *Partiya ekonomichnoho vidrodzhennya Krymu* (Party of Economic Revival of the Crimea) headed by Mykola Bagrov

PEV   *Partia ekonomichnoho vidrodzhennya* (Party of Economic Revival)

RDK   *Respublikanskoe dvizhenie Kryma* (Republican Movement of the Crimea) headed by Yury Meshkov

ZUBR   *Za Ukrayinu, Bilorusiyu, Rosiyu* (For the Union of Ukraine, Belarus and Russia [bloc])

SPS   *Soyuz Pravykh Syl* (Union of Right Forces)

# List of Tables

Table 2.1   Which Future Possibility for Ukraine Do You Prioritise?
(in per cent)                                                          47

Table 4.1   Changing Ethnic Composition of the Crimea (in per cent) 100

Table 4.2   Russian Parliamentary Votes on Ukraine
and the Crimea                                                        114

Table 5.1   1994 Crimean Opinion Poll (Referendum)                   136

Table 5.2   Votes in Ukrainian Parliament on Rejecting Legislation Upgrading Crimean Autonomy to Statehood (20 May 1994) 138

Table 6.1   Round One of Crimean Elections: 16 January 1994          155

Table 6.2   Round Two of Crimean Elections: 30 January 1994          155

Table 6.3   First Round of 1994 Ukrainian Presidential Elections
in the Crimea                                                         159

Table 6.4   Second Round of 1994 Ukrainian Presidential Elections
in the Crimea                                                         159

Table 6.5   Do You Support Autonomous Status for the Crimea?         171

Table 6.6   Should Crimea Have a Constitution?                       171

Table 6.7   Regional Attitudes to Abolishing the Crimean Presidency 173

Table 6.8   Do You Agree With Placing the Crimean Government
Under the Ukrainian Government?                                       173

Table 6.9   The 1998 Ukrainian Parliamentary Elections
in the Crimea (Proportional Party Lists)                              177

Table 6.10 The 2002 Ukrainian Parliamentary Elections
in the Crimea (Proportional Party Lists)                              177

Table 7.1   What should Ukraine do in answer to Russian demands
that Sevastopol become an exclusively Russian base?   219

# Introduction

The Crimea was the only region of Ukraine in the 1990s where separatism proved to be a problem. It was the only region where inter-ethnic conflict potentially could have taken place between the Ukrainian central government, ethnic Russians in the Crimea and Crimean Tatars. Such a conflict would have inevitably drawn in external actors. Russia had large numbers of troops in the Crimea within the Black Sea Fleet, a situation that will persist until at least 2017 when the twenty year lease expires on Sevastopol naval bays. Pro-Russian external paramilitary forces from Moldova's Trans-Dniestr and the northern Caucasus could also have become involved. This, in turn, would have had a domino effect on inciting Ukrainian nationalist paramilitaries. Until summer 1996 Ukraine possessed nuclear weapons, although it lacked the capability to launch them. This though, would not have represented a difficult problem to resolve considering Ukraine had built many of the Soviet nuclear weapons. Ukraine also had a high level of technical and scientific expertise, including in the military-industrial complex.

No inter-ethnic violence took place and the separatist challenge was resolved peacefully. This book seeks to answer two questions. First, the origins of the Ukrainian-Russian conflict over the Crimea. Second, how inter-ethnic violence was averted despite Crimea possessing many of the ingredients that existed that could have made a conflict possible.

The book is divided into seven chapters. Chapter 1 provides a theoretical introduction to the volume by focussing on the symbolic importance of borders to a country's sovereignty and national identity. It also investigates the potential threats to Ukrainian territorial integrity and public attitudes in Ukraine to its inherited Soviet borders.

Chapter 2 provides an analysis of regionalism and separatism in Ukraine. Besides investigating regionalism as a general factor influencing Ukrainian politics, it also analyses the second most important region, the Donbas, after the Crimea where pro-Russian influences are popular and autonomist ideas have been raised.

Chapter 3 provides a survey of the Ukrainian-Russian disputes in the 1990s over the Crimea and Sevastopol. The Crimea and Sevastopol cannot be treated in isolation from Russia's recognition of Ukraine's borders as they were the main factors holding up Russia's recognition of them until 1997. Recognition by the Russian executive in 1997 and ratification by its legislature in 1998-1999 of the Russian-Ukrainian border meant that Russia *de jure* recognised the Crimea and Sevastopol as belonging to Ukraine. It took a further three years between 1999-2002 to delimit the border, with the exception of the Azov Sea but Russia continues to refuse to demarcate its border with Ukraine.

Chapter 4 surveys the battle for ownership of the Crimea since the Tsarist empire occupied the Crimea and wrested control of it from the Ottoman empire in the late eighteenth century. The Crimea was disputed during the Russian revolution and Ukrainian drive to independence from 1917-1920 between the Bolsheviks and three Ukrainian governments. After three decades with autonomous status in the Russian SFSR from 1922-1945, the peninsula was downgraded to an *oblast*. The main factor which provided the reason for autonomous status – Tatars – was no longer the case after they had been ethnically cleansed in 1944. The Crimea remained an *oblast* within the Ukrainian SSR from 1954-1990, after which it returned to being an autonomous republic, but within Ukraine.

Chapter 5 provides an overview of Ukrainian policies towards the Crimea during the 1990s. Debate over what powers the Crimean autonomous republic should possess took between 1991-1998 to resolve. The chapter also looks at the role of the Crimean 'party of power' in assisting Kyiv in dealing with the separatist threat. The final section of this chapter analyses the impact of organised crime in the Crimea and, importantly, its links to political parties. Kyiv may have bought the loyalty of the Crimean 'party of power' to Ukraine's territorial integrity by effectively turning a blind eye to its rampant corruption.

Chapter 6 provides an analysis of the elections and constitution making in the Crimea from 1994 to the present. The rise and fall of separatist leader and President Yuriy Meshkov in 1994-1995 is covered, together with Crimean and Ukrainian elections in 1994, 1998, 2002, 2004 and 2006. In the first half of the 1990s the battle line in the Crimea was between Russian nationalist-separatists and the 'party of power'. After the marginalisation of Russian nationalism in 1995 the battle line became between Communists and the pro-presidential 'party of power'. The marginalisation of Russian nationalists permitted the Crimea to adopt a non-separatist constitution in 1998. This, in turn, had a positive impact on the ratification by both houses of the Russian parliament of the 1997 Ukrainian-Russian treaty.

Chapter 7 provides an in-depth study of the struggle in the Crimea over control over different branches of the security forces: army, navy, border troops, National Guard, Interior Ministry and Security Service. The last section of the chapter discusses the conflict over the division of the Black Sea Fleet and where it could be based. The security forces played an important role in the Crimea with Ukraine quickly taking them over and creating new s-tructures, such as the National Guard. This greatly strengthened its hands in dealing with Russian nationalist-separatists and with Russia. Permitting the Black Sea Fleet to be stationed in the Crimea moderated the demands of Crimean politicians and of Russia in their attitudes towards the Crimea and Sevastopol being recognised as part of Ukraine.

# 1 Borders: Theory and Practice

Boundaries are important in all our daily lives. They define the 'us' from the 'them', what is 'ours' from what is 'theirs'. Boundaries demarcate territories and regulate state sovereignty. Over time these boundaries and territories become 'natural'. They enclose peoples and nation-states. Boundaries and territories create and enclose environments that influence people's identities, cultures and traditions. They reinforce history, memory and myths while providing for rooted ties to the enclosed territory. As Penrose states, 'territory is fundamental to nationalist thought'.[1] Boundaries divide and separate nation-states.

The Russian-Ukrainian boundary is no exception. To Russians, boundaries between the three Eastern Slavs are absurd as the three peoples are closely bound together historically, culturally, religiously and linguistically. The majority of Russians believe that their fellow Eastern Slavs are merely wayward 'Russians' who should either be absorbed by Russia (a proposal made by Russia to Belarus in summer 2002) or function under Russia's wing as a 'little' or 'younger brother'.[2]

Belarus has accepted the Russian view that boundaries are unnecessary with Russia and in the proposed, but little advanced, union between both countries. Ukraine has always behaved differently, arguing that demarcated boundaries are required to establish state sovereignty and a right of ownership to territories. Russia prefers the Belarusian viewpoint and continues to oppose Ukrainian proposals for the demarcation of its border with Ukraine.

---

1    Jan Penrose, 'Nations, states and homelands: territory and territoriality in nationalist thought', *Nations and Nationalism*, vol.8, no.3 (July 2002), p.294.
2    See Taras Kuzio, 'Does Ukraine Return to Younger Brother Status?', *RFE/RL Poland, Belarus and Ukraine Report*, 4 February 2003.

This chapter is divided into four sections. The first deals with the disintegration of empires and their impact on the fate of national minorities. The second discusses the importance of borders as national symbols. The third discusses potential territorial disputes and the fourth section investigates the weakness of separatism in Ukraine and public attitudes towards borders.

### Empires, Minorities and Borders

Successful secessionist campaigns have been rare in the post-World War II era. Only Eritrea, Bangladesh and East Timor have managed to successfully secede from Ethiopia, Pakistan and Indonesia respectively. These regions were subsequently diplomatically recognised as independent states. The overwhelming majority of borders are not coterminous with ethnic groups. Connor found that less than ten percent of nation-states were ethnically homogenous in the early 1970s. One third of these nation-states possessed populations less than fifty per cent composed of the titular ethnic group.[3] The lack of congruence between ethnicity and nation-state borders has given way to a variety of territorial claims - not all of which will be necessarily followed by military action. Spain, Argentina and until the 1990s Eire all *de facto* harboured territorial claims towards Gibraltar, the Falkland island's and the UK's province of Ulster respectively. Although these sentiments may not be acted upon these claims nevertheless remain in place for psychological and nostalgic reasons.[4]

The psychological crisis brought into focus by the disintegration of empires has particular relevance for Ukraine and Russia, the subject of this chapter and book. Russian national identity had always been coterminous with empire and the state, rather than with an ethnic nation.

It has always therefore been difficult to locate where 'Russia' began and where it ended? 'Russia' or 'Russian' can refer to both the English-language translations of *Rossiya* and *Russkii,* yet both are different. Whereas the for-

---

3    Walker Connor, 'Nation-Building or Nation-Destroying?', *World Politics*, vol.24, no.3 (April 1972), p.320.

4    See James Mayall, 'Irredentist and Secessionist Challenges' in John Hutchinson and Anthony D. Smith (eds.), *Nationalism* (Oxford: Oxford University Press, 1994), pp.269-280.

mer refers to the Russian empire (for example, perhaps the closest equivalent would be 'British'), the latter refers to the Russian nation (or, maybe 'English'). Ukrainians and Belarusians are understood not as Scotland and Ireland but as the provinces of Yorkshire and Devonshire within England, with the English being the equivalent of *Russkii*. But, this division between *Rossia* and *Russkii* was only applicable to the non-Slavic nations of the Tsarist and Soviet empires. In the Tsarist empire, Ukraine and Belarus were both included within the definition of *Russkii*, who allegedly began their history together in the medieval state of Kyiv Rus and were therefore fated to 're-unite' in the future.

This confusion as to whether the three Eastern Slavic peoples are in fact separate nations, with the right to independent states, or merely branches of one *Russkii narod,* has a strategic significance for the question of ownership of the Crimea and borders. If a state adopts the latter view, as does Belarusian President Lukashenka and the majority of the Russian elites, then borders should not be established between three 'fraternal brothers'. If, on the other hand, a state adopts the former view, such as Ukraine (see later), borders cannot be divided into those which require delimitation and demarcation (i.e. 'external CIS') and those which do not (i.e. 'internal CIS').

The collapse of empires also leads to crises for the former dominant ethnic group. Russians, just as Turks in the Ottoman empire or Serbs in the former Yugoslavia, did not see their 'homeland' as purely their own republic. Instead, they looked to the entire multinational state or empire as their 'homeland'. In contrast, the non-Serbs and non-Russians of the former Yugoslavia and the USSR respectively, looked to their republics as their 'homelands'. For Russia to re-define its national horizons to those of the Russian Federation is therefore a traumatic experience.[5]

The fact that Yugoslavia and the USSR possessed clearly marked boundaries between republics was used by non-Serbs and non-Russians to demand their conversion into internationally-recognised borders. These states have supported policies which have largely been in favour of the territorial status quo (the exception was only Croatia). The Ottoman empire was

---

5      See David C. Rapoport, 'The Importance of Space in Violent Ethno-Linguistic Strife', *Nationalism and Ethnic Politics*, vol.2, no.2 (Summer 1996), pp.258-285.

not divided along such lines as Yugoslavia and the USSR and the newly independent Turkish state was immediately thrown into war to define its new
borders through territorial conquest and ethnic cleansing. Serbia and Russia
followed different paths after the collapse of Yugoslavia and the USSR.
Whereas the former backed irredentist claims on Bosnia and Croatia through
proxy forces and attempted to unsuccessfully halt the collapse of the Yugo-
slav state by force, the latter joined with Ukraine and Belarus in peacefully
dismantling the USSR and transforming it into the CIS.[6] Russia has not
launched military aggression against any former Soviet state to back up territorial claims. Nevertheless, it has remained difficult for it to reconcile 'Russian'
identity to only that encompassed within the borders of the Russian Federation.

Russia's psychological map of its 'borders' are not those of the Russian
Federation; many of its elites confuses the borders of the CIS with the USSR
and therefore look upon the CIS as a *de facto* 'Greater Russia'. This is especially true of institutions such as the Russian Orthodox Church and the Russian parliament in the 1990s. This has particular relevance for Ukraine, Belarus and Kazakstan. Not only do Russians traditionally not perceive Ukrainians
and Belarusians as anything but branches of one *Russkii narod*, but Russian
national identity itself is closely tied up with language, religion and culture.
The large number of ethnic Russians and Russian speakers in Ukraine, Belarus and Kazakstan therefore ensures that Moscow finds it difficult to come to
terms with the permanence of their independence or the need for borders between these four states.

One region, in particular, which has always remained a problem for
Russians is the Crimea. The Crimea has a particular relevance not only because of history, but because it has an ethnic Russian majority. Both of these
factors therefore mean Russia believes that the Crimea should be part of
'Russia'.

Historical experience has influenced Ukraine's prioritisation in obtaining
recognition of its borders by its neighbours. As Ukrainian Ambassador to

---

6    See Taras Kuzio, 'Russians and Russophones in the Former USSR and Serbs in
     Yugoslavia: A Comparative Study of Passivity and Mobilisation', *East European
     Perspectives*, vol.5, nos.15, 16, 17 (11 and 25 June, 9 July 2003). Available at:
     http://www.taraskuzio.net/journals/pdf/national-serbs_russians.pdf

Canada Yuriy Shcherbak pointed out, in the last one thousand years Ukraine was the object of 200 invasions, wars and foreign aggression which led to devastating foreign occupations. Although irrelevant if true,  the threat perceptions that arise from such commonly held views do have notable policy implications . The recognition of Ukraine's territorial integrity and security cooperation with the West were therefore important to forestall a repeat of what had often occurred in the past. This historical past had left a deep psychological scar in the Ukrainian national psyche and consciousness, making the Ukrainian elites highly sensitive about border conflicts. This was clearly seen during the 1990s when Ukraine was in bitter dispute with Russia over the Crimea.

### Borders as National Symbols

Ernest Renan said that France's frontiers in 1789 were not 'natural or necessary'.[7] Forsberg also argued that there was no 'legitimate borders' or 'natural frontiers'.[8] A century after the 1789 French revolution in the 1870s, France's frontiers had become, as do most borders, an additional national symbol. Between 1820-1945, 94 per cent of all wars took place between neighbours over borders. Territorial disputes only became a thing of the past from the 1960s onwards until flaring up again in the 1980s and 1990s. It is therefore, 'more difficult to explain neighbours who never go to war with each other than those who frequently do'.[9]

Borders are regarded as symbols of sovereignty[10] because one of the attributes of a sovereign state is bordered territory.[11] When former colonies or dependencies, such as the non-Russian Soviet republics of the former USSR,

---

7    E. Renan, 'What's in a Nation?' in Geoff Eley and Ronald G. Suny (eds.), *Becoming National. A Reader* (New York: Oxford University Press, 1996), p.46.

8    Tuomas Forsberg, 'Theories on Territorial Disputes' in Tuomas Forsberg (ed.), *Contested Territory. Border Disputes at the Edge of the Former Soviet Empire* (Aldershot: Aduard Elgar, 1995), p.36.

9    D.C. Raporport, 'The Importance of Space in Violent Ethno-Linguistic Strife', p.265.

10   Michael Mann, 'Nation-States in Europe and Other Continents: Diversifying, Developing, Not Dying', *Daedalus*, vol.122, no.3 (Summer 1993), p.123.

11   Robert H. Jackson, *Quasi States: sovereignty, international relations and the Third World* (Cambridge: Cambridge University Press, 1990), p.38.

obtained independence they invariably demanded the inviolability of their borders. This 'consecrates the ex-colonial boundaries',[12] no matter how they may have been arbitrarily formed at an earlier date. Boundaries provide additional significance to territory, sovereignty and borders, where, 'Even minor boundary disputes often prove difficult to resolve'.[13]

Nation and state building socialises the inhabitants of a former colony or dependency to a particular piece of territory. This is undertaken through the construction of a 'We' different to 'Others' beyond the borders.[14] Landscapes, monuments, culture, heritage, maps and history all become important factors for nation-state builders in their endeavour to forge a new 'We' from the peoples living on a clearly defined territory. They therefore dramatise the extent of state sovereignty and differences between those to whom this sovereignty is applicable and those who fall outside its jurisdiction.[15] Paasi argues that:

> Boundaries make a difference. Social life is full of boundaries which give direction to existence, and which locate that existence...The boundaries between nation-states hence receive their meanings in the continual nation-building process, in the social reproduction of the nation-state and in the socialization of the citizen into specific territorial frames.[16]

Borders are also symbols of modernity because pre-modern entities possessed no clear boundaries. These modern borders are established by power, 'maintained by the constitution and known readiness to defend them

---

12   *Ibid.,* p.41.
13   *Ibid.,* p.190.
14   On Ukraine see Taras Kuzio, 'Identity and Nation Building in Ukraine. Defining the 'Other'', *Ethnicities*, vol.1, no.3 (December 2001), pp.343-366 and Lowell Barrington, 'Views of the Ethnic 'Other' in Ukraine', *Nationalism and Ethnic Politics*, vol.8, no.2 (Summer 2002), pp.83-96.
15   See Fredrik Barth, 'Introduction' in Fredrik Barth (ed.), *Ethnic Groups and Boundaries. The Social Origins of Cultural Difference* (London: George Allen and Unwin, 1970), pp.9-38.
16   Anssi Paasi, 'Constructing Territory, Boundaries and Regional Identities' in T. Forsberg (ed.), *Contested Territory,* p. 59.

by arms'.[17] For the state and nation, borders are critical for their functionality as political communities with historical continuity.[18]

In the Ukrainian-Russian case, borders hold emotive significance. For Ukrainians their recognition by its neighbours was a paramount foreign policy priority after the disintegration of the former USSR in December 1991. 'Ukraine will defend its integrity, sovereignty in line with the Constitution, by all means available to it', then President Leonid Kravchuk warned.[19] As to attempts to forcibly change Ukraine's borders, Leonid Kuchma warned that, 'Separatism must be suppressed'.[20] After Ukraine became an independent state it sought to obtain recognition of its borders in international law from all of its neighbours.[21] An appeal to parliaments and peoples of the world by the Ukrainian parliament, issued less than a week after the Ukrainian referendum on independence in December 1991, stated that 'Ukraine considers its territory indivisible and inviolable, recognises the inviolability of existing state borders and has no territorial claims towards any state.'[22]

Kyiv therefore resolutely opposed Russia's concept of 'transparent internal' and 'jointly guarded external' CIS borders. If it agreed to these Russian proposals it would have meant Ukraine joining Russia's 'joint military-strategic

---

17    Elie Kedourie, *Nationalism* (London: Hutchinson, 1979), p.125.

18    Shmuel Sandler, 'Ethnonationalism and the Foreign Policy of Nation-States', *Nationalism and Ethnic Politics*, vol.1, no.2 (Summer 1995), p.263. See also Daniele Conversi, 'Reassessing Current Theories of Nationalism: Nationalism as Boundary Maintenance and Creation', *Nationalism and Ethnic Politics*, vol.1, no.1 (Spring 1995), pp.73-85, Steven Grosby, 'Territoriality: the Transcendental, primordial feature of modern societies', *Nations and Nationalism*, vol.1, no.2 (July 1995), pp.143-162 and Sun-Ki Chai, 'A theory of ethnic group boundaries', *Nations and Nationalism*, vol.2, no.2 (July 1996), pp.281-308.

19    Serhiy Kychyhin (ed.), *Leonid Kravchuk. Ostanni Dni Imperii...Pershi Roky Nadii* (Kyiv: Dovira, 1994), p.129. David R. Marples and David F. Duke believed that, 'Kravchuk had staked his presidency on the survival of his country within its existing borders'. See their 'Ukraine, Russia and the Question of Crimea', *Nationalities Papers*, vol.23, no.2 (June 1995), p.279.

20    Interfax, 6 October 1999.

21    See Taras Kuzio, *Ukrainian Security Policy*. Washington Paper 167 (Washington DC: Praeger and the Center for Security and International Studies, 1995) and Chapter Six, 'New Foreign and Defence Policies' in T.Kuzio, *Ukraine under Kuchma. Political Reform, Economic Transformation and Security Policy in Independent Ukraine* (London: Macmillan, 1997), pp.179-226.

22    *Holos Ukrayiny*, 5 December 1991.

space'.[23] Every independent state, in Ukrainian eyes, has a national anthem, flag, symbols, national airlines and borders. 'An independent country must have borders drawn on maps', then Ukrainian Foreign Minister Hennadiy Udovenko, argued.[24]

Borders do not require rows of barbed wire. These were only inherited on the former Soviet Western external borders with Poland, Slovakia, Hungary and Romania. On Ukraine's 'new' borders with Moldova, Belarus and Russia this is not envisaged. Delimitation of Ukraine's borders with its former Soviet neighbours would, in Ukrainian eyes, serve to:

1.  Define where the responsibility of the Ukrainian state ended;
2.  Define the border where there were instances of confusion (factories, farms and villages straddled the border);
3.  Establish a border regime favourable to both sides;
4.  Place markers every one kilometre on the delimited border and in each case where it turns.[25]

Only Russia and Romania dragged the process out of recognising Ukraine's borders until 1997. Russia found the very idea of a delimited or demarcated border with Ukraine to be unnatural and offensive.[26] Ukraine had submitted nearly twenty diplomatic notes to begin serious negotiations over the delimitation and demarcation of their common border but these had all been ignored prior to 1997.[27] A Russian commentary asked:

---

23    Yuriy Porokhniavyi, 'Problemy Kordony Ukrayiny', *Nova Polityka*, no.2, 1996, pp. 43-44. See also Chapter Five, 'The Strategic Significance of Borders' in T.Kuzio, *State and Nation Building in Ukraine* (London: Routledge, 1998), pp.100-118.

24    Interfax, 27 February 1997.

25    See comments by Colonel Leonid Osovalyuk, Chief of the State Border Committee's department on the Delimitation and Demarcation of the State Border, in *Ukrayina moloda*, 10 June 1997 and Vadym Dolhanov, head of the directorate on Foreign Policy of the Presidential Administration, in *Nezavisimost*, 27 December 1996.

26    See the interview with Russian Communist leader Gennadiy Zyuganov in *Sovetskaya Rossiya*, 21 February 1997.

27    *Holos Ukrayiny*, 4 March and *Ukrayina moloda*, 10 June 1997. See also the views of Viacheslav Zhyhulin, head of the Topographical directorate of the Ukrainian Ministry of Defence (*UNIAN news agency*, 16 December 1996), Leonid Osavoliuk, Deputy Head of the delegation to discuss the delimitation of the Russian-Ukrainian

> Really, do we need a border with Ukraine? After all, we have
> managed to come to an agreement with Belarus. We believe
> that many Russians pose the questions in just this way.[28]

Ukraine had previously signed treaties with Belarus and Moldova but the process of border delimitation was dragged out. Belarus had largely backed Russia's division of 'internal CIS non delimited/demarcated' and 'external CIS demarcated' borders. Nevertheless, in April 1997, after much Ukrainian persistence, Belarus became the first CIS state to agree to border delimitation with Ukraine. Nevertheless, Minsk has refused to ratify the Belarusian-Ukrainian treaty. This resembles Russia's approach to the three Baltic state's.

In June 1996, delimitation of the 1,200 kilometre Ukrainian-Moldovan border was begun based on the administrative border established by the USSR on 4 November 1940. It took until 2001 for delimitation to be completed. On 29 January 2003, the first demarcation point on the Moldovan-Ukrainian was installed in Chernivtsi *oblast* (formerly northern Bukovina). The demarcation of the entire Moldovan-Ukrainian border was completed in 2005.

Why then the long delay in the demarcation of the Moldovan-Romanian border? The border dispute between Moldova-Ukraine had always involved more than the issue of the exchange of territory. The Moldovan village of Palanca is located exactly on the country's border with Ukraine and the Odesa-Reni highway runs through the village. In return for seceding a 7.7 km. portion of the highway to Ukraine the village of Palanca was effectively split into two. In exchange, Ukraine initially transferred to the Moldovan state 100 kms of land which was to be followed by 1,000 sq. metres near the mouth of the Danube river. This allowed Moldova to begin building an oil terminal to import Trans-Casucasian oil (and resemble the Odesa Terminal constructed in the 1990s).

---

border (*Den*, 22 February 1997) and Deputy Foreign Minister Kostyantin Hryshchenko in *Dzerkalo tyzhnya*, 23 August 1996 and *Den*, 28 February 1997.

28    *Granitsa Rossii*, 41 (December 1995), p.2. See the official reply in *Narodna Armiya*, 13 December 1995.

The agreement on the transfer of territory was signed by Moldova and Ukraine in August 1999. Ukraine refused to withdraw its Border Troops from the Giurgiulesti region - the area seceded to Moldova to give it access to the Black Sea – until an agreement on state borders was ratified. This, in turn, halted the construction of the Moldovan oil terminal. The ruling Communist Party of Moldova (PCM), which returned to power in 2000, has always supported the territorial exchange. Opposition to it came from the People's Christian Democratic Party and other centre-right parties. These parties pointed to the constitution which only envisages a change in the country's territorial integrity through a referendum. In September 2002 their appeal opposing the transfer of land was ruled on by the Constitutional Court which decided that the transfer of land was constitutional.

An additional factor which complicated the Moldovan-Ukrainian border dispute was the separatist Trans-Dniestr enclave. Since coming to power in 2001 the PCM has been a staunch advocate of Moldova's territorial integrity hoping that its closer relations with Russia would lead to Moscow applying pressure on the Trans-Dniestr separatists to reach an agreement with Chisinau. Although Russia overtly and subsequently covertly backed the Trans-Dniestr separatists it has been unable (or unwilling) to force them to sit at the negotiating table. The PCM became quickly disillusioned with Russia because of its unwillingness to stop supporting the separatist Trans-Dniestr enclave in exchange for a pro-Russian oriented Moldova.

The recognition of Ukraine's borders with its last two neighbours - Russia and Romania – came in May and June 1997 respectively. This signified that Ukraine's territorial integrity was now recognised by all of its neighbours and territorial claims were a thing of the past (except on the part of radical right groups). The Black Sea Fleet agreement signed together with the Russian-Ukrainian treaty ended the last remaining Soviet institution on Ukrainian territory when Russian replaced Soviet naval flags on Russian naval ships in Sevastopol in June 1997. In January 1998 Soviet passports became invalid in Ukraine.

In 1998-1999 the Ukrainian parliament and both houses of the Russian parliament ratified the Ukrainian-Russian treaty. This signified that Russia had – reluctantly – accepted that the Crimea and city of Sevastopol were *de jure* part of Ukraine. Delimitation of the land border between Russia and

Ukraine took a further 5 years from 1999-2003. Nevertheless, Russia continues to refuse to agree to the delimitation of the Azov Sea and Kerch Straits, adjoining Crimea, or the demarcation of its land border with Ukraine. In addition, in autumn 2003, Russia re-opened the border question by laying claim to the island of Tuzla.[29]

The completion of the recognition of Ukraine's borders was given additional symbolism by being linked to the adoption of Ukraine's first post-Soviet constitution in June 1996. Both signified that Ukraine had established itself as a sovereign state. In addition to which there was, 'the introduction of the monetary unit or the approval of the Ukrainian state flag and emblem...'[30] On the eighth anniversary of Ukrainian independence then left-wing speaker of parliament Oleksandr Tkachenko said that Ukraine would not allow its borders to be infringed because they were 'sacred'.[31] Then Defence Minister Oleksandr Kuzmuk described the country's security forces as, 'guarantors of the sovereignty, territorial integrity, inviolability of national borders and social stability'. The military were always ready to, 'fulfil their constitutional duty with honour...'[32] The importance of Ukraine's security forces to the defence of Ukraine's territorial integrity was clearly seen in the conflict over the Tuzla island in autumn 2003.

These views by Ukraine's elites about the sanctity of Ukraine's territorial integrity have been made across the entire political spectrum from left to centre-right. There has always been, much to the consternation of Russian policy makers and the Russian parliament, a high degree of domestic consensus in Ukraine on the sanctity of country's inherited borders. The October 2003 par-

29    See Taras Kuzio, 'Russian-Ukrainian Strategic Partnership in Ruins', *RFERL Newsline*, 24 October and 'Behind the Tuzla Controversy', *Kyiv Post*, 30 October 2003.
30    *Ukrayina moloda*, 10 June 1997.
31    *Holos Ukrayiny*, 21 August 1999.
32    Ukrainian State Television, Channel One, 24 August 1999. This view was echoed by all state officials, 71 per cent of whom believed that one of their functions was the defence of Ukraine's territorial integrity. See *The Army in Domestic Politics in Russia and Ukraine*, Centre for Peace, Conversion and Foreign Policy of Ukraine, Kyiv, no.40 (November 2000) available at http://www.cpcfpu.org.ua. The same signal was given by the Security Service (SBU) which admitted it had under surveillance those who 'violated the constitution' (*Dzerkalo tyzhnya*, 5 February 2000). Meanwhile, the Foreign Ministry, 'is consistently defending the principle of territorial integrity' (ITAR-TASS, 17 August 1999).

liamentary decree was backed by 350 deputies from across the entire political spectrum.

## Potential Territorial and Border Disputes

The independent Ukrainian state inherited a large number of territorial conflicts and disputes which play a role in developing threat perceptions. Prior to world War II, territories with Ukrainian ethnographic majorities were divided between it's neighbours and were the source of various sharp disputes over the 'historical', ethnic and political rights to these lands. At one time or another therefore, Ukraine's borders have been contested by all of its neighbours, except Belarus.

A small number of Ukrainian national minorities live in Poland, Slovakia, Romania, Moldova and Belarus where they live contagious to the Ukrainian border. The exception is the case of Poland where Ukrainian minorities were ethnically cleansed in 1947 to northern and Western Poland in former German 'recovered' territories. The only major territorial threats to Ukraine are, first and foremost, with Russia and secondly Romania. In the Russian case the threat is made all the more dangerous because of the large number of Russians and russified Ukrainians living in Ukraine, the Crimean question and the belief among large numbers of Russians that Ukrainian independence is 'temporary'. The Crimean question is central and fundamental to the Ukrainian-Russian question.

Although eight million Russians live in Ukraine (a reduction of three million on the 1989 census), seven million Ukrainians also live in the Russian Federation. Russian complaints about forcible 'Ukrainianisation' are often matched by Ukrainian claims that their co-ethnics in Russia are also denied minority rights. Areas adjacent to Ukraine within Russia, such as the Kuban area of the Northern Caucasus, are regarded by Ukrainian nationalists as 'Ukrainian ethnographic territories' on the basis of historical and ethnic factors.

Russian territorial conflicts rest with Ukraine over Eastern Ukraine, Southern Ukraine (called *Novorossiya* by Russian nationalists) and the Crimea. In all of these regions only the Crimea has a Russian ethnic majority, a large part of which moved there after World War II when the Tartars were ethnically cleansed and the Crimean autonomous republic was abolished.[33] Since 1954 the Crimea has been a part of Ukraine and until December 1990 the peninsula had the status of an *oblast*. In January 1991 the Crimea was returned to the status of an autonomous republic within Ukraine, and between 1992-1998 negotiations were held with Ukraine over the sharing of power between Kyiv and the Crimea.

Although the Crimea declared sovereignty ('independence') in May 1992 this was less an attempt to fully break away from Ukraine than to use the step as a bargaining chip in its negotiations with Kyiv over the separation of powers. After all, the former communist leadership in power in the Crimea, which supported the August 1991 hard line *coup d'etat*, had more in common with national communist President Kravchuk than with then reformer President Borys Yeltsin. Although Ukraine successfully defused the situation in the Crimea by granting it a high degree of autonomy, Ukrainian and Russian nationalists are not content with the situation; albeit for different reasons.[34]

The only republic of the former USSR after Ukraine where Ukrainians outnumber Russians is Moldova. The Trans-Dniestr separatist enclave has been the scene of ethnic and political conflict with the Moldovan authorities since 1990, primarily over its refusal to grant it autonomy and the campaign for reunification with Romania. The Trans-Dniestr enclave was a part of Ukrainian SSR territory prior to World War II and historically it never belonged to Romania. Ukrainian-Romanian relations will continue to remain poor as long as extreme Romanian nationalists and others in Bucharest harbour territorial demands. The status of the Serpents Islands remains unresolved.

Ukrainian minorities lived within the Hungarian state and later in the Hungarian portion of the Austro-Hungarian empire in Trans-Carpathian and

---

33    According to the 1989 Soviet census, Ukrainians formed a low percentage of the population in Crimea (26 per cent), Donetsk (51 per cent), Luhansk (52 per cent), Odesa (55 per cent), Kharkiv and Zaporizhia counties (63 per cent). The remaining *oblasts* had greater than 70 per cent Ukrainian populations. By the 2001 census the proportion of Russians had declined in the Crimea from 65 to 58 percent due to out-migration of Russians and in-migration of Tatars. Within Odesa and Donetsk *oblasts* the proportion of Russians declined between 12-24 percent between the 1989 Soviet and 2001 Ukrainian censuses.

34    See Roman Solchanyk, 'The Crimean Imbroglio: Kyiv and Moscow', *RFE/RL Research Report*, vol.1, no.40 (9 October 1992).

Eastern Slovakia. These territories were removed from Hungary and given to the Czechoslovak state in the inter-war period. Trans-Carpathia, although geographically located in Western Ukraine, is home to strong demands for autonomy that have been resisted by Kyiv. Potentially, Hungary and Slovakia could lay claim to part, or all, of Trans-Carpathia.[35] In the case of Hungary, Slovakia and Poland the likelihood that territorial claims will re-surface is though unlikely. All three countries became members of the EU and NATO in 1999-2004.

The history of Polish-Ukrainian relations is dominated by conflict since the seventeenth century. With the disintegration of the Austrian-Hungarian empire in 1918, Poland attempted to reconstitute itself within its 'historic' borders, with little regard for the rights of ethnic minorities who lived there. The large discontented Ukrainian minority in Poland pursued their demands either through parliament or through acts of terrorism by Ukrainian nationalist groups.[36] During World War II, a Polish-Ukrainian civil war erupted again in Western Ukraine. Between 1945-1947, the Polish inhabitants of Western Ukraine, which was incorporated within the Ukrainian SSR, were deported to Poland. In order to ostensibly stop the struggle of Ukrainian nationalist partisans in South-Eastern Poland the Ukrainian population was ethnically cleansed in 1947 from the region to Poland's newly acquired German territories. The bloody conflicts of the inter-war period and 1940s left a bitter legacy that had to be initially overcome before relations could improve between both countries. Despite this historical legacy relations between Ukraine and Poland are good and the likelihood of territorial conflict between them is therefore, remote.

### Separatism and Public Attitudes towards Borders

Russian political parties and members of the Russian parliament and the executive have always been surprised at two developments in Ukraine. First, Russian-speaking regions of Ukraine heavily voted in favour of inde-

---

35    See Taras Kuzio, 'Rusyns in Ukraine: Between Fact and Fiction', *Canadian Review of Studies in Nationalism*, vol.32, nos.1-2 (December 2005), pp.17-29.

36    See Taras Kuzio, 'Commemorating 1943 events in Volyn', *Kyiv Post*, 10 April 2003.

pendence during the December 1991 referendum. Russian President Borys Yeltsin said to his Ukrainian counterpart, President Kravchuk: 'And you don't say - this is incredible! - What, and even the Donbas voted "yes"?'[37]

Second, Russians were surprised that the Russian-speaking regions of Eastern Ukraine and the Crimea did not create a Russian-speaking lobby which then proceeded to agitate for separation from Ukraine to Russia. This, in fact, only happened in the Crimea over a four-year period between 1992-1995.

The recognition by Russia of Ukraine's borders in May 1997 took the wind out of the former Crimean separatist movement. It then replaced its demands for union with Russia with defence of Russian-speakers and support for a pan-Eastern Slavic union.[38] The 1996 Ukrainian constitution banned regional parties, a step that forced Crimean parties to re-register as all-Ukrainian or regional branches of other Ukrainian parties. The collapse in support for Crimean separatism was also helped by three factors in Russia. First, the Chechen conflict provided Ukraine with a window of opportunity to peacefully deal with its own separatist challenge. Second, the re-election of Yeltsin as Russian President. Crimean separatists had pinned their hopes on Russian Communist leader Gennadiy Zyuganov winning the 1996 Russian presidential elections.[39] Third, interest in the Crimean problem within Russia had begun to decline.[40] In March 1995, Ukraine abolished the institution of the Crimean presidency which had served as the main vehicle for separatist agitation. This step by President Kuchma, elected primarily by voters within Russian-speaking Eastern Ukraine, was supported by nearly two thirds of Ukrainians, according to a poll conducted at the time. Even in the Crimea one third of respondents backed the abolishing of the institution of Crimean President.[41]

---

37    S.O. Kychyhin (ed.), *Leonid Kravchuk*, p.21.

38    See Taras Kuzio, *Ukraine. State and Nation Building in Ukraine*, pp.69-99.

39    Valentina Ivanova, a teacher in the Crimea, was quoted by Reuters (9 June 1996) as saying, 'Those able to vote in Crimea will be rooting for Zyuganov, the only one capable of restoring our shattered motherland (i.e. USSR)'.

40    See the views of Sergei Karaganov, head of the semi-official Council on Foreign and Defence Policy, on *Mayak Radio*, 29 May 1997.

41    The poll was conducted by SOTSIS-Gallup and cited in *Demokratychna Ukrayina*, 27 April 1995.

A separatist movement only existed in the Crimea during the first half of the 1990s after which it became marginalised. Public support for Ukraine's territorial integrity has always been high throughout the country, regardless of linguistic affiliation, inherited political culture or political beliefs. The Communist Party of Ukraine (KPU), a Russophile and Sovietophile party, has always been a staunch defender of Ukraine's territorial integrity. The KPU wants *all* of Ukraine to join a revived USSR, not individual regions such as the Crimea or Donbas. In the 1990s in the Crimea the KPU was an opponent of Russian nationalist separatists whom its leader, Leonid Grach, accused of being mere 'criminals'.[42] In 1998 the then left-wing leadership of the Ukrainian Parliament lobbied its Russian counterparts to successfully ensure that the Russian State Duma and Federation Council ratify the May 1997 treaty. KPU leader Petro Symonenko rejected accusations of support for separatism levelled against his party:

> Moreover, certain media are currently trying to portray the Communist Party of Ukraine as an enemy of the country's territorial integrity. I once again repeat that the Communists consider the Crimea and Sevastopol as inalienable parts of Ukraine.[43]

The survivability of the Ukrainian independent state in the 1990s was deemed doubtful both by the Russian leadership and by many Western scholars, experts, journalists and foreign governments. During 1993-1994 the view that Ukrainian independence was a temporary phenomenon was especially widespread. The *Strategic Survey (1994-1995)* of the well respected International Institute for Strategic Studies, argued that, 'In the past year, many outside observers have compared Ukraine to a state on the edge of collapse'.[44] In January 1994 a US National Intelligence Estimate, reflecting consensus among America's various intelligence organisations, predicted that Ukraine would split into two. Eastern Ukraine would allegedly clamour for 'uni-

---

42    Interview with L.Grach, Brussels, 15 September 1998.
43    *Veseukrainskiye vedomosti*, 15 January 1997.
44    'Ukraine: Rising from the Ashes', *Strategic Survey 1994-1995* (Oxford and London: Oxford University Press and the International Institute Strategic Studies), 1995), p.93.

fication' with Russia, something which would lead to civil war.[45] The London-based Royal United Services Institute also predicted that Ukraine was on the point of 'disintegration'[46], as did an internal report circulated to West European Christian Democratic parties.[47] In view of these pessimistic conclusions about Ukraine, Rand Corporation's Eugene B. Rumer concluded that the best solution for the West to forestall the security threat of Ukraine's impending 'collapse' would be its re-union with Russia.[48] Two years later the highly respected *Forbes* magazine predicted that, after Yugoslavia, Ukraine would become Europe's next ethnic and security crisis.[49] In 2003 *Forbes Magazine* again went off the deep end in its analysis of Ukraine when it included it together with Belarus as an unstable country.[50]

These prophesies of impending doom, separatist revolt and civil war in Ukraine proved to be wrong. In contrast to these prophets of doom, Ukraine has exhibited a high degree of stability and consensus regarding its inherited borders - both at the elite *and* at the public level. Pro-Russian separatism (in contrast to a pro-Russian cultural orientation) has never emerged in Eastern Ukraine.

All-national support for Ukraine's territorial integrity provides the Ukrainian elites with a strong bargaining hand for Ukraine's leaders when demand-

---

45    See 'U.S. Intelligence Predicts Ukraine Break-up Report', Reuters, 25 January, Daniel Williams and R. Jeffrey Smith, 'U.S. Intelligence Sees Economic Plight Leading to Break-up of Ukraine', *The Washington Post,* 25 January, Martin Fletcher, 'Spy agencies warn of Kyiv ethnic turmoil', *The Times,* 26 January and James Adams, 'West fears Ukraine is sliding towards war with Russia', *The Sunday Times,* 6 February 1994.

46    'Partnerships, National Interests and Defence Realities', *International Security Review* (London: RUSI, 1994), p.VI.

47    'L'Ukraine Aujourd'Hui. Rapport sur La situation economique, politique & sociale de l'Ukraine', Internationale Democrate-Chretienne, Bruxelles, le 6 decembre 1993. Copy in the authors possession.

48    E. B. Rumer, 'Eurasia Letter: Will Ukraine Return to Russia?', *Foreign Policy,* vol.96, no.3 (Fall 1994), pp. 129-144. See also 'The birth and possible death of a country, A Survey of Ukraine. Unruly Child', *The Economist,* 7 May 1994 and Paula J. Dobriansky, 'Ukraine: A Question of Survival', *The National Interest,* vol.36, no.2 (Summer 1994), pp.65-72.

49    Paul Klebnikov, 'Tinderbox. The world hasn't seen the last of ethnic turmoil in Eastern Europe. Keep your eye on Ukraine', *Forbes,* 9 September 1996.

50    Emily Lambert and Lhana R.Shoenberger, 'The Next Iraq, Atlas of Evil and Discord', *Forbes Magazine,* 17 March 2003. The article claims Belarus and Ukraine are 'Unstable states bordering new NATO members (which) could threaten the region'.

ing that its neighbours recognise these borders in international law. Support for Ukraine's territorial integrity remains high among ethnic Ukrainians, ethnic Russians and Russophone Ukrainians. Western and Russian misconceptions about the strength of separatism within Ukraine therefore proved to be highly exaggerated as public support for Ukraine's territorial has always been high. This has been used as a strong card by Ukraine's leaders to face off territorial challenges by its neighbours from domestic separatism.

The Crimea nearly became a 'hot spot' on two occasions in the 1990s among the many that engulfed the former USSR since its disintegration in December 1991. The two peaks of crisis in relations between Ukraine and the Crimea occurred in May 1992, when the peninsula declared sovereignty ('independence'), and during the first half of 1994, when Meshkov was elected Crimean President and the Russia bloc came to power in the Crimean Supreme Soviet.

The Ukrainian leadership refrained from adopting a violent solution to the Crimean problem. The use of a variety of non-violent methods by the Ukrainian leadership to bring the Crimea back within its sovereignty was successful. Within the space of only one year between Spring 1994-Spring 1995 support for pro-Russian separatism in the Crimea collapsed, and the leadership of the autonomous region was replaced by pro-Ukrainian local leaders from the 'party of power'. The credit for this change in political climate in the Crimea should also be given to the incompetence of the nationalist-separatist Russia bloc who came to power in early 1994 with a 'ragbag of promises' that they could not implement.[51]

### Conclusions

Borders are important markers of a countries identity and important components of national identity. As civic, territorial nation-states, they enclose the 'We' from the external 'Other'. If the nation-state is ethnically defined, these boundaries of the ethnic nation can be different to that of the interna-

---

51   See Tor Bukkvoll, "A Fall From Grace for Crimean Separatists", *Transition*, vol.1, no.21 (17 November 1995).

tionally recognised borders of the state. Four of Ukrane's neighbours in the former USSR – Moldova, Russia, Georgia and Azerbaijan – have separatist enclaves which complicates the issue of what constitutes boundaries. In three of these (Moldova, Georgia, Azerbaijan) the separatist enclaves have been *de facto* 'independent' for over a decade, although not *de jure* recognised as such. The Crimea was understood by Ukraine's central elites to be a special case and was given autonomous status in 1991, a step enshrined five years later in the Ukrainian constitution and two years later in a new Crimean constitution.

Ukraine has always stressed the importance of its territorial integrity and the recognition by its neighbours of its borders. Defence of Ukraine's inherited borders has always had a high degree of consensus at the elite and public levels. The most difficult problem rests with Russia which initially both refused to recognise the viability of Ukrainian independence and its sovereignty over the Crimea and port of Sevastopol. It took until 1997 for the Russian executive to recognise Ukraine's borders, another two years for its parliament to ratify the treaty and a further five for Russia and Ukraine to complete the delimitation of the land border. Nevertheless, Russia continues to refuse to delimit the Azov Sea and Kerch Strait or demarcate any portion of the border.

The marginalisation of the Russian nationalist-separatist movement in the Crimea after the ouster of Meshkov in March 1995 allowed other political forces to take control of the Crimea. Since 1995, and especially the 1998 elections, the only two political forces in the Crimea are Communists and pro-presidential 'party of power' centrists, both of whom respect Ukraine's territorial integrity. The defeat of Russian nationalist-separatists led to the adoption of the Crimea's non-separatist constitution in October-December1998. In 2004-2006, the Crimea voted overwhelmingly for Viktor Yanukovych and for the Party of Regions in presidential and parliamentary elections. Russian nationalists had become marginalised in the mid 1990s with Crimean politics then becoming dominated by the KPU and pro-Kuchma centrists. A decade later the KPU had lost one of its strongest bases of support as part of an all-Ukrainian trend that saw KPU support decline from 20 to 3.5 percent between the 2002 and 2006 Ukrainian parliamentary elections. Some of this former KPU support has migrated to the Party of Regions. By 2006 therefore, the

Crimea was no longer a base for pro-Russian separatism, but one for anti-Orange revolutionary forces who supported Ukraine's territorial integrity provided they were in the driving seat.

# 2    Regionalism and Separatism in Ukraine

Only after the conclusion of World War II were the bulk of territories where ethnic Ukrainians lived in a compact majority incorporated within the Ukrainian SSR, apart from small enclaves in Poland, Slovakia and Romania. Ukraine contains a wide diversity of regions with different histories, cultural outlooks and levels of national consciousness. In contrast to Western Ukrainians, inhabitants of Eastern Ukraine tend to look to independence only in terms of economic benefits. It is unlikely though, that a higher standard of living could in itself provide the long term loyalty to the newly independent state. This is required in order to maintain domestic stability and secure the legitimacy of the Ukrainian state in its current borders.

In Eastern Ukraine identity is grounded in 'multiple loyalties' traditionally found among subject peoples in multi-national empires. Kyiv's hegemony within Ukraine's large territory has never been completely certain, a factor which partly contributes to deep feelings of domestic Ukrainian insecurity because of manifestations of separatism and territorial claims. Although the Ukrainian SSR within its present borders existed for over half a century it was never governed as a single unit, but as regions in a larger empire. The residents of the Donbas and Crimea looked traditionally to Moscow - not to Kyiv - for support and instructions.

The newly independent Ukrainian state will be successful in maintaining control over its Eastern areas only if the inhabitants of the region increasingly adopt a Ukrainian identity, even if territorial and civic, rather than ethnocultural. The adoption of a Ukrainian identity is possible in Eastern Ukraine, where Russians have lived for centuries, have inter-married with Ukrainians and where Ukrainians are still the majority ethnic group. Although many Ukrainians in Eastern Ukraine are Russian speakers their attitudes to key issues, such as independence and armed forces, is still likely to be different to that of the ethnic Russian population.

But, such a re-identification will be dependent upon maintaining good relations with Russia and resolving the domestic political and economic crisis.

In 2000 the Ukrainian economy began to grow for the first time since the late 1980s, but Ukraine is still deeply mired in a political crisis.[52] By 2002 an opinion poll by the Kyiv International Institute Sociological Studies found that the number of adherents of Ukrainian independence had returned to their high level in the December 1991 referendum.[53] This was assisted by the overcoming of the socio-economic crisis and moderate nation building policies. This trend of support for independence returning to high levels has continued upwards, even though the 2004 and 2006 presidential and parliamentary elections widened regional divisions.

This chapter is divided into two sections. The first surveys regionalism in Ukraine and its impact upon Ukraine's politics. This investigates if regionalism can be considered a threat to Ukraine's territorial integrity and centre-periphery relations. The second section discuses the impact of a region similar to the Crimea, the Donbas, a region that contains ten per cent of Ukraine's population which entered central Ukrainian politics in 2002.

## Regionalism

### *Is Regionalism a Threat to Ukraine's Borders?* [54]

Ukraine inherited a disunited polity from the former USSR with a wide diversity of regions. This regionalism is compounded by weak traditions of statehood, few consolidating national ideas acceptable to the majority of the population[55], and until 1999 a severe socio-economic crisis. It also made the

---

52    See Taras Kuzio, 'Will Political Reform Lead Ukraine Out of Crisis', *RFERL Newsline*, 19 March 2003 and 'Party of power' in Crisis in Ukraine', *RFERL Newsline*, 8 April 2003.

53    See Taras Kuzio, 'Support for Independence Returns to 1991 Levels', *RFERL Poland, Belarus and Ukraine Report*, 21 January 2003.

54    On regional policy in Ukraine see V.A. Popvkin, *Do Kontseptsii Derzhavnoii Rehionalnoii Ekonomichnoii Polityky, no.37* (Kyiv: National Institute Strategic Studies, 1995), V.M.Kampo, *Misteve Samovriaduvannia v Ukrayini* (Kyiv: In Yure, 1997) and V.V.Tsvetkov (ed.), *Reformuvannia Derzhavnoho Upravlinnia v Ukrayini: Problemy I Perspektyvy* (Kyiv: Oriany, 1998).

55    Sven Holdar points out that there are no mass, all-Ukrainian parties. See his 'Torn Between East and West: The Regional Factor in Ukraine's Politics', *Post-Soviet Geography*, vol.36, no.2 (February 1995), pp.112-132.

resolution of the division of powers between Kyiv and Crimea more drawn out until the adoption of a new Ukrainian constitution in 1996 and laws on self-government and state administration in 1997 and 1999 respectively. A Crimean constitution acceptable to Kyiv was adopted and ratified in October-December 1998.

As the Ukrainian economy plummeted and the central authorities proved to be weak and inept, regional demands grew and reached their peak in 1993-1994.[56] Regional elite's saw their salvation in greater regional devolution, both as a means to enrich themselves as well as to overcome the poor economic policies promoted by the centre.[57] These developments were echoed in the media by a growing number of materials devoted to the need to revive ties to the CIS, grant greater regional economic autonomy and hold on to more of the locally generated budgetary receipts. These media debates were strongest in the Crimea, the Donbas and in Trans-Carpathia, three areas where regionalism and calls for federalism were the most acute in Ukraine during the 1990s.[58]

At the same time, regionalism in Ukraine, political analyst and Yulia Tymoshenko bloc MP Hryhoriy Nemirya argues, has less to do with ethnic divisions and should not be equated with separatism.[59] The population distrusts both local and national politicians, particularly the latter.[60] The weakness of both civil society and national identity in Eastern and Southern

---

56   See Taras Kuzio, 'Ukrainian Election Results Point to Growing Regionalism', *Jane's Intelligence Review Pointer*, no.6 (April 1994), p.3 and Gregory BV. Krasnov and Josef C.Brada, 'Implicit Subsidies in Russian-Ukrainian Energy Trade', *Europe-Asia Studies*, vol.49, no.5 (July 1997), p.840.

57   Nikolai Shulga, 'Federalism and Separatism in Ukraine: Historical Roots, New Realities and Prospects' in Klaus Segbers and Stephan De Spiegeleire (eds.), *Post-Soviet Puzzles. Mapping the Political Economy of the Former Soviet Union, vol. 11* (Baden-Baden: Nomos Verlag, 1995), pp.467-488.

58   Volodymyr Holotsvan, 'Pytannia Rehionalnoii Polityky ta Terytorialnoii Tsilisnosti Ukrayiny v Dzerkali Presy', *Politolohichni Chyttania*, no.4, 1994, pp.35-42.

59   Grigorii Nemirya, 'A Qualitative Analysis of the Situation in the Donbass' in K. Segbers and S. de Spiegeleire (eds.), *Post-Soviet Puzzles*, pp.58-59.

60   See Rainer Munz and Rainer Ohliger, *Die Ukraine nach der Unabhangigket. Natsionsbilding zwischen ost und west*, BIOST 5-1999.

Ukraine has traditionally meant that the socio-economic crisis in the 1990s did not lead to widespread calls for re-integration with Russia.[61]

Ukraine's regional divisions are mistakenly translated into separatist threats. This view is compounded by the standard - but simplistic – regional division of Ukraine into a 'catholic, nationalist, West' and a 'Russian-speaking, Orthodox, pro-Russian East'. Yet, four of the six Western Ukrainian oblasts' have more Orthodox than Catholic parishes.[62] Wise and Brown believe that eleven million Russians inhabit Eastern Ukraine while a previously unknown ethnic group, 'Ukrainian nationalists', seemingly populate the west.[63] Ukraine's regional divisions, according to Wilson, are 'deep' and based on ethno-linguistic and ideological differences. [64] Burant therefore believes that Eastern Ukrainians are more likely to see themselves as part of a *Russkii narod* than of a Ukrainian nation. [65] Russians in Ukraine allegedly therefore, 'would like to see Kremlin control restored in Ukraine'.[66]

The above rather simplistic divisions of Ukraine into a 'West' and 'East' fail to answer the question as to why Ukraine has remained so stable if its regionalism is so acute and in reality merely a disguised separatism? As Garnett points out, there is not one regional divide but many divides which overlap and are mutually reinforcing. [67] Using extensive survey data, Barrington found that the there was not an East: West divide in Ukraine because this failed to take into account the centre of the country. Regionalism in Ukraine is *not* along ethnic lines (as in, for example, Georgia, the Russian Federation or

---

61    Dmytro Vydryn and Dmytro Tabachnyk, *Ukrayina na prozi XXI stolittia. Politychnyi Aspekt* (Kyiv: Lybid, 1995), pp.79-80.

62    Stephen Shulman, 'National Integration and Foreign Policy in Multiethnic States', *Nationalism and Ethnic Politics*, vol.4, no.4 (Winter 1998), p.124. See also *Financial Times*, 27 November 1998.

63    Charles R. Wise and Trevor L. Brown, 'The Consolidation of Democracy in Ukraine', *Democratization*, vol.5, no.1 (Spring 1998), p.122.

64    Andrew Wilson, 'Ukraine: two presidents and their powers' in Ray Taras (ed.), *Post-communist presidencies* (Cambridge: Cambridge University Press, 1997), p.71.

65    Stephen R. Burant, 'Foreign Policy and National Identity: A Comparison of Ukraine and Belarus', *Europe-Asia Studies*, vol.47, no.7 (November 1995), p.1127.

66    Elaine Monaghan, 'Solana launches new era in NATO-Ukrainian relations', Reuters, 7 May 1997.

67    Sherman W.Garnett, *Keystone in the Arch. Ukraine in the Emerging Security Environment of Central and Eastern Europe* (Washington DC: Carnegie Endowment, 1997), pp.26-28.

Yugoslavia) but based on historical and economic factors. Barrington found that ethnic Russians in Ukraine are more nostalgic for the former USSR. They are also less supportive of independence and are less likely to see Ukraine as their homeland (rather than the former USSR) than either Ukrainophones or Russian-speaking Ukrainians. Barrington also found that Russian-speaking Ukrainians were closer to their fellow Ukrainians than ethnic Russians on these key questions. [68] As Barrington points out: 'What is clear is that if language and nationality are treated as separate variables,...there is little support for considering language when examining attitudes in Ukraine towards maintaining independence from Russia.'[69]

Barrington therefore believes that language is less important than region in deciding the domestic and foreign policy orientations of the population. This correlates with the findings of other authors who stress different regional political cultures which have arisen in Ukraine due to historic, climatic and economic factors.[70] There is little support for separatism throughout Ukraine, apart from in the Crimea for a brief period during the first half of the 1990s. The central issue therefore that faced Ukraine in grappling with its inherited regionalism was not any threat to its territorial integrity, although threats may be still *perceived*. [71] The key question was *never* if Ukraine would exist as a state but in what form and with what type of political regime.[72]

The Russian SFSR was never promoted as an ethnic Russian homeland in the USSR and some ethnic Russians in Ukraine therefore see the former USSR – not the Russian Federation – as their 'homeland'. There is little support for separatism in Ukraine. Russians, especially supporters of left-wing parties, tend to be either Slavophiles or Sovietophiles (the Commu-

---

68    Lowell Barrington, 'The Geographic Component of Mass Attitudes in Ukraine', *Post-Soviet Geography and Economics*, vol.38, no.10 (December 1997), p.611.
69    *Ibid.*
70    See Zenovia A. Sochor, 'Political Culture and Foreign Policy: Elections in Ukraine 1994' in Vladimir Tismaneanu (ed.), *Political Culture and Civil Society in Russia and the New States of Eurasia. The International Politics of Eurasia, vol.7* (Armonk, N.Y.: M.E.Sharpe, 1995), pp.208-226 and Taras Kuzio, *Ukraine. State and Nation Building* (London: Routledge, 1998), pp.43-68.
71    S. Shulman, 'Cultures in Competition: Ukrainian Foreign Policy and the 'Cultural Threat' from Abroad', *Europe-Asia Studies*, vol.50, no.2 (March 1998), p.288.
72    See T. Kuzio, *Ukraine. State and Nation Building*, pp.69-99 and 119-143.

nists or Progressive Socialist parties) and support either Ukraine joining the Russian-Belarusian union or a revived USSR, rather than separatism.

Regionalism in Ukraine therefore should *not* be equated with ethnic divisions or creeping separatism. Elite consensus in favour of a decentralised unitary state attempted to take this factor into account by rejecting what were regarded as two 'dangerous' extremes – a federal or centralised unitary state. A decentralised unitary state recognises two factors. First, the need to forge a united political community (i.e. civic nation) based upon shared values and common institutions which would to some extent overcome the wide regional disparities inherited from the former USSR. This would help buttress democratic consolidation and a market economy. Federalism, it is widely believed among Ukrainian elites, would not fulfil these two tasks.

Second, the concept of a decentralised unitary state implicitly rejects the French model of a highly centralised and homogenised nation-state. It accepts that Ukraine is composed of different regions due to historical, political cultural and economic factors. A de-centralised state supports integration without resorting to a nationalising project. Such a policy has been defined by myself elsewhere as 'unity in diversity' where pluralism is accepted and coupled with state support for integration.[73]

### Centre-Periphery Relations

Many outside observers have argued that support for federalism in Ukraine is widespread. Wilson, for example, argued forcefully that, 'the political and electoral weight of Ukraine's Russophone regions means that the federal question will remain on the political agenda for the foreseeable future'.[74] This view is based on two wrong assumptions. First, the 40-50 per cent of Ukraine's population who are Russophone, according to 'language of convenience' surveys ('native language' data from the 2001 census provides for fewer Russophones, with only 14.8 percent of Ukrainians giving Russian as their native language) would automatically support a federal structure for

---

73    See Taras Kuzio, 'Can Western Multiculturalism be Applied to the Post-Soviet States: A Critical Response to Kymlicka', *Journal of Contemporary European Politics*, vol.13, no.2 (August 2005), pp.217-232.

74    Andrew Wilson, *Ukrainian Nationalism in the 1990s. A Minority Faith* (Cambridge: Cambridge University Press), p.168.

Ukraine. This, of course, assumes incorrectly that Russophones have a developed, coherent and robust identity. In a subsequent article, Wilson accepts that this is not the case in the Donbas.[75] Second, Wilson also mistakenly extrapolates the views he found in the Donbas as representing the entire region of Eastern and Southern Ukraine (i.e. areas he defines as Russophone).[76] The Donbas and Crimea are unique regions and the political orientations and values found there are not necessarily the same as those found in other regions of Eastern and Southern Ukraine.

The reality is more complicated and far less divisive. During the March 1998 parliamentary elections, of the 30 blocs or parties which took part none advocated federalism. Even traditionally pro-federal parties, such as the Inter-Regional Bloc of Reforms or the Civic Congress (united in the 1998 Labour Ukraine [*Trudova Ukrayina*] election bloc) refrained from including federalism in their election manifestos. The Party of Muslims called for the Crimea to be converted into a Tatar national territorial-administrative unit. The Tatar language would become a third official language and Tatars would be recognised as the titular nation in the region. The pro-presidential Party of Regional Revival called for Ukraine's regions to be granted complete independence to decide socio-economic questions with the majority of locally collected taxes being left in the regions. It also called for the creation of more Free Economic Zones.[77] Nevertheless, none of these pro-devolutionary parties called for a federal territorial-administrative system. The Party of Regions is the succes-

---

75   Graham Smith and A. Wilson, 'Rethinking Russia's Post-Soviet Diaspora: The Potential for Political Mobilisation in Eastern Ukraine and North-east Estonia', *Europe-Asia Studies*, vol.49, no.5 (July 1997), pp.845-864. See also David J. Meyer, 'Why Have Donbas Russians Not Ethnically Mobilized Like Crimean Russians Have? An Institutional/Demographic Approach' in John S. Micgiel (ed.), *State and Nation Building in East Central Europe. Contemporary Perspectives* (New York: Institute on East Central Europe, Columbia University, 1996), pp.317-330.

76   For a different view see Louise Jackson, 'Identity, Language and Transformation in Eastern Ukraine: A Case Study of Zaporizhzhia' in Taras Kuzio (ed.), *Contemporary Ukraine. Dynamics of Post-Soviet Transformation* (Armonk, NY: M.E. Sharpe, 1998), pp.99-114.

77   The election manifestos are published in Mykola Tomenko and Oleh Protsenko (eds.), *Pravo Vyboru: Politychni Partii Ta Vyborchi Bloky* (Kyiv: Instytut Postkomunistychnoho Suspil'stva, 1998). For the 2006 elections, see Yuriy Marchenko, Oleh Telemko and Oksana Tudor (eds.), *Vybory 2006. Politychna Ukrayina Siohodni* (Kyiv: K.I.S., 2005).

sor to Regional Revival and it has refrained from openly advocating federalism, instead arguing for decentralisation and Free Economic Zones, in other words, economic and financial, rather than political, 'federalism'.

Polling data confirms the lack of public support for federalism. Miller, Reisinger and Hesli found that only 9 per cent of Ukrainians favoured federalism, ranging from as low as 4 in the West to 11 and 16 per cent in the East and South respectively.[78] Hesli also found that all of Ukraine' regions – including the East and South - were willing to delegate greater authority to the centre than maintain it at the local level. In fact, Hesli found that Western Ukrainians were more inclined to favour regional devolution than other regions[79]. A Galician Assembly had been created as an experiment by locally elected reformist leaders of the Democratic Bloc between 1990-1992. But, this fell into disfavour after regional divisions became pronounced during the 1993-1994 economic crisis and elections.

Another survey conducted simultaneously in Lviv and Donetsk found majorities against federalism. A clear majority in both cities believed that the unity of Ukraine was more important than regional issues, that regions would be worse off outside Ukraine and they linked the fate of their region to Ukraine.[80] As Table 1 shows, only 1.30-5.1 per cent of the inhabitants of both Lviv and Kyiv supported Ukraine's disintegration into regions.

---

78    See Arthur H. Miller, Thomas F. Klobucar, William M. Reisinger, 'Establishing Representation: Mass and Political Attitudes in Ukraine' in Sharon L. Wolchik and Volodymyr Zviglyanich (eds.), *Ukraine. The Search for a National Identity* (Lanham, MD: Rowman & Littlefield, 2000), pp.213-236.

79    Vicki L. Hesli, 'Public Support for the Devolution of Power in Ukraine: Regional Patterns', *Europe-Asia Studies*, vol.47, no.1 (January 1995), pp.91-121.

80    Yaroslav Hrytsak, 'Shifting Identities in Western and Eastern Ukraine', *The East and Central Europe Program Bulletin*, vol.5, no.3 (February 1995).

Table 2.1 Which Future Possibility for Ukraine Do You Prioritise? (in per cent)?

| Possibility | Lviv | Donetsk |
|---|---|---|
| Full independence | 62.2 | 13.3 |
| Federation with Russia | 5.4 | 57.0 |
| Member of EU | 25.2 | 18.0 |
| Federation with Central-Eastern Europe | 5.9 | 16.6 |
| Ukraine dividing regionally | 1.30 | 5.1 |

Source: Yaroslav Hrytsak, Oksana Malanchuk and Natalia Chernysh, 'Ukraiina: Skhid i Zakhid', *Sovremennoe Obshchestvo*, no.3, 1994, p.74

The federal question only began to become acute in Ukraine during the latter period of the Leonid Kravchuk era (1993-1994), at a time of deep socio-economic crisis and hyperinflation. These policy failures were compounded by a struggle between the centre and regions over divisions of powers not yet formulated in any post-Soviet constitution.

Classical federations consist of unions of lands or princedoms (e.g. Germany) which continue to preserve their separate identities. As we will see later[81], this is an important factor because the strongest supporters of federalism in Ukraine tend to also be supporters of four policies that dissuade Ukraine from giving its support to federalism and making ruling elites distrustful of the concept.

First, Slavophile and pro-Russophile foreign policy orientation ranges from a moderate call for a strategic partnership with Russia and economic integration (the view of small, centrist political parties) to full union (the view of the Communist Party [KPU]). Hesli found that perceived Russian-Ukrainian relations, 'will have an impact on decisions made about the territorial distribution of political authority'.[82] Khmelko and Arel also found that two questions polarised Ukrainian society – the status of the Russian language (i.e. if it is a 'foreign language'?) and relations with Russia (i.e. to what extent can Russia

---

81    On the application of the world experience of federalism to Ukraine see Serhiy Rymarenko, 'Federatyvna Derzhava? Chy Mozhlyvo Zapozychty Svitovyi Dosvid?', *Polityka i Chas*, no.8, (1994), pp.7-11.

82    V.L. Hesli, 'Public Support for the Devolution of Power in Ukraine', p.91.

be defined as Ukraine's constituting 'Other'?).[83] By the latter half of the first Kuchma term in office (1996-1999) both of these factors had been largely resolved. Evolutionary Ukrainianisation had been chosen over nationalising policies. Meanwhile, Russian-Ukrainian relations had been established on a new footing with the joint ratification of the border treaty and the resolution of the Black Sea Fleet question. In turn, these developments reduced support for federalism found earlier in the Kravchuk era.

Second, Russia has long proposed that its 'Near Abroad' introduce federal territorial-administrative systems, provide political autonomy to their regions and grant dual citizenship to ethnic Russians. Understandably, most 'Near Abroad' states have been reluctant to take this Russian advice. At the same time, such Russian strategic objectives have served to undermine support for federalism in countries such as Ukraine by allowing nationalists to blacken federalists as 'pro-Russian' and even 'treacherous'. Hesli believes that when Russian-Ukrainian relations improved – as they did between 1997-1999 – support for federalism would decline (as it in fact did). Russia has pressured Moldova to implement these policies since the Communists (PCM) came to power in 2001, but this pressure served to worsen Moldovan-Russian relations and the PCM retreated from federalism.

Russophile and Sovietophile political parties believe that Ukraine was jointly created by two people's and cultures (Russians and Ukrainians). Its identity is hence more Eastern Slavic than purely Ukrainian and therefore the state should be constitutionally defined with two titular nations. As Yulia Tymoshenko bloc deputy Mykola Tomenko points out, if you believe that Ukraine was created by different people's (and not only Ukrainians) then federalism, 'is the only logical path to dealing with the problems of the state system'. If, on the contrary, one argues that Ukraine was established as an independent state to allow Ukrainians to realise their right to self determination then federalism is not an option you are likely to consider.[84]

Third, Ukraine should also have two state languages (Ukrainian and Russian) with Russian also as an 'official language'. This question is continually raised by political figures and parties in the Donbas and the Crimea.

---

83    Valeri Khmelko and Dominique Arel, 'The Russian Factor and Territorial Polarization in Ukraine', *The Harriman Review*, vol.9, nos. 1-2 (Spring 1996), pp.81-91.

84    M. Tomenko, *Samooznazchennia Ukrayiny* (Kyiv: Institute of Politics, 1996), p.179.

Within the CIS the Russian language has been elevated to an 'official language' in Belarus, Moldova, Kazakhstan and Kirgizia.

The link between these four policies and federalism colours the entire debate within Ukraine. As a supporter of federalism, Vladimir Grynev, President Kuchma's former regional policy adviser, explains:

> The supporters of unitary, or, as it is fashionable to say in certain circles, united (*soborna*) state, regard the idea of federalism as such as one that harms the integrity of the state and is even hostile to the very idea of statehood.....federalism as the basis of the state is regarded as a potentially creeping separatism, and a unitary state as its 'suppression'.[85]

This is because, Grynev believes, federalists are seen as basically 'closet separatists' while unitarianism is perceived as a means with which to halt threats to Ukraine's territorial integrity. This sharp debate is, in of itself, influenced by the earlier disintegration of federal states, such as the former USSR, Yugoslavia and Czechoslovakia. Federalism would, it is argued by its opponents, also hinder the development of a uniform national identity throughout Ukraine as, 'without a unitary state it will not be possible to tie the remainder of the regions to their understanding of statehood'.[86]

Grynev, in contrast, supports federalism as a means of providing regional self government based on Ukraine's historic diversity of different regions. It would allow the budget to be divided between the centre and regions in a fairer manner (Grynev supports regions maintaining sixty per cent of their taxes[87]). In a federal system the regions would be able to 'protect' themselves from the Ukrainianising policies of the centre (thereby reducing conflict over linguistic issues), provide for local economic and cultural autonomy and ensure more rapid economic reform. It is ironic that Grynev's Inter-Regional Bloc of Reforms merged in 2001 with the People's Democratic Party (PDP) whose head, Valeriy Pustovoitenko, headed an anti-reform Ukrainian government between 1997-1999 that led Ukraine to bankruptcy.

---

85    V.B. Grynev, *Novaya Ukraina: Kakoy Ya Ee Vyzhu* (Kyiv: Abrys, 1995), p.27.
86    *Ibid.,* p.29.
87    See the interview with Vladimir Grynev in *Kyivska Pravda*, 7 September 1995.

Grynev argued that contrary to popular perceptions, the unitary state was far more of a threat to Ukraine's territorial integrity than federalism, especially if it attempted to implement an 'aggressive' Ukrainianisation policy.[88] Federalists in Ukraine believe that policies 'can only be formed and elaborated naturally, organically and comprehensively in the regions themselves'.[89] Although central laws would be higher than local decisions, the regions should, in Grynev's viewpoint, be granted wide ranging economic independence. He warns though that '[y]ou certainly understand that currently one cannot but be aware of the simple fact that if we speak about economic self administration, it inevitably entails political economic self administration.'[90]

The language question also remained an acute problem which should, on the Crimean model, be resolved at the local level, Grynev argued. Regions would, according to their specific historical features, resolve cultural, ethnic and educational questions.[91] Grynev's federal option for Ukraine also sought reform of the territorial-administrative system to one based on nine lands that largely followed historical, geographical and economic criteria. Soviet Ukrainian economists as early as the 1960s had divided Ukraine into nine economic regions which, supporters of a land system argue, could be the basis for a federal territorial-administrative system. They, like their nineteenth century forefathers, point to the historical basis for the unification of lands, according to historic and economic criteria, under Kyiv.

The reform of Ukraine's territorial-administrative system from the Soviet system of 25 *oblast's* and 2 cities into nine lands would allegedly reduce the number of bureaucrats and budgetary outlays. Such reforms are also credited with the ability to speed up economic reforms and take into account Ukraine's ethnic and regional differences. The nine economic regions which could form the basis of these lands are: Volyn (Volyn and Rivne *oblasts*), Donbas (Donetsk, Luhansk), Zaporizhzhia (Dnipropetrovsk, Zaporizhzhia, Kirovohrad), Carpathians (Trans-Carpathia, Ivano-Frankivsk, Lviv, Chernivtsi), Kyiv (Zhytomir, Kyiv, Cherkassy, Chernihiv), the Crimea, Podillia (Vynnytsia, Ternopil,

---

88    V.B. Grynev, *Novaya Ukraina*, p.35.
89    M. Tomenko, *Samooznazchennia Ukrayiny*, p.474.
90    *Kyivska Pravda*, 7 September 1995.
91    A critical response to Grynev and Inter-Regional Bloc of Reforms support for federalism can be found in Natalia Rudenko, 'Rozdumy z Pryvodu Terytorialno-Administratyvnoho Ustoroiu Derzhavy', *Narodna hazeta*, no.13 (March 1996).

Khmelnytskyi), Slobidska (Poltava, Sumy, Kharkiv), Chornomorska (Myko-laiiv, Odesa, Kherson).[92] Under these lands (zemlia or kraj's) there could be three tiers of local authority – counties (povit's), districts (volost's) and city re-gions (rayons).[93]

Grynev, Kuchma's main ally in the 1994 parliamentary and presidential elections, had long been an advocate of federalism and strong presidential power. His views though, proved to be too radical for both Kuchma and the majority of Ukraine's political parties (he left his presidential advisory post in 1996). Opinion polls since 2000, and during discussions on constitutional re-form in 2003-2004, have consistently shown that federalism has minority support and an upper house of parliament has only an average public back-ing of 30 percent. An upper house of parliament is understood in two ways: as the introduction of federalism and as an extension of presidential power.

A close examination of Grynev's views will therefore serve to illuminate some of the problems that federalists have in promoting their case in Ukraine:

- Inherent contradiction between federalism of the magnitude supported by Grynev and his backing for a presidential-style constitution modelled on Russia's. In addition, Ukraine's political culture is far closer to parliamenta-rism than to presidentialism. Parliament is capable of representing Ukraine's diversity and institution where compromise can be reached. Fol-lowing constitutional reforms voted on 8 December 2004 and introduced in 2006, Ukraine moved from a semi—presidential to a parliamentary-presidential system;

- Many Ukrainian elite's would support the creation of Free Economic Zones and greater economic powers devolved to regions. Nevertheless, this con-tradicts the creation of a unified national economy from the economic re-gions inherited from the former USSR. Free Economic Zones were abol-ished by the Tymoshenko government in 2005 because they had become a major source of corruption;

---

92    Ihor Vlasenko, 'Deviat Zemel - Osnova Novoho Terytorialnoho Ustroiu', Chas-Time, 8 September 1995.

93    Volodymyr Males, 'Derzhava I Rehiony (Do Formuvannia Rehionalnoii Polityku v Ukrayini)', Rozbudova Derzhava, no.9 (September 1994), pp.16-17.

- Greater economic autonomy for the regions would not necessarily assist the pace of economic reform, as Grynev argues. Many local elite's would see it as a means of personal enrichment, as seen in the Crimea and Donbas and in former Free Economic Zones;
- Grynev's admission that economic autonomy would inevitably lead to political demands is precisely the fear that many in Ukraine's elite's harbour about federalism. In other words, a slippery path towards separatism;
- Grynev's use of federalism freezes the national legacy inherited from the former USSR. The Ukrainian state is unlikely to launch a radical Ukrainianisation project along the lines Grynev is concerned about because there is neither public support nor a strong state available to undertake a nationalising project. At the same time, for any newly independent state, such as Ukraine, to not launch a civic nation building project would be rather unusual. Such a project would attempt to reduce – but not totally eradicate – the wide regional differences, provide affirmative action for Ukrainian language and culture, standardise educational policies and promote national consolidation and integration into a new political community. In other words, unity in diversity.
- Grynev believes that federalism can be used as an instrument to freeze the situation on the ground and thereby prevent these nation-state building policies from being implemented. It is therefore little wonder that his Inter-Regional Bloc of Reforms became so isolated from other centrist parties that backed Kuchma during his second term in office. (In 2001 Grynev's Inter-Regional Bloc of Reforms merged with the failed 'party of power' People's Democratic Party [NDP]). As Grynev was deserted by his centrist allies his only compatriots on the national question became marginal Pan-Slavic or centrist parties. Kuchma's centrist political allies, unlike Grynev's former Inter-Regional Bloc of Reforms, do *not* support federalism but a decentralised, unitary state which provides the devolution of socio-economic powers to the regions.[94] Grynev's allies included the Constitutional Democ-

---

94    Ihor Koliushko, then a parliamentary adviser, proposed a 'decentralised, unitary state' as a way of halting any slide towards federalism. See his 'Nasha Ukrayina Taka Rizna', *Holos Ukrayiny*, 13 February 1992. See also on the same theme, Mykola Yakovyna (head of the Ivano-Frankivsk *oblast* council), 'Unitarna, detsentralizovana', *Holos Ukrayiny*, 31 October 1992, Kostiantyn Maleyev, 'Ukrayina –

rats (who joined with his party to create the failed Social-Liberal alliance [SLON] in the March 1998 parliamentary elections), the Labour Party, the Party of Economic Revival of the Crimea (since discredited for possessing close links to organised crime) and the pan Slavic Civic Congress. Typically these parties are not popular with the public - SLON, Grynev's 1998 election bloc, for example, only polled a meagre 0.91 per cent.

Local self-government to preserve the cultural and historical traditions of the regions was backed by Kravchuk while he was President. Kravchuk drew the line at separatism and the promotion of inter-ethnic conflicts.[95] Kravchuk, who when out of office joined the Social Democratic United Party (SDPUo) and became a joint leader of Kuchma's October 1999 presidential election bloc Accord (*Zlahoda*), held similar views to Kuchma that opposed the introduction of a federal system in Ukraine. Their views coincided on the need for a decentralised, unitary state which possesses a vertical executive power chain and provides for local self government and greater regional devolution.[96] Their support for constitutional reforms, that transformed Ukraine from a semi-presidential to a parliamentary-presidential system, grew out of fear of Yushchenko being elected and inheriting the executive powers of the 1996 constitution. Members of the Ukrainian elites, including former President Kravchuk, also see federalism as, 'endangering the possibility of preserving the integrity of the state as such'.[97]

The moderate left (Socialists), led by Moroz, also support a decentralised, unitary state with broad powers, particularly economic, delegated to the regions. Like, the former 'party of power' (Kravchuk-Kuchma) the Socialists do not back political autonomy, fearing that this would lead to separatism along the lines of Moldova's Trans-Dniestr enclave or Russia's Chechnya. The left (either the Communists or Socialists), do *not* therefore back Grynev on the federal question (or an upper house of parliament).

---

Unitarna, Detsentralizovana', *Vechirnyi Kyiv*, 30 June 1993 and I.Kuras, 'Federatsiya Chy Unitarna Derzhava?', *Polityka I Chas*, no.6, 1993, pp.4-8.

95    Mykola Shpakovaty (ed.), Leonid Kravchuk, *Our Goal-A Free Ukraine* (Kyiv: Globus, 1993), pp.20 and 53.
96    M. Tomenko, *Samooznazchennia Ukrayiny*, p.191.
97    Radio Ukraine World Service, 6 April 1994.

The absolute majority of Ukraine's political parties see federalism as 'premature' which could be only possibly introduced after Ukraine is more fully consolidated as a nation and the socio-economic situation improves. Former Parliamentary Speaker Ivan Pliushch suggested that 'this process (towards federalism) needs to mature...the very nature of a democratic state implies its federal structure. However, it is necessary to proceed toward this in a civil and evolutionary manner and by no means a revolutionary one.'[98]

Other members of Ukraine's ruling elites also argued that federalism is currently 'impractical' because it is tantamount to a radical change in the state's territorial-administrative structure which would have short term negative effects upon economic and political processes in the state. Federalism as an institution requires a vibrant civil society to ensure active citizens at the local and national level. Civil society in Ukraine though, is weakest in precisely those areas of Eastern and Southern Ukraine where support for federalism is greater.

The centre-right have been the most vociferous opponents of federalism, accusing federalists such as Grynev of even being 'traitors' and of delivering Ukraine into Russian hands. One author argued, 'The idea of federalism, the idea of an autonomous-federal territorial system for Ukraine, is simply dangerous, harmful and destructive...'[99]

National democrats argued against federalism in three ways. First, they believe it would freeze the regional disparities in culture, language and ethnic relations from the Soviet regime. Second, it would convert Ukraine into a 'conglomerate' that would lead to a distancing of regions from one another, instead of their gradual coming together. Finally, federalism would provide Russia with the opportunity to 'annex' portions of Ukrainian territory, such as the Crimea and Donbas.[100] These fears may seem exaggerated, indeed highly so, but they have resonance in Western and Central Ukraine, two regions that voted for Yushchenko in 2004 and for Orange parties in 2006.

The fears of national democrats of federalism as a potential threat to Ukraine's territorial integrity are, to some degree, well founded. Federalism

---

98    *Holos Ukrayiny*, 5 May 1994.
99    Andriy Pashuk, 'Ideya Federatsii I Ukrayina', *Respublikanets*, vol.4, nos.3-4 (1994), p.126.
100   *Ibid.*

*does* institutionalise regional differences while providing resources to local elite's which could be used for mobilisation against the state.[101] A broad spectrum of opinion in Ukraine, ranging from the extreme right to the centre right (supporters of a unitary state) to the left and centrists (supporters of a decentralised, unitary state) see federalism as encouraging separatism.[102] This translated into opposition to an upper house of parliament proposed by Kuchma in his constitutional reform proposals in 2003-2004.

Potential separatist threats cannot be divorced from Ukraine's external environment, which only stabilised in 1997-1999. Prior to June 1997, Romania held territorial claims on Chernivtsi *oblast* (Northern Bukovina), parts of Odesa *oblast* and Serpents Island. The Russian Federation only finally recognised Ukraine's borders in May 1997, a treaty which was only then ratified by both of its houses of parliament between December 1998-February 1999. In both of these cases therefore, concerns were raised about devolving power to Odesa, the Donbas and the Crimea at a time when two external powers harboured territorial claims on these regions. In November 2004, Yanukovych organised a separatist congress in Severdonetsk to which he invited Moscow Mayor Yuriy Luzhkov. The congress discredited Yanukovych within the pro-Kuchma central elites.

In the Trans-Carpathian *oblast,* opponents of economic or political devolution have pointed to the support given to the Ruthenian (*Rusyn*) separatist movement by some Hungarian and Slovak politicians (*Rusyn's* regard themselves as a separate Eastern Slavic people and not as a regional branch of Ukrainians). Those who play the *Rusyn* card[103] 'are concerned not so much with the development of the so-called Ruthenian language and culture as with establishing a different identity and then secession of Trans-Carpathia (or, in their terms, Trans-Carpathian Rus) from Ukraine.'

A large spectrum of Ukrainian political and elite opinion is united in the view that the provision of autonomy to the Crimea is a negative example for other regions in Ukraine. The provision of institutions (such as a presidency)

---

101   See Philip G. Roeder, 'Soviet Federalism and Ethnic Mobilization', *World Politics,* vol.23, no.2 (January 1991), pp.196-233.

102   See the survey of political party opinion on federalism in 'Pretsedent Dvopartiynosti', *Post-Postup,* 30 March-5 April 1993.

103   See Taras Kuzio, 'Rusyns in Ukraine: Between Fact and Fiction', *Canadian Review of Studies in Nationalism,* vol.32, nos.1-2 (December 2005), pp.17-29.

and other federal arrangements (i.e. demands to have relations between the Crimea and Ukraine based on a treaty, as in the Russian Federation) led to escalating separatist demands.[104] As Tomenko points out, '[i]t [the Crimea] equips opponents of federalism with numerous arguments for considering it inexpedient to renounce unitarianism in general and during the period of nation-building and in the midst of a general economic crisis in particular.'[105]

It is noticeable that votes in the Ukrainian parliament against Crimean separatism have always obtained more than two thirds constitutional majorities (meaning that the left, centre and right have voted together)[106] The former Crimean Supreme Soviet chairman, Leonid Grach, leader of Crimea's KPU, has long been an arch opponent of local Russian nationalist-separatists. While rejecting federalism then President Kravchuk understood that the territorial-administrative system inherited from the former USSR could not be maintained and thereby he acknowledged that it required a degree of reform.[107] A middle ground was staked out between the twin opposites of a centralised, unitary state and federalism, a position which has been accepted by the majority of Ukraine's elites and parties as a decentralised unitary state based on a policy of unity in diversity. This middle ground of a decentralised, unitary state recognises the artificiality of the inherited Soviet territorial-administrative system while rejecting federalism as too 'dangerous' an experiment at this stage in Ukraine's state and nation building project.

Supporters and opponents of federalism in Ukraine tend to mistakenly link the question of a bicameral parliament to that of federalism, yet many countries have two-tier parliaments which are not federal (e.g. the UK, the Netherlands and Poland). Prior to the adoption of Ukraine's first post-Soviet constitution in June 1996 the question of whether the Ukrainian parliament should be transformed into a two-tier National Assembly was regularly de-

---

104    See T. Kuzio and D. Meyer, 'The Donbas and Crimea: An Institutional and Demographic Approach to Ethnic Mobilisation in Two Ukrainian Regions' in T. Kuzio, R.S. Kravchuk and P. D'Anieri (eds.), *State and Institution Building in Ukraine* (New York: St. Martin's Press, 1999), pp.297-324.
105    M. Tomenko, *Samooznazchennia Ukrayiny*, p.474.
106    On the Crimea see chapter three in Taras Kuzio, *Ukraine under Kuchma. Political Reform, Economic Transformation and Security Policy in Independent Ukraine* (London: Macmillan, 1997), pp.67-89.
107    Interview with L. Kravchuk in *Literaturna Ukrayina*, 26 November 1992.

bated.[108] President Kuchma had always backed the creation of a bicameral parliament while the centre-right and extreme left adamantly opposed it for two reasons. When Kuchma reintroduced bicameralism in his constitutional reform proposals in 2003-2004, bicameralism never received support within the central elites or more broadly within the public at large.

First, then parliamentary chairman Oleksandr Moroz, leader of the Socialist Party, believed it would encourage separatism.[109] These views are similar to those of the national democrats. Second, a second chamber composed of regional representatives would be inevitably pro-presidential (as was the Council of Regions[110]). This would give greater executive control over parliamentary affairs, reduce the possibilities of the left to halt or slow down economic reform and ultimately turn Ukraine into a presidential republic. Hence, the left have traditionally opposed the transformation of the Supreme Council into a bicameral National Assembly. Socialist Party head Moroz described an upper house of parliament as tantamount to creating a second presidential administration.

During the constitutional debate prior to the adoption of the Ukrainian constitution in June 1996, Ukraine's regions also increasingly became opposed to a bicameral parliament. Under the proposals supported by President Kuchma each region, regardless of its geographic size or population density, would send two senators to the upper chamber (the Senate). Such an arrangement would have diluted the influence of the more populated and urbanised Eastern Ukraine in favour of the more rural Western Ukraine. For example, the largely rural Ternopil *oblast* would have sent the same number of senators as that of the highly populated Donetsk *oblast*. This factor also helped to turn Eastern Ukrainians away from a bicameral National Assembly.

---

108   T. Kuzio, *Ukraine under Kuchma*, pp.90-136.
109   *Ukrayina moloda*, 5 May 1999.
110   See the support given by the Council to the government programme (*Narodna Armiya*, 4 October 1995).

## The Donbas

Two key Eastern Ukrainian Donbas *oblasts* bordering Russia - Donetsk and Luhansk - provide sixty of the deputies to the Ukrainian parliament, or 13.3 per cent of the total of 450 deputies. A large majority of the leftist deputies elected during the 1990s were from these two *oblasts*. By the 2002 elections the Donbas had become the stronghold of the Party of Regions, the local 'party of power'. In the 2004 and 2006 elections, the region voted overwhelmingly for Yanukovych and the Party of Regions.

In the first half of the 1990s much was heard about the strength, importance and the threat of the Donbas, home to a fifth of Ukraine's population and 60 parliamentary seats. Yet, the region remained relatively quiet and its integration into the Ukrainian independent state proved to be less problematical than at first thought. In the late Soviet era Eastern and Southern Ukraine remained passive during the evolution of Rukh from a platform of transforming the USSR into a confederation to out right state independence. Only in 1989 did Donbas coal miners go on strike and henceforth an uneasy alliance developed between them and the nationalist Rukh movement. This is not surprising as during the Soviet era, communist propaganda directed against 'bourgeois nationalists' and 'fascist collaborators' was collectively aimed at the Ukrainian Diaspora and Western Ukrainians. In the 2004 elections a similar tactic was used by the Yanukovych campaign, which fanned anti-Americanism and accused Yushchenko of being an American stooge and 'nationalist'.[111]

Ukraine's first Defence Minister, Konstantin Morozov, who was born in the Donbas, recalls in his memoirs that in the Soviet era a 'bourgeois nationalist' was anybody who dared to even speak the Ukrainian language. Morozov only found out that his family were ethnic Ukrainians after the USSR disintegrated; in the Soviet army he had always thought of himself as a Russian

---

111   See Taras Kuzio, 'Large Scale Anti-American Campaign Planned in Ukraine', *Jamestown Foundation, Eurasian Daily Monitor*, vo.1, no.102 (8 October 2004); 'UKRAINE: Anti-Americanism an election tool for Kuchma', *Oxford Analytica*, 8 January 2004.

from the Donbas.[112] This stereotype has left deep marks in Ukrainian politics to this day. A powerful regional Donbas identity and local patriotism exists alongside other identities. The Donbas, like the Trans-Dniestr separatist enclave in Moldova, was a 'mini USSR' where the fusion and russification of Soviet nationalities created a *Homo Sovieticus*. The Donbas, and to a lesser extent the Crimea, was the only region in Ukraine where in the 1990s up to half of its residents defined themselves as 'Soviet' (not as Ukrainian or Russian).

A local Donbas and Soviet identity existed alongside a territorial attachment to the former boundaries of the Ukrainian SSR. Separatism therefore, has not manifested itself to any great degree in the Donbas. The KPU and pan Eastern Slavic parties do not desire to break the Donbas away from Ukraine and join the region to Russia. Instead, they prefer to include Ukraine within a revived USSR or the Russian-Belarusian union.

51 per cent of the Donbas declared itself Ukrainian in the 1989 census, together with 44 per cent Russian. The 2001 census registered an increase in Ukrainians from 72 to 77 per cent in Ukraine as a whole and in the Donbas a change to 57 percent Ukrainian and 38 percent Russian. Surveys gave a different picture: 32 per cent Ukrainian, 27.5 per cent Russian and 36.5 per cent 'Russian-Ukrainian'. This latter group overlaps with that of the Soviet identity found in the Donbas in the 1990s. 'Russian-Ukrainian' or Soviet identities exhibit 'multiple identities' which over time may decline and become Ukrainian or Russian. The Soviet identity found in the Donbas in the first half of the 1990s is no longer seen, itself a reflection of the decline of the KPU and of the success of moderate nation-building policies.

Although Western Ukrainians continue to stereotype their Eastern Ukrainian brethren as 'separatists', separatism has always been weak in the Donbas. The Donbas demand for a separate status, seen in agitation in April and June 1993, aimed to obtain a greater share of the state budget, to which they allegedly contribute a majority, and maintain it in their region. The impact of the change in the fortunes of the Donbas can be seen in the transfer of Viktor Yanukovych from Donetsk governor to Prime Minister in November

---

112    Konstantin Morozov, *Above and Beyond. From Soviet General to Ukrainian State Builder* (Cambridge, MA: Harvard University, 2000).

2002.[113] The Donbas clan had the second largest faction in the 2002-2006 Parliament and its 'party of power', the Party of Regions, won the 2006 Ukrainian parliamentary elections with 32 percent of the vote.

The two Donbas *oblast* councils held simultaneous opinion polls during the 1994 elections (President Kravchuk had convinced them, like in the Crimea, to refrain from holding referenda which would be legally binding). These polls asked whether the new Ukrainian constitution should include references to Russian as a second state language and Ukraine as a federalised state. Both of these questions obtained high endorsements of 87.1 per cent and 79.7 per cent respectively in Donetsk oblast. The third question asked whether voters agreed with the view that Russian should be utilised as a second state language alongside Ukrainian in their two *oblasts*. The final question asked if voters were in favour of Ukraine's full membership of the CIS Economic Union and CIS Inter-Parliamentary Assembly. These questions obtained 89 per cent and 88.7 per cent endorsements respectively as well. A threatened poll with similar questions to be undertaken in January 2005, following the Sevrdonetsk separatist congress two months earlier, was not followed up on.

The 1994 poll results did not support the secession of the Donbas from Ukraine and had no legal force. But, as a source of pressure upon Kyiv their results were difficult to ignore. Secessionist tendencies in the Donbas are unlikely to appear unless an extreme nationalist comes to power in Kyiv which is unlikely; nevertheless, relations between Kyiv and Donetsk did worsen after Yushchenko, who was wrongly depicted as a 'nationalist', was elected president in January 2005.

The 1994 Donbas poll represented a victory for those political forces which favoured Ukraine's closer integration into the CIS. The polls also took some of the heat off the Crimean leadership which held its own separate polls at the same time. In the words of Yury Boldyrev, then deputy mayor of Donetsk and a leading force behind the polls, 'A new union of Russia, Belarus and Ukraine is inevitable'. Coal miners added further pressure on the new parliament and government with strikes in 1993-1994 which led to Kravchuk

---

113    See Taras Kuzio, 'Ukraine Replaces Prime Minister and Appoints a Possible Successor', *RFERL Poland, Belarus, Ukraine Report*, 26 November 2002,

agreeing to hold earlier presidential elections in July 1994 that he lost to Ku-chma. Pressure to join the CIS Economic Union as a full member grew in E-astern Ukraine, promoted particularly by members of the government who were from the Donbas, such as Prime Minister Yukhym Zvyahilskyy and Deputy Prime Minister Valentyn Landyk. At a Cabinet of Ministers meeting to discuss this question in March 1994, Marchuk warned against such a move because it would damage Ukraine's economic independence. Foreign Minis-ter Anatoly Zlenko also opposed such a move because it would signal that Ukraine was turning its back on the West after just signing an historic treaty with the EU. (The same arguments were used in 2002 against joining the Eurasian Economic Community).

The reaction of nationalist and national-democratic groups was hostile towards the polls conducted in these two *oblasts* and in 2005 in Kharkiv, Do-netsk and Odesa to elevate Russian to an 'official language'. In 1994, the centre-right Congress National Democratic Forces argued that these polls were 'rings in a chain used by the empire and chauvinistic orientated forces in their desire to tear Ukraine apart'. The Ukrainian Language Society Prosvita called the polls a provocation aimed at destroying Ukraine and provoking 'na-tional enmity'.

### Regional Clans

The Donbas elites are one of three large regional elite clans. In the So-viet era they and the 'Dnipropetrovsk mafia' (aka Nikita Khrushchev, Leonid Brezhnev, Volodymyr Shcherbytsky) as they were called, dominated Ukrain-ian SSR elites. In the post-Soviet era a third force has emerged as the Kyiv clan who are grouped in the SDPUo.

In the Kravchuk era the former 'sovereign communists' had not yet es-tablished political parties to represent their business interests. Kravchuk did have strong links to the then 'party of power' in the Donbas, the Liberals. In the 1994-1998 Ukrainian parliament, Kravchuk was a member of the Liberals faction (Social Market Choice) led by former Security Service (SBU) chairman Yevhen Marchuk. But, the Liberals were never able to fully take control of the Donbas, even though half of its members were based there. Social Market Choice did not become a united and influential faction. Marchuk was also not able to take over the Liberals and he and Kravchuk shifted their allegiance to the SDPUo in the 1998 elections. When the SDPUo backed Kuchma – and not Marchuk – in the 1999 presidential elections, Marchuk left to create a Social Democratic Union.

The Liberals and another Donbas 'party of power', the Labour Party, joined forces in the 'Together' (Razom) bloc in the 1998 elections, but they only obtained 1.89 per cent. Another Donbas regional force, the Party of Regional Revival of Ukraine, did even worse with 0.9 per cent. Since then the Liberals, Labor and Regional Revival have declined in influence and the Donbas lost political influence in Kyiv in the late 1990s. The Donbas was therefore ripe for the creation of a new 'party of power' - Regions of Ukraine - for the 2002 elections and 2004 succession to the post-Kuchma era. A new 'party of power', the Party of Regions, was created in March 2001 through the unification of five parties: the Party of Regional Revival of Ukraine, Petro Poroshenko's Party of Ukrainian Solidarity, the Beautiful Ukraine party, the Party of Pensioners, and the Labour Party. When the newly united party created its own parliamentary faction, Regions of Ukraine, Oleksandr Volkov was forced to change the name of his own Regional Revival faction to that of his party's name, Democratic Union.

After Kuchma was elected in July 1994 the 'Dnipropetrovsk mafia' returned to power in Ukraine and dominated key positions in Kyiv. The pinnacle of their power was under Prime Ministers Pavlo Lazarenko (1996-1997) and Pustovoitenko (1997-1999), both of whom were from Dnipropetrovsk (the two previous prime ministers were the Donbasite Zvyahilsky and Marchuk, who had links to the Donbas Liberals). In the ensuing conflict over control of business interests the Donbas lost out to Dnipropetrovsk, complimenting the decline of its political influence in Kyiv. The stakes were high. According to the State Prosecutor, Lazarenko allegedly paid $US 2 million to a criminal group to murder Donetsk regional governor Yevhen Shcherban in October 1996. The Liberal Party joined Yushchenko's Our Ukraine bloc in the 2002 elections but Liberal Party members, such as Volodymyr Shcherban, quickly defected to the pro-Kuchma coalition in parliament. Shcherban fled to the US in spring 2005 fearing imprisonment for abuse of office as governor of Sumy oblast. In autumn 2006 he returned to Ukraine, presumably less concerned at the threat of imprisonment following the return of Yanukovych to government.

Until the appointment of Yanukovych as Prime Minister in November 2002 the Donbas lacked political clout in Kyiv and had few media outlets, despite possessing a powerful economic-financial base. One wing, Systems Capitol Management, is led by Ukraine's wealthiest oligarch Rinat Akhmetov with interests in energy, manufacturing and mining. An alternative group, the Industrial Union of Donbas (ISD), began life as a gas monopoly in the Donbas through which it accumulated large financial reserves that were then invested in local privatisations. Systems Capital Management invested in the Party of Regions and Akhmetov was first elected to parliament in March 2006. The ISD has taken a different route by not investing in Ukrainian political parties. In autumn 2006, senior ISD leaders Valeriy Chalyi and Vitaliy Haydiuk were brought into the presidential secretariat and National Security and Defence Council. The Party of Regions has politically legitimised the economic power of the Akhmetov wing of the Donbas clan that includes the former head of the Tax Administration Mykola Azarov, former Donetsk mayor Volodymyr Rybak and former Prime Minister Zvyahilskyy. Former Donetsk governor and Prime Minister Yanukovych became head of the Party of Regions in April 2003 leading it to victory in the 2006 elections.

In November 2002, 234 deputies who comprised the pro-presidential parliamentary majority from the eight factions that grew out of the For a United Ukraine (ZYU) election bloc and the SDPUo, supported President Kuchma's candidate - Yanukovych - as Ukraine's tenth prime minister. All four opposition groups on the left (Communists, Socialists) and the right (Our Ukraine, Yulia Tymoshenko) voted against Yanukovych, except for two deputies. The other two candidates for Prime Minister were also from Ukraine's largest and wealthiest Donbas clan.

The model that the Party of Regions brought from the Donbas was of a corrupt, 'social regulated market economy' combined with paternal authoritarianism. Stability is seen by the ruling elites as of paramount importance. The opposition is marginalised by the authorities whose refusal to compromise with them denies them any semblance of legitimacy. Their right to protest is condemned as creating instability and threatening the independent state. Such policies combined with the SDPUo's authoritarianism to produce democratic regression in the last two years of the Kuchma era when Viktor Medvedchuk and Yanukovych headed the presidential administration and government respectively. The For a United Ukraine bloc and the SDPUo only elected 54 deputies on the proportional lists in the 2002 elections. Although this meant that pro-presidential forces had lost the elections they were able to change the results by incorporating deputies elected in majoritarian districts and those bribed to defect from the opposition (such as the Liberal Party and trade union leaders in Our Ukraine). This increased their original 54 deputies to the 234 that comprised the parliamentary majority. SDPUo senior MP Kravchuk admitted that deputies were paid on average $5,000 per month to defect to the pro-presidential majority.[114]

In the Donbas all political life remains controlled by the local 'party of power', the Party of Regions, a fact that has not changed since Kuchma's departure from office in 2004. This allowed Kuchma to reduce the local base of support of his Communist opponents in the 1999 and 2002 elections. In the 2002 elections, Yushchenko's Our Ukraine failed to cross the four per cent threshold in only Donetsk and Luhansk *oblasts*, where it obtained 2.69 and 3.62 per cent, and the city of Sevastopol, where it reached 2.99. In comparison, Donetsk was the only *oblast* where the For a United Ukraine bloc came first with 36.83 per cent, a victory that must have been assisted by then governor Yanukovych. In the 2006 elections, Our Ukraine received even fewer votes in Donetsk (1.41) and Luhansk (2.04), perhaps reflecting its overall worse performance compared to the 2002 elections.

Opinion polls during the last two years of Kuchma's rule gave Yushchenko popularity ratings of 20-30 per cent. This was far higher than any pro-Kuchma oligarch but insufficient on its own to win a presidential election. Ukraine's regional and linguistic divisions negatively impacted on raising Yushchenko's popularity in Eastern Ukraine. In the 2004 presidential elections Kuchma drew upon Yanukovych's Donbas experience of electoral fraud. Yanukovych's appointment as Prime Minister, coupled with the failure to adopt constitutional reform in spring 2004, led to Ukraine's worst election fraud that, in turn, served to provoke Ukrainian citizens to protest in what be-

---

114    *Den*, 17 September 2002.

came known as the Orange Revolution.[115] The choice of Yanukovych as the regime's candidate led to widespread negative voting against him.

International observers reported that the worse election fraud took place in Donetsk Oblast in the 2002 and 2004 elections. Although the KPU obtained 29.78 percent in Donetsk oblast in 2002, the other three opposition blocs and parties (Our Ukraine, Yuliya Tymoshenko, Socialists) were blocked by the local authorities from crossing the 4 percent threshold in Donetsk oblast. The two Donbas oblasts (and city of Sevastopol) were the only regions of Ukraine where Our Ukraine failed to cross the 4 percent threshold.

### Conclusions

Ukraine's inherited regionalism is a product of empire and totalitarianism. It has though, not produced sustained support for separatist movements or elite and public backing for federalism. A separatist movement did exist in the Crimea in the first half of the 1990s and its leader, Yuriy Meshkov, was elected Crimea's President in January 1994. After the removal of the Crimean presidential institution, the separatist movement became progressively marginalised. Ukraine's nationality policies permitted the upgrading of the Crimea from oblast to autonomous republic, a decentralised unitary state and unity in diversity policies towards national minorities.

Regionalism is most acute in the Donbas and the Crimea. Although the latter produced secessionist movements in the first half of the 1990s these have become marginalised since 1995-1998. Regionalism has not therefore led to separatism and domestic instability in post-Soviet Ukraine. After the marginalisation of Crimean separatism it is the Donbas, with its far larger population, that may in the long run have the greatest influence over Ukrainian politics. A sign of this growing power was in the 2002-2006 Parliament, where the Donbas had the second largest faction and in the power base of Eastern-Southern Ukraine which voted for Yanukovych in the 2004 elections

---

115    See Anders Aslund and Michael McFaul (eds.), *Revolution in Orange. The Origins of Ukraine's Democratic Breakthrough* (Washington, DC: Carnegie Endowment, 2006), Askold Krushelnycky, *An Orange Revolution. A Personal Journey Through Ukrainian History* (London: Harvill Secker, 2006 and Andrew Wilson, *Ukraine's Orange Revolution* (New Haven, CT: Yale University Press, 2006).

(44 percent) and the Party of Regions in the 2006 elections (32 percent). These twin votes reflected a powerful base of support that, coupled with strategic mistakes made by President Yushchenko, assisted in the return of Yanukovych to government in August 2006 as head of the Anti-Crisis coalition.

Regionalism has also not led to popular support for federalism. A federal structure for Ukraine is only backed by a small section of the marginalised political centre while the left and right remain opposed to federalism. There is also low support for a bicameral parliament which was understood as strengthening the discredited Kuchma presidency and bringing in federalism through surreptitious means. Kuchma supported a bicameral parliament in his 2000 or 2003-2004 constitutional reform proposals. The creation of a new upper house did not receive support from the left or right opposition, as well as from the majority of pro-presidential centrist parties.

# 3   Russia–Ukraine: The Border Issue

This chapter surveys the difficulties in the 1990s of Russia coming to terms with both Ukrainian independence and Kyiv's sovereignty over the Crimea and Sevastopol.[116] It took between 1991-1997 for both executive's to sign a treaty, between 1997-1999 to have both parliaments ratify it, and a further five years until 2003 for the border to be delimited. Three outstanding issues remain. First, Russia continues to refuse to delimit the Azov Sea and Kerch strait, both areas adjoining the Crimea.[117] Second, Russia also continues to refuse to demarcate any part of its border with Ukraine. Finally, Russia continues to apply pressure to extend its 20 year lease on three Sevastopol naval bases beyond 2017 in order for them to become a permanent forward military base. All of these factors have a direct bearing on Ukraine's strategic objective of integration into NATO and the EU.

The chapter is divided into five sections. These survey Ukraine's insecurity vis-à-vis Russia, territorial conflict with Russia (including the Crimea, Sevastopol and island of Tuzla), Ukraine's responses to Russian territorial claims, and Russia's approach to the its border with Ukraine.

### Ukrainian Insecurity

In August and November 1990, Russian-Ukrainian treaties were drawn up between democratic parliamentary blocs and at the level of the then heads of Soviet republics. These were then mainly directed against the Soviet centre and Soviet President Mikhail Gorbachev. Both treaties recognised the inviolability of current borders and renounced territorial claims against one an-

---

116   A survey of Russians territorial claims can be found in 'Sevastopol – misto Rosiyskykh Zazikhan. Analiz terytorialnykh pretenziy z boku Rosiyskoii Federatsii shchodo Krymu', *Narodna Armiya*, 27 February 1997.

117   This issue of Ukraine seeking to divide the Azov Sea into sectors and Russia supporting joint jurisdiction goes back as far as 1997. See ITAR-TASS, 13 May 1997 and *Holos Ukrayiny*, 17 June 1999.

other. Demonstrators in Kyiv even shouted 'Glory be to Yeltsin!' after the signing of the November 1990 treaty. But after Ukraine's declaration of independence in August 1991, Russia claimed that these provisions only applied if Ukraine remained within the USSR (or later the CIS). In August 1992, Russia proposed a Treaty on Friendship, Cooperation and Partnership, but it was rejected the following month by Kyiv. The main Ukrainian objections included the provisions for dual citizenship, the establishment of a common military and foreign policy, inability to join another alliance without the consent of the other party, Russian/CIS bases in Ukraine, joint customs, taxation and trade policies as well as a 'single regional military-strategic space'. The treaty would have created a *de facto* Ukrainian-Russian union or confederation, which was unacceptable to Kyiv.[118] The bulk of the provisions of the treaty were included in the January 1993 CIS Charter, which the Ukrainian parliament has never ratified, and the 1994 CIS Economic Union.

The main threats perceived by Ukraine in the formulation of its security policy have remained primarily linked to Russia. The reality of the Russian threat became abundantly evident in the dispute over the island of Tuzla in fall 2003. Separatism, energy pressure, territorial claims, and nuclear blackmail (until 1996) were threats understood as linked to Russia. In contrast, Ukrainian security policy repeatedly emphasised defence of its territorial integrity and promotion of the status quo in Central-Eastern Europe.

Unlike Russia, which inherited the bulk of the former Soviet foreign and military apparatus and expertise, Ukraine had to formulate a new security policy during which it would define its national interests. Russian-Ukrainian relations have remained central to the formulation of this security policy. Ukraine has sought to place its Russian problem in an international context, increasing bilateral relations with all of the former Soviet republics, searching for allies to jointly deal with Russia, increase Ukraine's integration with Central Europe and Euro-Atlantic structures, build up its state apparatus (especially diplomatic missions and security forces) and make Ukraine's presence known on the international stage. Ukrainian insecurity encouraged Kyiv towards demanding 'security guarantees' for nuclear disarmament as well as proposing the creation of a Zone of Stability and Cooperation in Central Europe. The

---

118    *Vechiriy Kyiv*, 21 September 1992; *The Guardian*, 23 September 1992.

'security guarantees' were to be all-encompassing against nuclear and conventional attack, economic and political pressure as well as in defence of Ukrainian territorial integrity.[119] In 1994, in return for nuclear disarmament, Ukraine only obtained 'security assurances' from the nuclear powers which fell far short of security guarantees.

President Kravchuk's Central European Zone of Security and Cooperation was to stretch from the Baltic to the Black Seas by widening existing structures, such as the Visegrad group.[120] The zone was to have ensured that Ukraine was not completely sucked into a Russian-dominated CIS confederation, balancing the interests of different political constituencies within the country (pro and anti-Russian). Ukraine also proposed that its future lies in an, 'all European system of collective security' while its contribution lies, 'in the construction of a single, peaceful space on the continent'. The proposal was reincarnated in the late 1990s in the GUUAM (Georgia, Ukraine, Uzbekistan, Azerbaijan, Moldova) CIS regional group and in the Viktor Yushchenko era as the GUAM (GUUAM minus Uzbekistan) and the Community of Democratic Choice.[121] Its historical analogies were the Polish inter-war plans for a *Miedzymorze* group of countries lying between Russia and Germany and under Polish influence.

The Basic Principles of Ukrainian Foreign Policy were ratified by parliament in 1993 and have not been updated since then.[122] They do not specify any particular country as a threat to Ukraine but only point to unspecified countries with territorial claims. The Military Doctrine adopted in October 1993 (which was updated in the late Leonid Kuchma era) did state that, 'Ukraine will consider as its potential adversary to be a state whose consistent policy constitutes a military danger to Ukraine'. This could refer only to Russia. The Foreign Policy Basic Principles outlined Ukrainian national interests, foreign policy objectives and the mechanics for pursuing them. While arguing in favour of cooperation with the CIS and bilaterally with Russia it also balances

---

119   See Taras Kuzio, 'Ukrainian Security Policy', *Jane's Intelligence Review*, December 1993.

120   See Foreign Minister Zlenko on Ukrainian security policy in *Holos Ukrayiny*, 10 July 1993.

121   See Taras Kuzio, 'Geopolitical Pluralism in the CIS: The Emergence of GUUAM', *European Security*, vol.9, no. 2 (Summer 2000), pp.81-114.

122   *Holos Ukrayiny*, 24 July and *Nezavisimaya Gazeta*, 30 July 1993.

this by the need to cooperate in other sub-regions and with other institutions. The Basic Principles also object to the location of foreign troops on its territory and their location in other countries, 'without their clearly formulated agreement'. This was a clear reference to Sevastopol and Russian bases in Moldova and Georgia. Ukraine considers itself as an equal successor with the other post Soviet republics to the Soviet legacy.

### Territorial Conflict with Russia

In November 1990 the Russian SFSR and Ukrainian SSR signed a treaty respecting each others territorial integrity 'within the framework of the USSR'.[123] Yet, only three days after Ukraine declared independence on 24 August 1991 President Yeltsin's press secretary Pavel Voshchanov challenged Ukraine's borders.[124] The most commonly heard view in Russia stated that the November 1990 treaty would not be honoured if Ukraine seceded from the USSR. This problem remained in limbo until the 1 December 1991 referendum endorsed Ukraine's independence and the creation of the CIS that month. A day after the CIS was created the November 1990 condition of Russia recognising Ukraine's border was now changed from 'within the USSR' to being conditional on Ukraine remaining within the CIS. Under Kravchuk the dominant view was that the CIS was a temporary structure designed to facilitate a 'civilised divorce'. This view of Ukraine's temporary relationship to the CIS changed during Kuchma's second term in office to a more permanent relationship between Ukraine and the CIS.[125]

Only agreeing to recognise Ukraine's borders if she remained within the CIS was Russia's way of fudging the issue of having to introduce delimited and demarcated borders with Ukraine. There is within Russia a, 'psychological aversion to the idea of a legally fixed Ukrainian-Russian border'.[126] The issue was also complicated by the views of some Eastern Ukrainians who

---

123   *Radyanska Ukrayina*, 21 November 1990.
124   Roman Laba, 'How Yeltsin's Exploitation of Ethnic Nationalism Brought Down an Empire', *Transition*, 12 January 1996, p.10
125   See Taras Kuzio, 'Ukrainian President Revamps CIS, Obtains Russian Backing for 2004 Elections', *RFERL Newsline*, 27 February 2003.
126   UNIAN, 20 August 1996.

also did not wish to see a demarcated border between both states.[127] Russia continues to refuse to consider the demarcation of its border with Ukraine. Throughout the 1990s it was therefore Ukraine which continually pushed the question of legalising the Russian-Ukrainian border through its delimitation and demarcation.[128] Between 1991-1995 the Russian side had not submitted any proposals to legally formulate the Russian-Ukrainian border.[129] Russia preferred to maintain the borders in the same symbolic manner as in the Soviet Union because it considers the borders of the Russian Federation 'un-Russian'. In the USSR the Russian psyche understood 'Russia' and the 'USSR' to be one and the same.

What were Russia's real borders to be then after 1992?[130] Russian Communist leader Gennadiy Zyuganov said, 'We do not need any demarcation lines with a country with which we have fraternal relations'.[131]This particularly applied to Ukraine and Belarus. It is unclear how a 'fraternal country' can be one that has territorial claims against another, such as Russia towards the Crimea, Sevastopol or Tuzla.

The most radical comments came from Russian politicians such as Vladimir Zhirinovsky, head of the extreme right Liberal Democratic Party. In a 1995 book by Zhirinovsky an entire chapter was devoted to the Crimea which not only insisted that the Crimea belonged to 'Russia' but that the Donbas

127   'To divide these two peoples, especially here, in Eastern Ukraine, is simply impossible'. Many on both sides of the border could not accept 'that they are representatives of different peoples' (*Holos Ukrayiny*, 13 March 1993). Lieutenant-Colonel A.N. Borodenko, head of the Donetsk section of the south-Eastern Ukrainian Border region, said, 'it will be necessary to get used to the fact...that the fields of Donetsk region and the Rostov and Kuban steppes are already divided by a real state border and that we live in an oblast that is adjacent to the border' (*Aktsent*, 10 January 1996).

128   Comments by Viacheslav Zhyhulin, head of the Topography directorate of the Armed Forces General Staff (UNIAN, 16 December 1996).

129   *Narodna Armiya*, 13 December 1995 and comments by then Deputy Foreign Minister Kostyantin Hryshchenko in *Dzerkalo tyzhnya*, 23 August 1996. By early 1997 Ukraine was at the end of its tether and was contemplating unilateral demarcation (Holos *Ukrayiny*, 4 March 1997). See *Problems of the Borders of Ukraine, Occasional Paper 39* (Kyiv: Ukrainian Center for Peace, Conversion, Conflict Resolution Studies, 1997).

130   See Alexander Goncharenko, *Ukrainian-Russian Relations. An Unequal Partnership.* Whitehall Paper 32 (London: Royal United Services Institute, 1995).

131   *Sovetskaya Rossiya*, 21 February 1997.

and Kyiv also was 'Russian'. Zhirinovsky has always had close relations with the Russian authorities and worked as a close ally of President Vladimr Putin in the Russian State Duma elected in December 2003 where he had the third largest faction. For Russians the idea that the Crimea now lay in 'foreign territory' was difficult to accept.[132] To Zhirinovsky and most Russians their claim towards the Crimea rested on the right to ownership through conquest in the 1780s and in the shedding of blood in defence of it in the mid nineteenth century Crimean war and during World War II. To accept such arguments means to accept that the Crimea had no Ukrainian or Tatar history prior to the 1780s or since 1954.

Other Russians were far more condescending. Konstantin Zatulin, chairman of the State Duma Committee on CIS Affairs, criticised Ukraine's infatuation with the recognition of its borders 'that never existed in history'. These borders now belonged to 'a state that never existed in history'.[133] Again, this assumes that Kyivan Rus was not a proto-Ukrainian state but actually 'Kievan Russia'. If Kyiv Rus was a proto-Ukrainian state, as Ukrainian national historiography asserts, the Crimea was part of 'Ukraine' long before it was annexed by the Tsarist empire.[134] What of Greek settlements in the Crimea prior to Slavs in Kyiv Rus?

Other Russians also made radical demands. Moscow Mayor Yuriy Luzhkov wrote to Yeltsin demanding that the Russian executive support claims made by the Russian parliament over Sevastopol.[135] In Luzhkov's view, the city had never been transferred to Ukraine in 1954 alongside the Crimea and had continued to have all-union jurisdiction. Sevastopol was, 'Russian land. It has always been and always will be Russian land', Luzhkov wrote.[136] He continued, 'Sevastopol was never transferred to Ukraine by any

---

132    Vladimir Zhirinovsky, *Poslednii vagon na sever* (Moscow, 1995), pp.56, 58.
133    *Nezavisimaya Gazeta*, 1-7 April 1995.
134    See Taras Kuzio, 'Nation-State Building and the Re-Writing of History in Ukraine: The Legacy of Kyiv Rus', *Nationalities Papers*, vol.33, no.1 (March 2005), pp.30-58.
135    'Moscow mayor Luzhkov says Ukraine city is Russia's', Reuters, 31 October 1996. See also Luzhkov's interviews in *Obshchaya Gazeta*, 19-25 February 1998 and *Krymskaya Pravda*, 3 August 1999.
136    *Rossiyskaya Gazeta*, 22 October 1996. See the reply by Odesa Mayor Eduard Gurfits in *Izvestiya*, 6 November 1996 reprinted in *Flot Ukrayiny*, 16 November 1996. Other open letters were from the Hetman of the Ukrainian Cossacks in Sevastopol and the Ukrainian navy (*Molod Ukrayiny*, 3 December 1996), and Bohdan

document, even in Khrushchev's time, when he, in a drunken state, transferred Crimea'.[137] Luzhkov was third on the list of Unified Russia in the 2003 elections, Putin's 'party of power'. Luzhkov was also invited to the Severdonetsk separatist congress on 28 November 2004 where he presented Putin's support for Viktor Yanukovych's presidential candidacy.

The Moscow city council built apartments, kindergartens and schools for Black Sea Fleet officers.[138] Such steps served to embolden the Black Sea Fleet to not negotiate compromises with Ukraine. Black Sea Fleet commander Admiral Viktor Kravchenko adamantly stated 'we are staying'.[139] This was because the Russian Black Sea Fleet was not, in his view, in foreign territory but 'at home'.[140] This resembled Moscow Mayor Luzhkov's definition of Sevastopol as 'Moscow's 11th prefecture'.[141] Luzhkov also made totally false allegations of mass Ukrainianisation of Russians in the Crimea. 'What is happening is the forcible Ukrainianisation of the Russian population, but we are pretending not to notice anything', Luzhkov claimed. [142] The plates of cities and villages had been allegedly changed into Ukrainian while Russian language television and radio programmes were being curtailed.[143]

The reality was very different. In 1995, 85 per cent of all television and 88 per cent of all radio broadcasts in the Crimea were in Russian. Of the remainder only 1.7 and 3 per cent were in Ukrainian on television and radio respectively.[144] The situation in the printed media was as bad. Of 363 publica-

---

Yaroshynsky, head of the Republican Party (*Molod Ukrayiny*, 15 November 1996). The Ukrainian Foreign Ministry also issued a statement (*Uriadovyi Kurier*, 14 November 1996). The parliamentary committees on Defence and State Security and Foreign Policy and CIS Ties held a joint meeting and issued a combined statement (*Tserkva I Zhyttia*, 18-24 November 1996). A joint statement by the Union of Ukrainian Officers, Congress of Ukrainian Intelligentsia and Ukrainian Cossacks was published in *Vechirnyi Kyiv*, 13 November 1996.

137    Reuters, 17 January 1997.
138    120 apartments were built as early as 1997 for Black Sea Fleet officers. They were also provided with access to Moscow television via satellite (*Krymskaya Pravda*, 24 February 1998).
139    *Trud*, 30 April 1997.
140    *Rossiyskaya Gazeta*, 5 March 1997.
141    Interfax, 30 July 1996.
142    *Obshchaya Gazeta*, 19-25 February 1998.
143    *Krymskaya Pravda*, 3 August 1999.
144    *Krymska Svitlytsia*, 24 February 1996.

tions in the Crimea, 2 were in Ukrainian, 16 in Tatar, Bulgarian or Greek and 345 are in Russian.[145]

According to Luzhkov, 85 per cent (on another occasion he said 78 per cent[146]) of the Crimean population are Russians. In reality Russians accounted for 65 per cent in 1989 and now only make up 58 per cent of Ukraine's population, according to the 2001 census. Luzhkov, like most Russians, confused Russian-speakers ('compatriots') for ethnic Russians which meant his figures are inflated by including Ukrainians and other russified non-Russians. As Luzhkov said: 'There must be no forced Ukrainisation of Russian people torn apart from their Motherland. Russian people want to speak their own language and teach their children Russian history and Russian literature.'[147]

At the time Luzhkov made these unsubstantiated remarks there were 586 Russian-language schools in the Crimea. The Ukrainian and Tatar minorities had two Ukrainian-language and 15 Tatar language schools respectively.[148] Complaints about forced Ukrainianisation were not the only area Luzhkov commented upon. He also demanded that Russians should be constitutionally recognised as a second titular nation and the Russian language upgraded to a second state language.[149] Luzhkov also demanded dual citizenship for Crimeans.[150]

Did Luzhkov act independently or was he acting covertly for the Russian executive and government which continued to officially distance itself from the State Duma, Federation Council and Mayor Luzhkov. After all, Luzhkov and then Foreign Minister Yevgenny Primakov created a joint political bloc for the 1999 State Duma elections (Fatherland-All Russia bloc). The Ukrainian Foreign Ministry considered banning Luzhkov from visiting Ukraine

---

145 *Krymskaya Pravda*, 31 March 1999. NTV (27 January 1999) gave 392 publications in the Crimea. Of these 338 were published in the Russian language.
146 *Krymskaya Pravda*, 3 August 1999.
147 Interfax, 21 February 1998.
148 In 1995 there were 300 schools in the Crimea of which one used Ukrainian and two used the Tatar language (*Krymska Svitlytsia*, 24 February 1996). By 1998 there were 582 schools of which 572 were Russian, 1 was Greek, 4 Ukrainian and 6 Tatar language (NTV, 27 January 1999).
149 Interfax, 19 March 1999.
150 *Krymskaya Pravda*, 3 August 1999.

but then refrained from taking this step (it actually banned Zatulin). Speaking about Luzhkov the Foreign Ministry stated:

> His statements do not correspond to the spirit and letter of the treaty on friendship, cooperation a partnership between Ukraine and Russia, are confrontational and unfriendly toward Ukraine, and are detrimental to the development of Ukrainian-Russian relations. Certain statements of Yuriy Luzhkov can be regarded as interference into internal affairs of Ukraine and a sign of a lack of respect toward its sovereignty.[151]

The Russian executive refused to openly back territorial claims on the Crimea and Sevastopol made by its parliament.[152] At the same time, these radical claims were useful to the executive to maintain pressure on Ukraine to reach compromises in its favour over the Black Sea Fleet. As one large analysis of Russian policy towards Sevastopol concluded, the idea that the Russian executive was opposed to its parliament applying claims towards the Crimea and Sevastopol 'is too weak to be taken seriously'.[153] The Russian executive regularly distanced itself from State Duma resolutions. At the same time, Security Council secretary Nikolai Lebed wrote an article for the Crimean media entitled 'Sevastopol is a Russian City'.[154] The Federation Council, which brought together regional governors appointed by Boris Yeltsin and Putin, also supported the State Duma's resolutions. Federation Council chairman Yegor Stroyev said, 'Sevastopol is a town of Russian glory. So they

---

151  *Dzerkalo tyzhnya*, 31 August 1998. See the critical response by Petr Fechep, 'Krymskiye "Bortsyi s Ukrainskym Natsional-Separatyzmom', *Flot Ukrayiny*, 10 January 1998.

152  Interfax, 17 December 1996.

153  'Sevastopol - misto Rosiyskykh zazikhan. Analiz terytorialnykh pretenziy z boku Rosiyskoii Federatsii shchodo Krymu', *Narodna Armiya*, 27 February 1997.

154  *Flag Rodiny*, 5 October and *Krymskaya Pravda*, 10 October 1996. As *Den* (24 January 1997) pointed out, Russia does not have any territorial pretensions, but, at the same time, it wants to lease the entire city'. For other discussions see Valeriy Samovalov and Kononenko of the National Security and Defence Council in *Uriadovyi Kurier*, 4 January and *Krymska Svitlytsia*, 16 May 1997, 'Konflikt v Krymu', *Flot Ukrayiny*, 2 August 1997, and Vitaliy Palamarchuk, 'Sevastopol: Vektory, Stanu I Rozvytku', *Narodna Armiya*, 28 May 1997. See also Nikolai Savchenko, *Anatomiya Neobiavlennoy Voynyi* (Kyiv: Ukrainian Perspectives, 1997).

voted correctly'.[155] The Russian executive had to walk a tightrope. If it openly backed its parliament the Ukrainian side threatened to demand the immediate withdrawal of the Black Sea Fleet. Such a step was outlined in a 22 October 1996 Ukrainian parliamentary appeal .[156] At the same time, Luzhkov and the Russian parliament applied pressure on Ukraine that the Russian executive found useful in its strategy of obtaining its strategic priorities in the Crimea.

### Territorial Claims

The vote in December 1996 by 110:14 in the Russian Federation Council, the upper house of the Russian Parliament, to issue a statement and resolution declaring the city of Sevastopol 'part of Russian territory' marked a dangerous stage in the six-year row with Ukraine over Crimean territory. The resolution arrogantly condemned, 'Ukraine's refusal to recognise Sevastopol's Russian status'[157] This followed a vote by 334:1 in October 1996 by the State Duma to halt the division of the Black Sea Fleet and obtain exclusive Russian basing rights in Sevastopol. A vote the following day by 282:0 sent an appeal to the Ukrainian Parliament declaring Sevastopol to be exclusively Russian territory. The Federation Council resolution mandated the creation of a Russian commission involving the presidency, the Cabinet of Ministers, the Federation Council and the state Duma to draft a law on Sevastopol's status.

Four dangerous trends were evident from the Federation Council vote by a wide margin claiming Sevastopol as 'Russian territory'. First, claims on Ukrainian territory by the Russian Parliament were nothing new. In May and December 1992 the Russian Parliament had already questioned the 'legality' of the 1954 transfer of both the Crimea and Sevastopol; in July 1993 it went further and actually declared Russian jurisdiction over the city of Sevastopol. Neither of these three resolutions were denounced by the Russian State Duma's elected in December 1993 or December 1995. The new resolutions adopted in 1996 laying claim to Ukrainian territory therefore built upon a legacy of previous claims which soured relations with Ukraine and re-confirmed Kyiv's mistrust towards its Russian neighbour.

---

155   *Argumenty I Fakty*, January 1997.
156   *Holos Ukrayiny*, 22 October 1996.
157   Reuters, 5 December 1996.

Second, the Russian executive and Western governments condemned these parliamentary resolutions as having no juridical significance. In other words, they had no legal force because the Russian parliament had little effective power according to the 1993 constitution which transformed Russia into a super presidential regime. Nevertheless, by 1996 there was a convergence of the views of the nationalist/communist wing of Russian politics with that of the centre-right in power ('pragmatic nationalists' or statists). This has continued under Putin since 2000 with United Russia allied to *Rodina* (Motherland) and the Liberal Democratic Party.

In the State Duma and the Federation Council in the 1990s the then 'party of power' Our Home Russia faction of the political party led by then Prime Minister Viktor Chernomyrdin, also usually voted with the nationalist/communist wing to provide constitutional majorities in favour of hard-line policies on the 'Near Abroad'. These included support for the Trans-Dniestr separatist enclave of Moldova, union with Belarusian President Alyaksandr Lukashenka, Abkhazian separatism and territorial claims upon Sevastopol. Putin's alliance with the extreme right built on an earlier alliance that had been cultivated under Yeltsin in the 1990s. Therefore, there was an increasingly dangerous convergence of support for hard-line policies vis-à-vis Ukraine, and other regions of the 'Near Abroad', between the legislature and the executive. The Federation Council was largely staffed by President Borys Yeltsin's allies. Prime Minister Chernomyrdin, not for the first time, demanded in December 1996 that Ukraine recognise the 'illegality' of its sovereignty over Sevastopol, using nationalist language and rhetoric usually reserved for the extremist wing of Russian politics. In addition, both Yeltsin and Chernomyrdin referred to parliamentary initiatives to back up their case of demanding exclusive long-term, Russian basing rights in Sevastopol. Russian Public Television, in which the state still had a majority stockholding, began including Sevastopol in October 1996 within its daily weather reports of the 'Russian Federation'.

Third, the step towards officially recognition that a territorial dispute existed between Ukraine and Russia over the city of Sevastopol, backed by the legislature and executive, did not prove to be the end of the matter. The city of Sevastopol was only the thin edge of a territorial wedge towards the Crimea as a whole. In the second half of the 1990s and since 2000 the rise of pragmatic Russian nationalism, first under Foreign Minister Yevgenny Prima-kov and later under President Putin has led to a convergence with the imperi-alism espoused by 'red-brown' nationalism. The 'red-brown' alliance that President Yeltsin had been in conflict with in 1993 in the Russian parliament became allied to Putin's Unified Russia in the State Duma. The democratic opposition has been marginalised during Putin's second term.

Russia's parliamentary elections are held according to a 50:50 formula whereby half of the seats are elected according to proportional voting for party lists and the remaining half are elected in first past the post single man-date districts. Of the 23 parties and blocs registered for the 2003 elections, only four managed to cross the five percent threshold in the proportional half of elections. Three of these four are pro-Putin, meaning the opposition will be reduced to only an enfeebled Communist Party. Putin's 'party of power', Uni-fied Russia, won 37 per cent of the vote. Putin's Unified Russia is Russia's first serious 'party of power' uniting Russia's elites after two failed preceding attempts to create similar 'parties of power' in the 1990s – Russia's Choice (1992-1995) and Our Home is Russia (1995-1999). Unified Russia was cre-ated in 2001 through the merger of the pro-Putin Unity party and Moscow Mayor Yurii Luzhkov's and former Foreign Minister Yevgenny Primakov's Fa-therland-All Russia. In 1999-2000 Fatherland-All Russia was Primakov's ve-hicle for the March 2000 presidential elections. But, it was faced with a choice of merger or disbandment by Putin who wanted to remove electoral competi-tion within the Russian elites.

Two pro-Putin parties and blocs also crossed the threshold. Zhiri-novsky's Liberal Democratic Party obtained a similar showing to the Commu-nists at 12 percent. The Liberal Democratic Party was registered in the USSR in 1990 as a satellite party of the Communist Party for then Soviet President Mikhail Gorbachev to prove that the USSR was becoming a 'multi-party de-mocracy'. In Russia during the 1990s it has always backed the authorities, acting as a 'sponge' to soak up critical nationalist votes. The Liberal Democ-ratic Party plays a similar role to the 'loyal nationalist' Serbian Radical Party which was allied to Slobodan Milosevic's Socialists. A second pro-Putin bloc is *Rodina* which combines Communist and nationalists in what in Russia has been termed a 'red-brown' alliance. Unified Russia, the Liberal Democratic Party and *Rodina* together command 68 per cent of the vote in the Duma.

This provided Putin with the ability to adopt whatever legislation he proposed without facing any opposition. Putin was re-elected for a second term in March 2004 but his successor in 2008 will undoubtedly be as nationalist and imperialist. Russia's two main democratic parties – the centre-left Yabloko and the liberal Union of Right Forces (SPS) failed to cross the threshold, even though they had both in recent years attempted to mellow their opposition to Putin. This was therefore the first Russian parliament since Soviet republican elections in March 1990 where there were no pro-reform parties represented in the Russian parliament.

### Tuzla

The dispute over the island of Tuzla in the Kerch Strait, the entrance to the Azov Sea, should not have theoretically happened. The Ukrainian-Russian 'strategic partnership', which was devoid of real content during President Kuchma's first term in office and under President Yeltsin, was beginning to be finally filled with some substance during Kuchma's second term and under Putin. As the Kuchmagate crisis unfolded after November 2000 and the reformist government of Prime Minister Viktor Yushchenko was removed in April 2001, Ukraine's multi-vector foreign policy reoriented toward Russia and the CIS. For Moscow, the crowning achievements of this reorientation came in 2002 which was designated 'The Year of Russia in Ukraine' and in January 2003 Kuchma became the first non-Russian CIS leader to be elected head of the CIS Council of Heads of State. On 17 September, Ukraine, Russia, Kazakhstan, and Belarus signed the CIS Single Economic Space (YES). Ukraine's reorientation toward Russia and the CIS seemed set to continue. Kuchma desperately needed Putin's support in the 2004 presidential elections in order to ensure a suitable successor is elected.

The Tuzla conflict damaged these trends favourable to Russia's geopolitical environment in the CIS. Pro-Kuchma Crimean Prime Minister Serhiy Kunitsyn lamented that, 'I don't know whose idea it was to build the dam, but I do know that it is ruining everything achieved during the Year of Russia in Ukraine'. As the crisis escalated, calls from within Ukraine's elites to speed up steps to join NATO, an objective first outlined in a presidential decree in July 2002, became more frequent. In a secret presidential decree dated 21 October 2003, Kuchma outlined steps to be taken to defend Ukraine's territorial integrity. Those steps included Ukraine quitting the YES if Russia attempts to encroach on its territory. Other non-military steps included appealing to the declared nuclear powers, which provided 'security assurances' in return for Ukraine's nuclear disarmament in 1994-96, the UN Security Council, NATO, and the OSCE. A further step outlined in the decree was for the Foreign Ministry to unilaterally declare the Kerch Strait and the Azov Sea internal Ukrainian waters. Different approaches to the status of these waters lie at the heart of the conflict. Ukraine has always been a territorial-status-quo power and defends its territorial integrity based on everything it inherited from Soviet Ukraine.

Ukrainian officials reminded their Russian colleagues that copies of Soviet documents showing Ukraine's right to Tuzla existed in both Kyiv and Moscow. The Ukrainian side was infuriated by Russia's claims that it does not possess and is unaware of any such documents. Russia has also always insisted that there are no legal documents proving that the port of Sevastopol was transferred together with the Crimea to Soviet Ukraine in 1954. Rusian Foreign Minister Igor Ivanov compared the conflict to that between the UK and Spain over Gibraltar.

Kuchma was criticised in Ukraine in spring 2003 for succumbing to Russian pressure on the Azov Sea. By agreeing that the Azov Sea is joint internal waters, he might have sent the wrong signal to Russia over the entrance to the Azov Sea. Ukraine's control of Tuzla and the Kerch Strait gives it the ability to control the entrance to the Azov, from which it obtains $150 million per year in fees from ships. This then explains the incomprehension of both sides at the speed with which the conflict escalated. During Kuchma's second term, Putin and he had regularly met for 'no neck-tie summits'. Nevertheless, Kuchma and Putin failed to contact each other until after Kuchma had left for Latin America on 20 October 2003. Kuchma returned from what was to be a 10-day tour after two days to oversee the handling of the Tuzla dispute and Prime Minister Viktor Yanukovych similarly cancelled a visit to the Baltic states. Kuchma visited Tuzla on 23 October to check its defences and that day construction of the dam was halted just 100 meters from the island.

The Russian leadership miscalculated in two respects. First, Ukraine's reorientation eastward did not mean Kuchma or his oligarch allies entertained the idea of vassal status. Similar miscalculations had thwarted attempts to integrate Russia and Belarus. Second, Russia has continually underestimated Ukraine's readiness to defend its territorial integrity, first by diplomatic and second by military means. A border-guard unit was hastily deployed on Tuzla Island immediately after the construction of the dam began. They were backed up by Interior Ministry special forces (*spetsnaz*) with naval units on standby. An air-defense exercise was also held on the Kerch Strait. Support for Ukraine's territorial integrity has always existed across the entire political spectrum from left to right. Communist Party leader Petro Symonenko even accused Kuchma of being a 'traitor' for leaving Ukraine during the Tuzla crisis. The standoff reflected the degree to which any talk of a Russian-Ukrainian 'strategic partnership' would remain devoid of real content until both sides overcame barriers put up by conflicts arising from their national identities.

### Ukrainian Responses

Ukraine had five policy options which were utilised in response to these concerted territorial claims. First, the territorial claims were raised at the United Nations and within the OSCE. This step was undertaken in summer 1993 after the then Russian Parliament laid claim to Sevastopol. The United Nations backed Ukraine's territorial integrity in 1993 and then again in 1996 by referring to the November 1990 Ukrainian-Russian treaty which recognised current borders (Russia argued that this became legally invalid after the USSR disintegrated).

Second, Ukraine used its NATO card. Three high ranking Ukrainian officials (Foreign Minister, Deputy Foreign Minister and the Secretary of the National Security and Defence Council) stated that Ukraine would seek future NATO membership, a step partly conditioned upon relations with Russia. If the Yeltsin leadership backed up the territorial claims advanced by both houses of the Russian Parliament, then Ukraine threatened to drop its declared non-bloc status and neutrality in favour of opting earlier for NATO membership (Ukraine first declared its interest in NATO membership only in May 2001 that became officially outlined in a July 2002 decree[158]).

Third, Ukraine could have sought the support of the four declared nuclear powers in its territorial dispute with Russia. These five declared nuclear powers provided security assurances to Ukraine in December 1994, a demand that Ukraine had raised as a *quid pro quo* for its ratification of the Nuclear Non-Proliferation Treaty three months earlier. These security assurances (which the Ukrainian leadership and media always referred to wrongly as 'security guarantees') uphold Ukraine's territorial integrity and sovereignty. Four of the declared nuclear powers (the UK, USA, France and China) have continually upheld Ukraine's position on the Crimea and Sevastopol.

Fourth, Ukraine could have demanded that the two issues of the Black Sea Fleet and recognition of Ukraine's borders be un-coupled. Russia had refused to sign an inter-state treaty recognising Ukraine's borders in international law until the Black Sea Fleet question was resolved. This was a question Moscow would only have regarded as resolved if it had been granted long-term, exclusive basing rights in Sevastopol. This was finally agreed in May 1997 for a twenty year lease.

Finally, Ukrainian nationalist parties and parliamentary factions obtained additional support from centrist and even some left-wing members of parliament who felt outraged by Russia's actions. Some members of the Communist and Socialist parliamentary factions, which chaired respectively the two committee's on Defence and Security and Foreign Affairs and CIS Ties, felt betrayed by their left-wing colleagues within the Russian parliament over the Sevastopol question. This cross-party support strengthened Ukraine's hand in its territorial disputes with Russia.

In November 1996 the Ukrainian parliament issued a statement which outlined a number of 'guidelines' for Ukrainian negotiators which were insisted upon by the Ukrainian parliament. The statement also insisted that members of the Ukrainian legislature be henceforth included in negotiating teams on the Black Sea Fleet. These 'guidelines' laid claim to the entire infra

---

158   See Taras Kuzio, 'Ukraine decides to join NATO at last', *Kyiv Post*, 13 June 2002; 'Ukraine Hopes for NATO Membership in the Post-Kuchma Era', *RFERL Newsline*, 11 June 2002; 'Ukraine and Georgia in Riga and Beyond', *Kyiv Post*, 22 December 2006.

structure of the Black Sea Fleet, thereby refusing to divide it 50:50. They refused to allow Russia to infringe the CFE Treaty by stationing higher than the permitted numbers of its troops in the Crimea. It also insisted on Russian bases being regulated by a lease (which would amount to Russia's *de jure* recognition of Ukrainian sovereignty over Sevastopol) as well as arguing that, 'the location of Ukrainian military bases is non-negotiable'. The 'guidelines' also called upon the Foreign Ministry to deny entry to Russian citizens who held territorial claims against Ukraine (this ruling was used against Zatulin in the 1990s and under President Yushchenko).

Both national democrats and Communist Party member Borys Oliynyk, then Chairman of the parliamentary committee on Foreign Affairs and CIS Ties, warned before the Federation Council vote that they could introduce two additional pieces of legislation in the Ukrainian parliament. First, they would call for the removal of the clause in the chapter on Temporary Provisions in the Ukrainian Constitution which allows for the 'temporary' stationing of foreign bases on Ukrainian territory. Second, they would call for a law to be adopted outlying the complete withdrawal of Russian military forces from Ukrainian territory by the year 2,000.

### Russia Recognises Ukraine's Border

In May 1997 Yeltsin finally visited Ukraine after his visit had been postponed on seven occasions. Kuchma had staked his reputation in the 1994 elections on doing what he claimed the incumbent, Kravchuk, had been unable to do; namely, 'normalise' relations with Ukraine. No 'normalisation' of relations could though, take place until Russia recognised Ukraine's border and this did not take place until three years after Kuchma was elected. One factor which encouraged Yeltsin to visit Kyiv in 1997 was the impending NATO Madrid summit two months later. Russia, however unrealistic, was fearful that Ukraine would move into a far closer relationship with NATO up to, and possibly including membership. Between 1994-1997 Ukraine had deliberately flirted with NATO by being the most active CIS member of NATO's Partnership for Peace Programme (PfP) as a way of pressurising Russia to 'normalise' relations. This tactic worked. Ukraine signed a Charter on Distinctive Partnership with NATO at the July 1997 Madrid summit.[159] Ukraine was invited by NATO to Intensified Dialogue on Membership Issues in May 2005 but its upgrading to a Membership Action Plan will be a drawn out process following the return of Yanukovych to government in summer 2006.

The 1997 treaty recognised that Sevastopol was *de jure* 'part of Ukraine's territory'. Nevertheless, as Russian Deputy Prime Minister Valeriy Serov said at the same time, this did not mean that Russia stopped recognising Sevastopol as no longer a 'Russian town'.[160] One way of Russia reinforcing this would be to ensure that the Russian Black Sea Fleet stayed based in Sevastopol after the twenty year lease expired in 2017. After the treaty was signed in Kyiv it took until December 1998 for the Russian State Duma to ratify it and then two months more for the Federation Council to follow suit (Ukraine ratified it earlier in March 1998). Russia's parliamentary ratification was conditioned on the Crimea's adoption of a constitution which took place in October 1998 that came into force after its ratification by the Ukrainian parliament in December. As then Ukrainian parliament chairman, Peasant Party member Oleksandr Tkachenko, said, these steps were significant as they were the first time Ukraine had been recognised by Russia since the 1654 Russian-Ukrainian Treaty of Pereiaslav.[161]

After the 1997 treaty was signed Russia continued to express no interest in the delimitation, let alone demarcation, of the border.[162] Mayor Luzhkov accepted that the border treaty was signed but ruled out any 'official borders between our states'.[163] Then Prime Minister (since May 2001 Ambassador to Ukraine) Chernomyrdin agreed, 'we are not advocates of putting poles on the border – there will be no fence'.[164] Russian Foreign Minister Ivanov ruled out not only demarcation but also the introduction of visas.[165] Already in 1997 Russia made plain its opposition to any delimitation and division of the Azov

---

159    See Taras Kuzio, 'NATO Membership for Ukraine Not Likely Before 2012', *RFERL Newsline*, 21 February 2003.
160    NTV, 2 June 1997.
161    *Holos Ukrayiny*, 6 May 1999.
162    *Moskovskiy Komsomolets*, 3 June 1997.
163    *Trud*, 13 February 1997.
164    ITAR-TASS, 28 May 1997.
165    ITAR-TASS, 23 October 2000.

Sea and Kerch Straits (see later).[166] The Russian side put forward its case that the Azov Sea-Kerch Strait be maintained as a 'single economic and natural complex jointly used in the interests of Russia and Ukraine'.[167] Russia ruled out the Azov Sea being divided and therefore opened up 'to unrestricted access by third countries'.[168]

Some Russian commentators continued to be concerned that recognising Ukraine's borders would let Ukraine join NATO, as countries with border disputes were not allowed into this international organisation. This was a reason given by Ukrainian commentators why Russia unexpectedly launched a claim on Tuzla.[169] Luzhkov began to claim that although Sevastopol was *de jure* part of Ukraine he would ensure Russia's indefinite presence there. Luzhkov began to finance the building of apartments for officers of the Black Sea Fleet, something he has never done for the Baltic or Far Eastern fleets. The delimitation of the border (except for the Azov Sea and Kerch Straits) was completed between 1999-2003.[170]

### Border Demarcation with Ukraine

When Ukraine and Russia signed a treaty in Kyiv, and after both houses of the Russian parliament ratified it, the border question continued to bedevil both countries. By 2003 Russia had agreed to delimit on maps the former Soviet internal administrative frontier between itself and Ukraine, but it has continued its opposition to land border demarcation. Ukraine and Russia continue to hold opposing views as to how the border should be defined. The Ukrainian side believes that the border should be the same as any other international border where delimitation on maps is followed by physical demarcation by natural objects or signs arranged at regular intervals. Such an arrangement would be very different to that which continues to exist on

---

166    *Vechirnyi Kyiv*, 16 May; *Ukrayina moloda;* 10 June, *Rossiyskaya Gazeta*, 21 June and *Den*, 2 September 1997
167    Comments by Sergei Shishkarev, deputy head of the Duma Cmmittee on International Affairs (ITAR-TASS, 16 November 2000).
168    *Rossiyskaya Gazeta*, 23 November 2000.
169    K. Zatulin and Andranik Migranyan in *Sodruzhestvo NG*, no.1 (December 1997).
170    ITAR-TASS, 27 February 1998.

Ukraine's Western border where Ukraine inherited Soviet-style watch towers and barbed wire. Russia, in contrast, continues to insist that borders within the CIS should be divided into 'internal' and 'external' borders. CIS 'internal' frontiers are, in effect, the same as those that existed in the USSR, except that they may be now delimited on maps for greater clarity. 'External' frontiers represent former Soviet external borders.

These opposing views on borders reflect different understandings of nation building and identity within Russia and Ukraine. Since its Declaration of Sovereignty in July 1990, state and nation-building in Ukraine has always been understood to understand borders – wherever they might be – as integral to a country's sovereignty and territorial integrity. Ukraine has therefore not signed the majority of border agreements adopted by CIS institutions. Russia has always remained confused as to whether it is building a nation-state, which would lead to Moscow having similar views on borders to Ukraine. Or Russia understands the CIS to be the successor to the USSR (i.e. 'USSR-light'), or more simply as an extension of 'Russia'. These views mean that the CIS, like the USSR, would have no need for demarcated borders between 'fraternal' republics. Such a view is accepted by Russophile states in the CIS, such as Belarus and Kazakhstan and follows from Russia's view of the CIS as a 'Near Abroad' with limited sovereignty, greater than in the USSR but still less than in the 'Far Abroad'. Within the 'Near Abroad', Russia views Ukraine and Belarus as having the least sovereignty, the graphic example of which is Russia's gross intervention in the 2004 Ukrainian presidential elections.[171]

The Ukrainian position became confused itself in July 2002 when Oleksandr Kupchyshyn, Director of the Treaty and Legal department of the Ukrainian Foreign Ministry, stated that demarcation would not be necessary because this would violate the, 'historic traditions of living together and coexistence of our countries and nations'. This sounded suspiciously similar to the position of the Russian Foreign Ministry which rejected demarcation because the Russian-Ukrainian border, 'should be the one of friendship, accord and communication, uniting rather than separating our two nations'. The Ukrainian

---

171    See Taras Kuzio, 'Russian Policy to Ukraine During Elections', *Demokratizatsiya*, vol.13, no.4 (Fall 2005), pp.491-517.

media reported that Kupchyshyn was officially reprimanded for his statement. Support for demarcation into a fully fledged international border with Russia was again re-stated as the official view by then Foreign Minister Zlenko and State Secretary Yuriy Serheyev. Serheyev, the president's representative in the Foreign Ministry, confirmed that Ukraine's approach to borders remained delimitation through protocols and separate agreements on maps, followed by demarcation with special signs or boundary posts, and finally, agreeing to a border regime. Explaining this position to Russia, Serheyev said that it, 'coincides with our constitution', conforms to the 'national will' and, 'fully corresponds to the standards of international law'.

In an opinion poll among foreign policy elites by the Centre for Peace, Conversion and Foreign Policy of Ukraine (CPCFPU), a Kyiv-based Think Tank with close links to the Ukrainian Foreign Ministry, 87.5 per cent supported a demarcated border with Russia and 53.1 per cent believed the lack of demarcation prevented Ukraine from integration into Europe. 59.4 per cent of those polled believed it forced Ukraine's Western neighbours to introduce visas on Ukrainians while 56.3 per cent thought it contributed to illegal migration, organised crime and contraband.

Ukraine placed Border Troops on its 2,292 km. Russian border in January 1993 and its status still continues to differ from that on Ukraine's Western (former Soviet) borders. Although delimitation on land was completed by 2003, Russia's position on the Azov Sea, the Kerch Strait and the Black Sea are again influenced by national identity considerations. Non-Russian former Soviet republics, such as Ukraine, Azerbaijan, Turkmenistan and Kazakhstan, view the Azov Sea, Kerch Strait and Caspian Sea as international waterways. These should be delimited into country sectors with exclusive economic zones. Russia (backed by Iran in the Caspian) disagrees, because the Soviet legacy continues to influence its attitude that they should remain 'internal seas' (as in the USSR).

Besides national identity, the CPCFPU think tank pointed to three strategic motives for Russia's rejection of border demarcation. First, the continuation of Soviet internal administrative frontiers in the form of 'internal' CIS borders would allow Russia to continue to exert influence and apply pressure on other CIS states. Delimitation of the Kerch peninsula and Azov Sea is opposed by Russia because they are directly linked to the Crimea question. The same is true of Tuzla which Russia believes could be jointly divided. Second, a non-demarcated border would continue the confusion surrounding energy deliveries to Ukraine. Russia has always refused Ukrainian requests to sell gas at the border where meters could be installed so that it would be clear as to exactly how much Ukraine has imported. Third, Russia has always had irrational fears that Ukraine would slip from its sphere of influence by integrating into the EU and NATO. Unresolved borders would prevent Ukraine's integration westwards as the resolution of border questions is a prerequisite for membership in the EU and NATO. The CPCFPU therefore argues that accepting Russia's position (as Kupchyshyn briefly did) would, 'cast doubts on the realisation of Ukraine's European choice'.

The Russian-Ukrainian border has enhanced importance for European security in the wake of the 11 September 2001 terrorist acts in the USA. Ninety percent of illegal migrants and two thirds of contraband, including narcotics and weapons, enter Ukraine from Russia and from Ukraine are trafficked into the EU. A demarcated border with Russia has therefore importance not only for Ukraine, but also for an enlarged EU. Support for the demarcation of Ukraine's Eastern border and improving security on it came during a June 2002 meeting between Prime Minister Anatoli Kinakh and the EU's Security Chief, Xavier Solana, who promised EU funds for improving security on the Russian-Ukrainian border which could only be provided if the border is demarcated, a step which Russia continues to hold up.[172]

It took Russia five years to sign a treaty with Ukraine in 1997 and then a further two for both houses of its parliament to ratify the treaty. Three years later Russia's actions in a number of areas show that although Ukraine's borders might be no longer in question it still finds it extremely difficult to recognise Ukraine as an equal and sovereign state.

---

172    See Taras Kuzio, *EU and Ukraine: A Turning Point in 2004? Occasional Paper 47* (Paris: Institute Strategic Studies-EU, November 2003). Available at http://www.iss-eu.org/

## Russia Steps Up Its Influence in Ukraine

Chernomyrdin was appointed Ambassador to Ukraine and 'Special Presidential Envoy for the Development of Russian-Ukrainian Trade and economic Ties' in May 2001. Since then his actions show he is confused as to whether he also has a third position, that of Regional Governor. Chernomyrdin's appointment was meant to consolidate the Russian vector in Ukraine's 'multi-vector' foreign policy as the primary one after the West's growing disenchantment with Ukraine. During the March 2002 elections Chernomyrdin openly interfered in favour of pro-presidential parties and helped fan the flames of an 'anti-nationalist' campaign against pro-Western political forces. He also chided Ukrainian Foreign Ministry state secretary Oleksandr Chaly as an 'obtuse man' when he outlined Ukraine's goals as joining the EU, not the alternative Eurasian Economic Community. Chaly and Vitaliy Haydiuk, both senior leaders of the Industrial Union of Donbas, were brought into the presidential secretariat and National Security and Defence Council during Yushchenko's second year in office.

Chernomyrdin's governoral style is due to two reasons related to Russian national identity. First, since the creation of the CIS in December 1991 Russia has looked upon it as a loose commonwealth or confederation guided and led by Russia. CIS members only possess partial sovereignty as the 'Near Abroad'. Chernomyrdin and the Russian elite were hostile to Our Ukraine's 2002 election foreign policy platform of integration into the EU and NATO because this is seen as an attempt at breaking ties with Russia. This hostility to Our Ukraine and Yushchenko was evident in both the 2002 and 2004 elections. Russia openly supports the Russophile Communist Party of Ukraine, which seeks to revive the USSR, and oligarchic centrist parties, such as the Party of Regions, who prefer a foreign policy strategy of 'To Europe with Russia'.[173] Unified Russia and the Party of Regions signed a cooperation agreement in 2005.

Second, Russia still finds it difficult to accept Ukraine (and Belarus) as separate nations with independent statehood. Russian Foreign Minister

---

173    See Taras Kuzio, 'To Europe with Russia! Ukraine's 'Little Russian' Foreign Policy', *RFERL Newsline*, 4 June 2002.

Ivanov told the *Rossiyskaya gazeta* newspaper that Ukraine and Russia were slated to be close 'strategic partners' because of, 'our shared linguistic, religious, cultural, and historical legacy, our kindred mentality...' Although only the extreme left support Ukraine's membership of the Russian-Belarusian union, Russia still holds out hope that this will change. Interviewed in the *Trud* newspaper Chernomyrdin was asked if a union of the three Eastern Slavs was possible? His reply was indicative: 'When Ukrainian society matures to this point it will opt for such a step'.

According to a March 2002 poll by the Russian Public Opinion Fund, almost half of Russian citizens would like Russia and Ukraine to unite. Another 35 per cent believe Ukraine and Russia should remain independent but remove border restrictions and have no visas or customs controls. Russian elites are therefore in touch with popular feeling, eighty per cent of whom see no need for a border with Ukraine.

When Russia equates demarcation with erecting a 'fence' between both countries it is not referring to normal practice as this kind of border demarcation was only undertaken by the USSR, not in the West. In an age of globalisation and the internet super highway such views on the ability of borders to isolate country's is impossible. In Russia's eyes, the only difference between frontiers in the USSR and those within the CIS are that they can be now delimited on maps. But, this is as far as Russia will go. Demarcation should only be applied – as it was in the USSR – to the 'external frontiers' of the CIS. Chernomyrdin, whose views have been echoed by other Russian officials, said that 'demarcation is out of the question' because it is allegedly being imposed on Ukraine and Russia by the West (i.e. the US, EU and NATO). Russia continues to view demarcation as leading to a Soviet-style fence between both countries. 'We are not ready for that (demarcation) and do not intend to put up a fence between Russia and Ukraine', Chernomyrdin said.[174] To some extent this is true. Ukraine cannot make good on its rhetoric in favour of aspiring to become an Associate and then full member of the EU if it has not demarcated its long Eastern border with Russia (Ukraine's 2,600 km. Western border was demarcated in the Soviet era). To accept Russia's division of borders in the CIS into only delimited 'internal' and delimited-demarcated 'exter-

---

174    www.forUm.ua., 29 April 2002.

nal' ones would be to accept a status of only partial sovereignty. The security of the Russian-Ukrainian border cannot be therefore resolved without demarcation, former secretary of the National Security and Defence Council and former Defence Minister Yevhen Marchuk, pointed out.

As is common with Russian officials who seek to speak on behalf of the CIS, Chernomyrdin claimed that not going ahead with demarcation was by 'mutual agreement'. This is not the case. Ukrainian Foreign Ministry First Deputy State Secretary Volodymyr Yelchenko responded by saying demarcation is an integral part of the legalisation of national borders. During Putin's visit to Ukraine in January 2003 to launch the 'Year of Russia in Ukraine' and to attend the Kyiv CIS summit the delimitation of Ukraine's borders was finalised. Discussions over its delimitation had been taking place since winter 1998-1999 when both houses of the Russian parliament ratified the 1997 treaty. Putin said in Kyiv that Russia, 'has been knowingly working towards the signing of an agreement on the border with Ukraine'.[175] During Putin's visit to Kyiv, Russia and Ukraine signed a treaty on the Ukrainian-Russian border.[176] The delimitation question only resolved the Russian-Ukrainian land border; it did not resolve that of the Azov Sea to the East of the Crimea and the Crimea's Kerch Strait. Foreign Minister Zlenko believed it was necessary to sign a separate agreement on the division of the Azov Sea.

Ukraine favoured the division of the Azov Sea's basin and waters while Russia prefers to maintain it as joint internal waters. Russia knew that if the Azov Sea was divided, Ukraine would obtain sixty per cent. This would damage its fishing industry and a potential share of future oil and gas deposits. Since then Russia has raised a territorial claim on the island of Tuzla. Article 5 of the newly signed treaty defined the Azov Sea according to the Russian standpoint,[177] that the current status of the Azov Sea and Kerch Strait 'as internal marine territories of the two countries' would remain in force.

Was Zlenko deliberately misinforming the Ukrainian public so as not to show that Ukraine had made a major concession to Russian demands? As one commentary wrote: 'even the most enthusiastic advocates of that document wondered whether it was really worth signing, if it meant an end to the

---

175    ITAR-TASS, 28 January 2003.
176    *Ukrayinska Pravda*, 28 January 2003.
177    ITAR-TASS, 28 January 2003.

idea of dividing the Azov Sea'.[178] In reality, political instability in Ukraine and a crisis in relations with the US were used by Putin to force Kuchma to make wide ranging concessions on the Azov Sea and Kerch Strait. This confused Ukrainian approach may have led to Russia raising Tuzla as another area that should not be delimited.

Ukraine conceded on these territorial issues in order to ensure Kuchma's election as Head of the CIS Council of Heads of State at the January 2003 Kyiv CIS summit. This was the first occasion that a non-Russian CIS leader had ever held this position. The irony was that Kyiv was not *de jure* a CIS member as the Ukrainian parliament had never ratified the CIS Charter. Ukraine had always therefore described itself as an 'Associate Member' of the CIS - even though no such status exists. The correct term for Ukraine was 'participant' in the CIS. Only in an entity where there is such nihilism towards the rule of law as the CIS could a country which is a 'participant' of the CIS nevertheless lead the same structure. The same is true over Sevastopol and Tuzla which Russia claims there are no Soviet legal documents to prove that Ukraine obtained sovereignty over them in the USSR. These Russian territorial claims also show the contempt with which Russia regards the 'security assurances' it, together with the USA, UK and France, gave to Ukraine in 1994-1996 in exchange for de-nuclearisation. The central aspect of these 'security assurances' was the sanctity of Ukraine's territorial integrity.

## Conclusions

Because most Russians never looked upon Ukrainians and Belarusians as anything but wayward 'Russians' throughout the 1990s it proved difficult for Moscow to first, accept Ukraine's independence as a permanent factor and second, to recognise Eastern Ukraine and the Crimea as territories lying in a foreign country. The Sevastopol and Crimea questions proved to be the main stumbling blocks to signing the 1997 inter-state treaty which replaced those signed in 1990 in the USSR. Even after the treaty was signed by the

---

178   Vladimir Kravchenko, 'Sea of Azov: Invisible Reefs', *Dzerkalo tyzhnya*, 22-28 February 2003.

executives and ratified by both parliaments, Russia still refuses to divide the Kerch strait and Azov Sea into national sectors. Ukraine's concessions on the Azov Sea and Kerch Strait ensure Russia's continued presence and influence in the Crimea, where it has naval bases until 2017 that it seeks to extend. In addition, Russia still refuses to take the next step, border demarcation. Russia's refusal to delimit the Kerch Strait and Azov sea, or demarcate it's border with Ukraine, attempts to extend the lease of naval bases to the Black Sea Fleet are inter-connected aspects of a more assertive Russian security policy towards Ukraine during President Putin's terms in office.

# 4   Ukraine-Crimea-Russia: Triangle of Conflict

This chapter is divided into seven sections that span the history of the Crimea and how it is differently perceived by Tatars, Russians and Ukrainians. The common theme running through all of the sections is the conflict over the historical legacy and territory of the Crimea. The first surveys the manner in which these three ethnic groups perceive the Crimea through how history is perceived. The second looks at the history of Tatar statehood between the fourteenth-eighteenth centuries and Russian occupation from the eighteenth to the twentieth centuries. The third and fourth sections analyses the history of the Crimea within the Russian SFSR and Ukrainian SSR in the former USSR. The last three sections are a study of the return of the Tatars to Ukraine after 1989. They survey the conflict between Ukraine and Russia throughout the 1990s over the historical right to ownership of the Crimea.

### The Impact of History

After the Tatars were ethnically cleansed in 1944 the history of the region was re-interpreted in a way that built upon past prejudices against Tartars since the late eighteenth cerntury. Russian historiography claims that the Crimea was inhabited by few people with a low level of culture and civilisation. Crimea history was therefore written only from the perspective of the 1783 occupation through Russian victories and defeats (e.g. Crimean war of 1854-1855 and German siege of 1942). In all of these events the Tatars are either marginal or collaborators with Russia's enemies. Three competing views of history therefore exist:

1.   *Tatar View*: Tatar statehood between the fifteenth-eighteenth centuries signifies to them that they are the only indigenous Crimean people. The Crimea is their only homeland.

2. *Russian View*: the Crimea is naturally part of the Russian world, while the Tatars were part of the Mongol invasion and collaborators. The Crimea is an important component of the glory of Catherine the Great and the Tsarist Russian empire.

3. *Ukrainian View*: the Crimea was always linked to Ukraine through geography, culture and ethnically prior to, and including the medieval Kyiv Rus state. As Kyiv Rus was a proto-Ukrainian state the Crimea was historically part of 'Ukraine' far ahead of the Tatars or Russians. The Crimea is included as part of Ukrainian history in all standards textbooks of Ukrainian history published after 1992.

Historical disputes greatly influence the triangle of conflict between Ukraine-Crimea-Russia. Tatar-Russian relations are strained by the Treaty of Kalinarjii of 1775 which transferred sovereignty over the Crimea from the Ottoman Turks to the Russian empire. Ukrainian and Tatar historians dispute Russian nationalist claims that the Crimea has been 'Russian land from time immemorial', pointing to Kyivan Rus, Zaporozhian Cossack, Tatar and Ottoman influence prior to 1775. Turkey and Russia fought 13 wars in the eighteenth and nineteenth centuries.[179] Central-Eastern Ukraine and the Crimea were never separate entities in the Russian empire but merely divided between eleven *gubernias*. Russians point to its 'glorious' association with Russian history (incorporation of the Crimea into the Russian empire, defeat of the Turks, Sevastopol as a naval base). Ukrainians meanwhile, who are eager to establish their earlier claim, argue that prior to the Russian conquest of the Crimea in the eighteenth century, Cossacks and Kyiv had long established contacts to, and ties with, the Tatars and the Crimea.

The injustice of the ethnic cleansing of Tatars has left a profound mark upon the Tatars (in the same way as it has upon the Chechens). Mass rallies are annually held in Simferopol that demand the reinstatement of the rights of the Crimean Tatar people and for the 1944 ethnic cleansing to be defined as 'genocide'. These rallies also demand the replacement of Tsarist street names and the erection of a monument to the 1944 ethnic cleansing. A reso-

---

179    AP, 19 June 1994.

lution adopted at the 2003 rally stated: 'There can be no legal reason to justify seizing the land of Crimean Tatars, resisting them in opening Crimean-Tatar schools and refusing to give the Crimean Tatar language official status in Crimea.'[180]

The rally was attended by Crimean Prime Minister Serhiy Kunitsyn and Hennadiy Udovenko, the former head of Rukh and Foreign Minister, in his capacity as head of the parliamentary committee for human rights, Rukh has a long standing record of supporting the Tatar cause. It came as no surprise that Leonid Grach, leader of the Crimean Communists, was absent. Grach and the Communist Party still uphold the Soviet view that the ethnic cleansing was justified on the grounds of Tatar alleged collaboration with the Nazis. Communist hostility to the Tatars is as deeply racist as that found among Russian nationalists.

This legacy of the dispute over ownership of the Crimea continues to influence contemporary Turkish-Russian relations. The Turkish chief of staff commented that, 'Russia has become a serious danger... Today, there is a Russia which behaves with a Czarist motivation'. Turkish and Ukrainian apprehensions about Russian neo-imperialism propelled them into becoming strategic allies in the 1990s.[181]

The dispute over the Black Sea Fleet has its own historical conflict. After the disintegration of the Tsarist Russian empire in 1917, pro-Ukrainian independence officers and sailors transferred their allegiance to the Kyiv authorities. In March 1918 the Ukrainian Hetmanate government adopted a law placing the Black Sea Fleet under Kyiv's control. Over a month later the Fleet raised the Ukrainian flag. The bulk of the Fleet was scuppered by the Bolsheviks rather than let it fall into Ukrainian hands.

In 1954 then Soviet leader Nikita Khrushchev, himself a Russian from Ukraine, arranged the transfer of the Crimea from the Russian SFSR to Ukraine. The transfer was adopted in law by the USSR Supreme Soviet on 26 April 1954. Khrushchev's reasoning was that the Crimea was geographically connected to Ukraine, not to Russia. The Crimea remained within the Ukrainian SSR as only an *oblast* until 1991 when it was upgraded into an autono-

---

180   Interfax-Ukraine, 18 May 2003.
181   See Taras Kuzio, 'Turkish-Ukrainian Relations given a Boost', *RFE/RL Newsline*, 3 July 2002.

mous republic.

Russophone Slavs migrated to the Crimea in the post-war era in large numbers. This changed the ethnic balance even more against the Tatars who no longer resided in the Crimea after 1944. As well as worsening future inter-ethnic relations, many of the new migrants were retired high ranking Soviet military officers and Communist Party members who believe that the Tatars had indeed been 'Nazi collaborators' and that they were 'historical enemies of Russia'.

One of many Ukrainian resentments against Russian nationalists rests over the subsidies provided by the Ukrainian SSR to the Crimea over four decades between the 1950s and 1980s (the Crimea has a budget deficit). In addition, there has always been fear that loss of the Crimea would lead to a domino effect over Russian claims to other regions of Ukraine. A third re-sentment points to additional Soviet acts which transferred territory in Eastern Ukraine to Russia and asks rhetorically if these acts should also be annulled? Finally, Ukraine also backs the view of the bulk of European countries that post-Yalta borders should remain intact to prevent continent-wide instability if demands for border changes were acted upon, as in the former Yugoslavia.

Russian, Tatar and Ukrainian historians and commentators therefore approach the Crimean question from a variety of incompatible angles. Rus-sia's attempts at inheriting the great power status of the former USSR - but not the negative aspects of the Soviet past - is one of the factors that has contributed to damaging its relations with the former Soviet republics, particu-larly with Ukraine. As one author has pointed out,

> [t]he discontinuity between the Soviet past and the [Ukrain-ian] present is most apparent in Crimea...acceptance of Cri-mea's status as a part of Ukraine has been half-hearted at best and quite often implicitly challenged.[182]

In the May 1994, during Russian celebrations of the end of World War II the Russian military press suggested that because Sevastopol was liberated by them fifty years ago this entitled them to a voice in its future today. Like-

---

182    John W.R. Lepingwell, 'The Soviet Legacy and Russian Foreign Policy', *RFE/RL Research Report*, vol. 3, no.23 (10 June 1994), p.3.

wise, even then President Boris Yeltsin described the city as, 'one of the national sacred places for all Russians'.

### Tatar State and Tsarist Empire

The Tatars trace their origins to the thirteenth century when their ethnic group was created as a consequence of the inter-mingling of the remnants of the Golden Horde and the local nomadic tribes. Their main geographic location was the Crimea and the southern shore of Ukraine. The Crimea was united by Khan Haci Giray in the mid fifteenth century who claimed descent from Gengis Khan. The dynasty he created ruled the Crimea until the Tsarist occupation of 1783. They had accepted the protection of the Ottoman Turks who arrived in the wake of conquering Byzantium and Constantinople in the 1470s. The Tatars retained many of the traditions inherited from the Mongol empire, including the Kurultai assembly. Besides Ottoman influences the Tatars absorbed Greek and Genoese traditions which were also prevalent in southern Crimea. Their identity is firmly rooted in the Crimea making them distinct from Tatars in Tatarstan and Astrakhan in Russia.

Russian hegemony was established over the Crimea in 1783 when the Tsarist empire destroyed the Crimean Tatar state. Prior to Russia's occupation the region had been known for several centuries as the Crimean Khanate. One of the major impacts of the Tsarist occupation was the emigration of Tatars. 100.00 Tatars out of a total Tatar population of half a million left the Crimea in 1783-1791 (see Table 4.1). Turkey is home to a large and influential Tatar minority.

Table 4.1 Changing Ethnic Composition of the Crimea (%)

| Nationality | 1783 | 1897 | 1937 | 1989 | 2000 |
|---|---|---|---|---|---|
| Tatars | 83.0 | 34.1 | 20.7 | 1.5 | 15.0 |
| Russians | 5.7 | 45.3 total | 47.7 | 67.0 | 61.6 |
| Ukrainians | 2.9 | for Eastern Slavs | 12.8 | 25.8 | 23.6 |

Note: The Remaining Balance up to 100% consists of smaller nationalities. Source:Andrew Wilson, *The Crimean Tatars. A Situation Report on the Crimean Tatars* (London: International Alert, 1993), p.36.

By the second half of the nineteenth century the Crimean population had declined to 200,000 of which half were Tatars. This proportion continued to decline as Slav in-migration continued in the next century as a consequence of industrialisation, the building of the Black Sea Fleet and tourism. By the 1897 and 1926 censuses the Tatar share of the population had declined to 34 and then to 26 per cent respectively.

### The Russian Revolution and Ukrainian Drive to Independence

The Ukrainian historian Doroshenko believed:

> But, Ukraine could not have renounced Crimea. She could not for a number of reasons; political – not wishing to have at hand some sort of Piedmont for the rebuilding of 'one and indivisible Russia', strategic – Sevastopol, the key to Black Sea supremacy, could not have been left in unknown hands; ethnographic – a high percent of Crimea's population was Ukrainian, and finally – purely economic conditions bind Crimea to Ukraine so closely that it could not be viable without Ukraine.[183]

The Third Universal of the Central Rada of 1917 led by President and historian Mykhailo Hrushevsky did not include the Crimea within its under-

---

183    Dmytro Doroshenko, *History of Ukraine. 1917-1923* (Winnipeg-Toronto-Detroit: np, 1993), p.260.

standing of 'Ukraine'. The Central Rada also did not claim the Kuban, Kholm, Kursk or Voronezh regions now inside the Russian federation. The 1918 Hetmanate did claim the Crimea which it believed should be tied to Ukraine on a federal basis. The Hetmanate also put forward claims to the Black Sea Fleet. This resulted in the raising of the Ukrainian flag on 29 April 1918 on the majority of the naval vessels. Those vessels that refused to raise the Ukrainian flag moved to Novorossiysk. The Ukrainian state created in the 1990s followed many of the steps earlier undertaken by the Hetmanate. On both occasions economic, political, historical and ethnographic arguments were made to lay claim to the Crimea.

An economic blockade and pressure was utilised in August 1918 and in 1994-1995 against Russian separatists. In 1918, 'This forced the Crimean government to look at the state of play in a realistic manner'. The same could be said about the 1990s.[184] On both occasions, local Ukrainian-language newspapers and pro-Ukrainian groups were financed by Kyiv.[185] On both occasions in 1917-1920 and in the 1990s Kyiv offered autonomous status to the Crimea.[186] The Directory from 1919 continued to lay claim to the Crimea and offered to provide it with full autonomy. The Ukrainian historian Shapoval therefore concluded that Ukraine has historically seen the Crimea as a part of Ukraine's territory.[187] The 1918 Hetmanate[188] offered similar provisions for autonomous status to those proposed in the 1990s:

- Crimea should be allowed to station soldiers from the Crimea in the peninsula (this demand was rejected in the 1990s);
- A Crimean Cabinet of Ministers (government);

---

184   Vasyl Boechko et al. (eds.), *Kordony Ukrayiny: Istorychna Retrospektyvna ta Suchasnyi Stan* (Kyiv: Osnovy, 1994), p.33.

185   *Pravda Ukrainy* and *Nazavisimost*, two Russian-language newspapers published in Kyiv, were subsidised for distribution in the Crimea. Interview with Valerii Bebyk, Press Service, Presidential Administration, Centre for Russian and East European Studies, University of Birmingham, 5 February 1996.

186   Igor B. Torbakov, 'Russian-Ukrainian Relations, 1917-1918: A Conflict Over Crimea and the Black Sra Fleet', *Nationalities Papers*, vol.24, no.4 (December 1996), pp.679-690.

187   Yuriy Shapoval, 'Istorychnyi dosvid derzhavnosti', *Holos Ukrayiny*, 11 February 1997.

188   V. Boechko et al. (eds.), *Kordony Ukrayiny*, pp.114-117.

- A Crimean Supreme Soviet (parliament);
- Ukrainian legislation supersedes Crimean legislation;
- Crimea controls its economy, budget and trade but delegated foreign and defence affairs to Kyiv;
- Crimea would use Ukrainian currency;
- Crimean language policy would be determined according to local preferences.

During the Russian revolution the (Tatar) National Party campaigned for an independent Crimean state. The first Kurultai of Tatars was held in Bakhchisarai in December 1917 which elected a Crimean Tatar government. This had to compete with the Crimean Provincial Assembly where the Socialist Revolutionaries dominated. In December 1917 the Bolsheviks established a Crimean Soviet. The following month the Bolsheviks overthrew the Tatar and Provincial Assemblies. During the civil war of 1917-1921 the Crimea was claimed by the independent Ukrainian state, which obtained the peninsula under the terms of the 1918 Brest Litovsk Treaty. But, the Crimea was also the scene of conflict between the Whites and Bolsheviks. From 1919 the Crimea came increasingly under the influence of the Bolsheviks. Ukraine's hold on the Crimea was therefore tenuous following the collapse of the Tsarist empire.

### Soviet Rule

On 18 October 1921, the Crimean ASSR was included within the Russian SFSR as an autonomous (non-ethnically designated) republic with two cities (Sevastopol and Evpatoriia) under all-union jurisdiction. This administrative division was to continue until 1944-1945 when the Tatars were ethnically cleansed after which the region became a Russian *oblast*. The Crimean ASSR included Tatar as one of its official languages.

The indigenisation policies of the 1920s increased the number of Tatars in institutional positions in the Crimea, where they were over-represented, and promoted their language and culture. Similar policies took place in the

Ukrainian SSR. These policies of indigenisation and Ukrainianisation were reversed in the 1930s and in 1938 the Tatar language was converted into Cyrillic. The Ukrainian and Tatar elites were decimated in the Stalinist Great Terror with 10.000 Tatars dying in the purges.[189] Large numbers of Tatars left the Crimea for abroad. The Crimea's ethnic composition again changed in May 1944 when nearly 200.000 Tatars were ethnically cleansed to Central Asia together with 60.000 other minorities. It is estimated that up to 40 per cent of the Tatars died during the ethnic cleansing. A year later on 30 June 1945, Crimean autonomy was formally abolished and the peninsula became an *oblast* (region) of the Russian SFSR. Most vestiges of the Tatar legacy were removed. The following year the Crimea's status was changed when it was downgraded to an *oblast* of the Russian SFSR. The Crimea was progressively russified and all traces of Tatar identity removed. This policy of russification was strengthened by the deliberate influx of Russian settlers after World War II, many of whom were Soviet military personnel.

### Transfer to Soviet Ukraine

In 1954, Sevastopol and the Crimea were transferred to Ukraine. Article 77 of the 1978 Ukrainian SSR constitution placed Sevastopol (and Kyiv) under all-Ukrainian jurisdiction.[190] This judicial and constitutional status was argued by Sevastopol Mayor Viktor Semenov to counter Russian territorial claims in the 1990s.[191] Post-Soviet Russia strenuously disagreed. Secretary of the Russian Security Council Aleksandr Lebed claimed Sevastopol was subordinated to Moscow as the capital of the USSR right up until 1991.[192] The 1978 Russian SFSR constitution only included Moscow and Leningrad with all-republican status. Sevastopol was only included within the annual

---

189    Mustafa Cemiloglu, 'A History of the Crimean Tatar National Liberation Movement: A Sociopolitical Perspective', in Maria Drohobycky (ed.), *Crimea. Dynamics, Challenges, and Prospects* (Lanham, MA: Rowman & Littlefield, 1995), p.92.
190    Eduard Ozhiganov, 'The Crimean Republic: Rivalries for Control' in Alexei Arbatov *et al.* (ed.), *Managing Conflict in the Former Soviet Union: Russian and American Perspectives* (Cambridge, MA: The MIT Press, 1997), p.123.
191    *Obschaya Gazeta*, 9-15 January 1997.
192    Interfax, 1 November 1997.

Russian SFSR budget until 1953; thereafter it was funded by the Ukrainian SSR budget. Sevastopol was also included in Crimean election districts.[193] The then chairman of the Presidium of the Supreme Soviet of the Russian SFSR, M.Tarasov, commented:

> ...Crimea is an undeniable natural continuation of the south-ern steppes of Ukraine. Economically the Crimean *oblast* is closely tied to the economy of the Ukrainian republic. For geographic and economic reasons the transfer of the Cri-mean *oblast* to the ranks of brother Ukraine certainly reflects the general interests of the Soviet state.[194]

The Crimea's status was changed in 1954 when then Soviet leader Khrushchev transferred it to the Ukrainian SSR. It remained an *oblast* within the Ukrainian SSR until 1991 when a popularly supported referendum re-turned its status to an autonomous republic, this time within the Ukrainian SSR and then in independent Ukraine.

The justification for the transfer of the Crimea was common territorial and close economic and cultural links between the *oblast* and Ukrainian SSR. Marples and Duke concluded that it was, 'a purely internal administrative mat-ter which, it would seem, did not have much significance in political or eco-nomic terms'.[195] None of the official documents at the time mentioned the transfer as part of the 1954 Soviet official anniversary celebrations of the 1654 Treaty of Pereyaslav.[196] In earlier decades Ukrainian territories had been transferred to Russia (Kursk, Belgorod and Voronezh *oblasts*).[197] What this tells us is that the issue of Sevastopol was a conflict based around his-torical myths that had little basis in historical fact. Similar historical myths

---

193    Information supplied by the directorate on Treaties and Legal Issues of the Ukrain-ian Ministry of Foreign Affairs (*Flot Ukrayiny*, 30 November 1996).
194    V. Boechko *et al.* (eds.), *Kordony Ukrayiny*, p.92.
195    David R. Marples and David F. Duke, 'Ukraine, Russia, and the Question of Cri-mea', *Nationalities Papers*, vol.23, no.2 (June 1995), p.272.
196    V. Boechko *et al.* (eds.), *Kordony Ukrayiny*, p.93.
197    *Nezavisimaya Gazeta*, 3 September 1991.

sparked the conflict in Kosovo and the rise of Slobodan Milosevich to power in Serbia.[198]

### Tatars Return to the Crimea

Tatars had begun to return to the Crimea in the Mikhail Gorbachev era but they still only accounted for 15 per cent of the population by the late 1990s. The remainder of the population was divided between Russians and russified Ukrainians. Approximately half of the estimated 500-600.000 Crimean Tatars have returned to the Crimea since 1989. This followed the first official condemnation of the 1944 ethnic cleansing of Tatars in a November 1989 USSR Supreme Soviet resolution.

The status of the Crimea, the city of Sevastopol and the division of the Soviet Black Sea Fleet stationed on the peninsula were the object of acrimonious dispute between Ukraine and Russia throughout the 1990s. The Russian parliament repeatedly voted to demand that Ukraine return both the Crimea and Sevastopol and argued that legally they were Russian territory. They claimed that Russia, as the successor state to the USSR, had the right to inherit Sevastopol and the Black Sea Fleet, both of which had not been under Ukrainian jurisdiction. This dispute was not resolved until May 1997 when Ukraine and Russia signed an inter-state treaty at the executive level that recognised each other's borders. The treaty was quickly ratified by the Ukrainian parliament in January 1998 with 317 votes and 27 voting against. Both houses of the Russian parliament only ratified it after intense lobbying from Ukraine in October 1998 and February 1999.

The resolution of the question of the ownership of the Crimea and Sevastopol between 1997-1999 also assisted in the division of the Black Sea Fleet. Russia, which inherited 80 per cent of the fleet, leased two Sevastopol bays for twenty years until 2017. The local situation was also stabilised by the

---

198    See Taras Kuzio, 'Russians and Russophones in the Former USSR and Serbs in Yugoslavia: A Comparative Study of Passivity and Mobilisation', *East European Perspectives*, vol.5. nos.15, 16, 17 (11, 25 June and 9 July 2003). Available at http://www.taraskuzio.net/journals/pdf/national-serbs_russians.pdf.

adoption by the Crimea of a constitution in October-December 1998 which for the first time recognised Ukraine's sovereignty.

Between 1991-1993 the former communist leadership of the Crimea, led by Nikolai Bagrov, attempted to obtain significant concessions from Kyiv in an attempt to maximise the Crimea's autonomy. This autonomist position was sidelined by a pro-Russian secessionist movement which was the most influential political force between 1993-1994 after its leader Yuriy Meshkov was elected Crimean president in January 1994. The secessionist movement collapsed in 1994-1995 due to internal quarrels, lack of substantial Russian assistance and Ukrainian economic, political and military pressure. The Crimean presidential institution was abolished by presidential decree in March 1995.

Within the Crimea the Tatars have been able to mobilise large demonstrations that have at times been successful in applying pressure. The small size of the Tatar population, coupled with racist hostility from Russian and Soviet nationalists, has reduced their ability to extert influence on the peninsula's politics. In September 1990 the second Kurultai was held in the Crimea, deliberately entitled so as to show continuity to the first meeting held in 1918. The Kurultai passed the 'Declaration of National Sovereignty of the Crimean Tatar People'. The declaration stated that the: 'Crimea is the national territory of the Crimean Tatar people, on which they alone possess the right to self government.' It continued: 'the political, economic, spiritual and cultural rebirth of the Crimean Tatar people is only possible in their own sovereign national state.'[199]

The Tatars look upon the Kurultai as their own parliament which elects a Mejlis to function as a working body between assemblies. As a 'parliament' it is therefore a rival power center to the Crimean Supreme Soviet. The Kurultai has adopted a flag, hymn and returned the Tatar language to the Latin script.

On a visit to the Crimea in March 1992 the OSCE delegation welcomed the advances made in both the regions autonomy and the rights of ethnic minorities. The Crimean republic is an example of the peaceful solution of its

---

199   Andrew Wilson, *The Crimean Tatars. A Situation Report on the Crimean Tatars for International Alert* (London: International Alert, 1994), p.13.

potentially explosive ethnic imbroglio and the tug of influence between three competing parties - Ukraine, Russia and the Tatars. In the former USSR, the peaceful resolution of the Crimea stands in contrast to Chechnya, Trans-Dniestr, Abkhazia, South Ossetia and Nagorno-Karabakh.

Crimean Tatars placed high hopes in the election of Viktor Yushchenko in January 2005 after a decade of neglect under Leonid Kuchma. These high hopes remain unfulfilled in seven outstanding Tatar demands. Violence continues on a regular basis between Russophone Slavs and Tatars in the Crimea. Tatar activist houses have been bombed, Tatar journalists have been murdered and Tatars have been sentenced to lengthy prison sentences for acts of civil disobedience. The most serious violence has erupted over historic Tatar sites that are now misused by Russophone Slavs. Violence between Tatars and Russophone Slavs have clashed over attempts to build apartments and business dwellings on ancient Tatar sites, such as the former imperial seat of the Tatar Khans in Bakhchisarai and old Moslem cemeteries used as flea markets. In 2006, private security guards working for the large development firm Olbi-Krym evicted Tatars encamped on a city plot in Simferopol. Dozens were injured in the fighting and the police made six arrests.

Tatars have also undertaken acts of civil disobedience to bring attention to their plight. In January 2007, thousands of Tatars protested outside Crimean government buildings banging metal drums. The Crimean Tatars were protesting at the lack of land allocated to them by the local authorities and recent changes to the criminal code giving severe punishments for illegal seizures of land. The Tatars have seven unfulfilled demands:

1.  *Land*: 75 percent of Tatars live in rural areas but they only possess half of the land allocated to Russophones. Prior to 1944, Tatars accounted for 70 percent of the population along the south coast, an area that today they are barred from because of its high value to tourism and developers.

2. *Employment*: although Tatars account for 12.1 percent of the population, according to the 2001 Ukrainian census, they only account for 4 percent of the official working population in the Crimea. Many Tatars are forced to work in the shadow economy which has led to violence with organised crime groups who often control markets.

3. *Allocation of Housing*: the number of Tatars in the Crimea has grown 6.4 times between the 1989 Soviet and 2001 Ukrainian censuses. Numbering today 243,000 another 150,000 remain in Uzbekistan. Tatars find that their former homes are occupied by Russian settlers, creating demands for property restitution. The authorities have failed to allocate sufficient resources for returning Tatars to build new accommodation which has led to the growth of shanty towns.

4. *Religion*: Prior to the absorption of the Crimea into the Russian empire in the late eighteenth century, the peninsula had 21,000 mosques. This number declined to only 1,700 by the 1944 deportation. The number has dwindled to 160 mosques that are in very poor condition and 9 madrasahs (religious schools). Tatars complain that the local authorities and Ukrainia Orthodox Church (Moscow Patriarchate) are hostile to the building of new mosques.

5. *Cultural and Educational Needs*: 13 Tatar-language schools with poor resources and under-qualified teachers are sufficient to only serve 14 percent of Tatar children. 86 percent of Tatar children attend Russian-language schools that leads to accusations of continued Soviet era russification. Tatars demand that the Crimea return to the policy in place prior to 1944 whereby the Tatar language was recognised as an additional official language. Insufficient funds are provided for renovating Tatar historical sites, even though these could bring in tourist revenue to the Crimea.

6. *Legal Demands*: that Tatars be recognised as an indigenous national group in the Crimea, not as a national minority. That their 1944 deporta-

tion be recognised as an act of 'genocide' and to adopt a legislative base for the rehabilitation of Tatars. In summer 2004 a law 'On the Re-habilitation of People Deported on Ethnic Grounds' was adopted by the Ukrainian parliament but it was vetoed by President Kuchma.

7.    *Guaranteed Representation in the Crimean Supreme Soviet:* Tatars were allocated 14 seats in the 1994-1998 Crimean parliament but this was revoked from the 1998 elections. The 2004 revised law on elections only provides for full proportional elections to local councils and the Crimean parliament. This makes it difficult for Crimean Tatars to be elected in the Crimea as local Communist and pro-Russian forces are hostile to Tatars who can only seek seats within national democratic groups in the Ukrainian parliament.


The potential for conflict in the Crimea existed in the first half of the 1990s because of the presence of two factors. First, the Tatar minority who have historical grievances of ethnic cleansing as well as contemporary griev-ances over racial, socio-economic and political discrimination. Second, a large Russian minority, most of whom settled in the Crimea after World War Two, now finds itself 'abroad' in independent Ukraine in a country it does not believe has the moral right to sovereignty over the peninsula. A major factor that worked in favour of a peaceful resolution of the Crimea was the weak-ness of Russia ethnic nationalism, a factor that led to its rapid marginalisation after 1995.[200] A stronger Russian nationalist base may have led to violent conflict within the Crimea and between the Crimea and Kyiv. Russian nation-alists were also at a distinct disadvantage in two areas compared to other CIS conflicts. First, Russia provided little support beyond rhetoric. Second, the Ukrainian authorities controlled the security forces stationed in the Crimea, with the exception of the Black Sea Fleet. Ukraine's control over the security

---

200    See Alexander J. Motyl, 'Chapter 11: The Myth of Russian Nationalism', in his, *So-vietology, Rationality, Nationality. Coming to Grips With Nationalism in the USSR* (New York: Columbia University Press, 1990), pp.161-173; Anatol Lieven, 'The Weakness of Russian Nationalism', *Survival*, vol.41, no.2 (Summer 1999), pp.53-70.

forces proved to be an important deterrent against extremists.

### Russia and Ukraine: Dispute Over the Crimea

Between 1991-1993 the former communist leadership of the Crimea, led by Bagrov, attempted to increase the power of local elites by obtaining additional sovereignty for the peninsula, while stepping short of demanding out right secession. In 1993-1995 this pro-Ukrainian, autonomist orientation was over-shadowed by the growing popularity of the separatist Russian Bloc which became the most influential political force. In January 1994, Russian Bloc separatist leader - Yuriy Meshkov - was elected Crimean President. The separatist movement sought to separate the Crimea from Ukraine and integrate with Russia. From a Tatar point of view, the Crimea's secession to Russia was the worst case scenario.

From 1998-2002 the Crimean regional Supreme Soviet was led by Communists who were as antagonistic towards the Tatars as were Russian nationalists in the Crimea. In the 1998-2002 Crimean Supreme Soviet there was no allocation of seats for Crimean ethnic minorities, unlike in the 1994-1998 Crimean Supreme Soviet which was held under a majoritarian election law that allocated 14 seats to Tatars.

The view that the Crimea and Sevastopol historically and ethnically belong to 'Russia' is very widespread within the elites of the Russian Federation, even among many democrats. Seventy per cent of Russians polled in early 1997 supported the transfer of Sevastopol to Russia.[201] One Ukrainian commentator pointed out that:

> It would be a mistake, however, to boil down the 'Crimean' activities of Moscow to a method of scoring points by Russian politicians because those who want to see the Crimea as Russian prevail among the helmsmen of the Kremlin's course.[202]

---

201    Russian TV Channel, 21 January 1997.
202    *Vseukrainskiye Vedomosti*, 18 January 1996.

Territorial claims against Ukraine were launched by Yeltsin's press secretary immediately after Ukraine declared independence in August 1991[203] The Russian Supreme Soviet then began to initiate them itself almost immediately in early 1992, particularly vis-à-vis the Crimea and the city of Sevastopol. Vladimir Lukin, former Russian Ambassador to the US and a leading member of the centre-left Yabloko, initiated the first votes in the Russian Supreme Soviet in favour of using the Black Sea Fleet to exert pressure upon Ukraine vis-à-vis the Crimea.[204] Moscow Mayor Luzhkov became an ardent supporter of territorial claims against Ukraine.[205] Luzhkov was backed by Boris Nemtsov, the respected reformist former Governor of Nizhni Novgorod and Deputy Prime Minister, who also regarded Sevastopol as a 'Russian city acquired with Russian blood'.[206] Nemtsov was head of the centre-right Union of Right Forces and became an adviser to President Yushchenko. Grigory Yavlinsky, head of Yabloko, had always considered Sevastopol to be historically a Russian town.[207] Russia's marginalised democratic opposition – Yabloko and Union of Right Forces – harboured imperialist views towards the Crimea.

The degree to which these imperialist views by democrats have elite consensus could be seen in the comments of Aleksei Mitrofanov. Mitrofanov, Chairman of the State Duma Geopolitics commission and a member of the extreme right Liberal Democratic Party, said that, '...Luzhkov behaves very correctly, he is increasingly resembling Zhirinovsky'.[208] The radical left and right within Russia both backed these territorial claims.[209] On these questions there was strong elite consensus within the Russian Federation.

---

203   *Robitnycha Hazeta*, 27 August 1991.
204   *Komsomolskaya Pravda*, 22 January 1992.
205   See his open letter to Yeltsin in *Moskovskaya Pravda*, 22 October 1996 and his views in *Literaturnaya Gazeta*, 22 January and *Trud*, 13 February 1997. An open letter in response was sent by Odesa Mayor Gurfits (*Izvestiya*, 6 November 1996).
206   ITAR-TASS, 20-21 January 1997.
207   Mayak Radio, 1 June 1997.
208   ITAR-TASS, 20-21 January 1997.
209   Georgii Tikhonov, head of the State Duma commission on CIS Affairs and Ties to Compatriots believed, 'Sevastopol was, is, and will be Russian' (ITAR-TASS, 30 September 1996). See also the views of Yegor Stroyev, speaker of the Federation Council, the upper house of the Russian Supreme Soviet, in *Komsomolskaya Pravda*, 25 February 1997.

The Russian executive officially reiterated its view that Sevastopol and the Crimea belonged to Ukraine.[210] Yet, prior to 1997 the Russia is Our Home faction in the State Duma, the 'party of power', and the Yeltsin appointees in the Federation Council both supported resolutions staking claims to the Crimea and Sevastopol.[211] As Marples and Duke pointed out, Yeltsin always 'sent mixed signals to Kiev'.[212]

The Russian Scientific Fund met in the Crimea in January 1992 and outlined hard line policies for Yeltsin and the Russian government. It concluded:[213]

- Crimea is vital to Russia for historical, cultural, ethnic and economic reasons (the same reasons were outlined by Ukraine);
- Annul the 1954 transfer to Ukraine;
- Ensure a three way (Crimea-Russia-Ukraine) discussion over the future of the Crimea;
- Establish Russian protection over the Crimea;
- Force Ukraine to agree to concessions.

Russian military means to re-take Sevastopol were ruled out because Ukraine had nuclear weapons and controlled the peninsula's security forces (see Chapter 7). One Russian official newspaper pointed out, sovereignty could only be reversed in the case of Sevastopol by, 'turning the city of our glory into a city of shame, into Grozny-2?'[214] President Leonid Kuchma had repeatedly refused to countenance any transfer of Sevastopol to Russia because Ukraine would then lose its independence.[215]

The Russian executive, according to the 1993 constitution, maintains for itself the prerogative of foreign policy. There was nothing therefore to stop

---

210    See the comments by Russian Foreign Ministry spokesman Gennadiy Tarasov in Interfax, 17 December 1996.
211    ITAR-TASS, 1 March 1997.
212    D. Marples and D. Duke, 'Ukraine, Russia and the Question of Crimea', p.275.
213    *Literaturna Ukrayina*, 14 May 1993.
214    *Rossiyskiye Vesti*, 3 June 1997.
215    Interview with President Kuchma in *Dzerkalo tyzhnya*, 25 December 1996. Three years later Kuchma said, 'Sevastopol is, and will remain, Ukrainian and I am not negotiating on the subject with anyone' (ITAR-TASS, 25 July 1999).

the Russian executive from implementing its alleged official policy of recognising Ukraine's borders by signing an inter-state treaty with Ukraine shortly after Kuchma was elected in 1994. The draft of the treaty was initialled by the then Ukrainian Prime Minister, Yevhen Marchuk, and the then Russian Deputy Prime Minister, Oleg Soskovets, as early as February 1995. In addition, the Russian executive were no doubt aware that the Black Sea Fleet command gave covert support to separatist forces in the Crimea in the form of the, 'most ardent supporters of anti-Ukrainian activities by the Russian Communities'.[216]

Between 1992-1996 Russia's leaders had refused to sign a draft treaty with Ukraine until it was given the entire city of Sevastopol as a naval base on a long term lease. Russian pressure upon Ukraine to accept this position rested upon five areas. First, the November 1990 Russian-Ukrainian treaty and the CIS founding acts of December 1991 only respected borders if the contracting parties remained within the former USSR or CIS respectively. The November 1990 treaty therefore, in Russian eyes, had lost its legal validity. Second, at the crudest level some Russians argued that Ukraine had never existed as a state prior to the creation of the former USSR. It was therefore an 'artificial' construct of the Soviet era.[217] Third, while grudgingly accepting the Crimea as part of Ukraine the Russian authorities focused upon the city of Sevastopol, arguing that it, unlike the Crimea, had never been legally transferred to Ukrainian jurisdiction in 1954. Therefore, Sevastopol was legally Russian territory and Russia could not therefore lease land from itself Fourth, Russia promoted the idea of an international status or joint administration over the city of Sevastopol by Kyiv and Moscow. Such an argument was also made over Tuzla in autumn 2003. Finally, although officially distancing itself from parliamentary votes on the Crimea and Sevastopol the Russian execu-

---

216  *Vseukrainskiye Vedomosti*, 12 April 1997.

217  See the views of Konstantin Zatulin, former head of the State Duma commission on CIS Affairs and Ties with Compatriots, in *Nezavisimaya Gazeta*, 1-7 April 1995 and those of the Russian historian, Yevgenniy Kisilov. Transcript of interview with Kisilov on SBS, Sydney Radio, 4 and 8 December 1996 is in the possession of the author. Anatol Lieven claims that only forty per cent of Ukraine is historically Ukrainian. The remainder was settled jointly by Ukrainians and Russians. Independent Ukraine's borders are therefore primarily a Soviet creation. See his *Ukraine and Russia. A Fraternal Rivalry* (Washington: US Institute of Peace, 1999).

tive indirectly utilised them as an additional form of pressure that was brought to bear upon Ukraine (see Table 4.2). As a Ukrainian military commentator pointed out, 'this explanation (by the Russian executive) is too weak to be taken seriously'.[218] These votes were backed by some democrats (including the 'party of power' Our Home is Russia faction) as well as the radical left and right, who remained heavily in favour of territorial changes:

Table 4.2 Russian Parliamentary Votes on Ukraine and the Crimea

| | |
|---|---|
| 315:001 | (14 February 1996) State Duma overrode Federation Council veto to halt division of the Black Sea Fleet to Ukraine; |
| 334:001 | (23 October 1996) State Duma vote to halt division of the Black Sea Fleet and demand exclusive basing rights in Sevastopol; |
| 282:000 | (24 October 1996) State Duma appeal to Ukraine on the Black Sea Fleet and Sevastopol as legally Russian territory; |
| 110:014 | (5 December 1996) Federation Council vote in favour of Sevastopol as Russian territory. |

Ukraine rejected these votes by Russia and the Ukrainian Supreme Soviet and regularly replied to Russian territorial ambitions in parliamentary resolutions adopted by large constitutional majorities.[219] Nevertheless, Luzhkov remained unconvinced:

> Sevastopol, as an independent entity, has never in any context whatsoever been supplied or financed by the Ukrainian republic. No document has ever indicated that when Crimea was transferred, Sevastopol was also handed over to Ukraine.[220]

President Kuchma held a different view. He argued that, 'Truth is on our side and everyone should proceed from this fact'.[221] But he forgot to mention that those Russian political leaders who backed territorial claims on Ukraine

---

218  *Narodna Armiya*, 27 February 1997.
219  See the comments by Deputy Foreign Minister K.Hryshchenko as carried by ITAR-TASS, 22 April 1997.
220  Russian Public TV, 21 October 1996.
221  Radio Ukraine, 14 December 1996.

also argued that 'truth is on their side'. The November 1996 vote by 110:14 in the Russian Federation Council claimed that the city of Sevastopol was Russian territory. They blamed Ukraine's unilateral actions which were, 'tearing away from Russia a part of its territory' which was, 'not only illegal under international law, but also directly damaged Russia's security'.[222] Russia's territorial claims on Ukraine were not therefore the cause of a deterioration of Russian-Ukrainian relations. Incredibly, Russia claimed it was Ukraine's stubbornness that was at fault in not conceding to Russia's 'legal demands' regarding territory which it allegedly owned in international law. Ukraine, on the other hand, believed Russia's actions to be, 'simply aggressive', according to Volodymyr Horbulin, then Secretary of Ukraine's National Security and Defence Council.[223] In Ukrainian eyes, regardless of the fact that these territorial claims were only officially made by the legislature, they nevertheless were still tantamount to territorial pretensions, 'anti-Ukrainian actions' and an infringement of international law.[224]

### Crimean Conundrum

Whereas Ukraine has always refused to discuss the status of the Crimea with Russia, believing it to be a purely internal matter, a wide spectrum of Russian thinking argued along the lines of former vice President Alexander Rutskoi: 'The Crimea must never be allowed to be Ukrainian. Because from time immemorial it has been Russian land and it is soaked with the blood of our ancestors'. Baburin, the key instigator in the move to open the Crimean question in the former Russian Supreme Soviet, announced that he would be among those who would conduct the third defence of Sevastopol.[225] Some Russian nationalist groups developed close working relations with extremist groups in the Crimea, such as the Russian Party, or established regional

---

222   Reuters, 5 December 1996.
223   Reuters, 6 December 1996. See also the large document prepared as a reply to the Russian Supreme Soviet by then Minister of Justice Serhiy Holovatiy entitled 'Sevastopolska Ahresiya', *Narodna Armiya*, 26 December 1996).
224   See *Holos Ukrayiny*, 19, 22 and 25 October 1996. Horbulin called the vote by the Russian Federation Council 'aggressive' (Reuters, 6 December 1996).
225   *Moscow News*, no.7, 1992.

branches of the National Salvation Front.

Throughout 1992-1993 the Russian Supreme Soviet escalated its demands towards the Crimea and Sevastopol. The then chairman of the Russian parliamentary committee on international affairs and former Ambassador to the US, Lukin, argued that Ukraine should be faced with a tough choice - relinquishing either the Black Sea Fleet or the Crimea. Lukin also suggested that the Russian Supreme Soviet should look into the legality of the transfer of the Crimea in 1954 from Russia to Ukraine.[226] The Russian Supreme Soviet and Ministry of Foreign Affairs condemned the transfer on 23 January 1992. This illicited a strong protest from Ukraine claiming that it violated previously signed Ukrainian-Russian treaties in 1990 and CIS agreements in December 1991.[227]

Ukrainian-Russian relations continued to worsen over the Crimea. Former vice President Alexander Rutskoi visited the Crimea in April 1992 where he called for its secession from Ukraine and a month later the Russian Supreme Soviet passed a resolution declaring the 1954 transfer of the Crimea 'illegal' to a Ukrainian storm of protest. The Ukrainian parliamentary resolution replied that it had 'no legal significance and no legal consequences for Ukraine' as Ukraine was recognised by many countries, including Russia, within its current borders that included the Crimea. The Foreign Ministry pointed out: 'Accordingly, the issue of the Crimea's status is an internal affair of Ukraine and in no way can be the subject of negotiations with any other state'.[228] On the initiative of 12 factions the Russian Supreme Soviet debated the status of Sevastopol on 7 December 1992. In their opinion, Sevastopol should be the main base for the Black Sea Fleet, have a special status and not be under Ukrainian sovereignty.

The Ukrainian response to the new claim on Sevastopol was sharp, although not strong enough for national democratic political groups which argued that the issue should have been raised in the UN Security Council. The then deputy head of the Ukrainian parliamentary committee on foreign affairs,

226    *Komsomolskaya Pravda*, 22 January 1992.
227    *Silski Visti*, 11 February 1992. An opinion poll at the time found 42 per cent in favour of the Crimea staying with Ukraine, 22 per cent staying in the CIS, 15 per cent going to Russia and 8 per cent becoming independent (Radio Kyiv, 10 February 1992).
228    *The Ukrainian Weekly*, 7 June 1992. See also the protest sent to the North Atlantic Assembly in *Holos Ukrayiny*, 5 June 1992.

Bohdan Horyn, argued that it should be regarded as an 'undeclared state of war'.[229] The Ukrainian Foreign Ministry and parliament issued condemnations, while parliamentary chairman, Ivan Pluishch, condemned the move as an attempt to, 'reanimate the old empire and old imperial policies'.[230]

The Russian leadership persisted in its two track approach to the Crimea. While President Yeltsin distanced himself from the Supreme Soviet resolutions he continued to argue, through the Russian ambassador to Ukraine, that Sevastopol should be leased to Russia. Questionnaires were distributed to Crimean deputies on the status of Sevastopol by the Russian Supreme Soviet.

Many Russian democrats may not have sympathised with the aggressive tone of the Russian Supreme Soviet resolutions. Nevertheless, they supported the denunciation of the 1954 transfer of the Crimea from Russia to Ukraine. Anatoly Sobchak, mayor of St.Petersburg and a leading member of the Movement for Democratic Reforms, argued that 'the Crimea has never belonged to Ukraine. There are no legal or moral grounds for Ukraine to lay claim to the Crimea'.

The next salvo across Ukraine's bows came in mid July 1993 when the Russian Supreme Soviet gave instructions to prepare a draft law, 'on enshrining the federal status of the town of Sevastopol in the Russian Federation constitution'.[231] The vote was passed by 166 in favour with only one voting against it in the Russian Supreme Soviet, itself an indication of the deep emotions surrounding the question. The decision was condemned by the Ukrainian executive and parliament, Crimean Supreme Soviet, Crimean Tatars and all Ukrainian political parties (including Communist and centrists). The resolution would only serve to, 'aggravate the relations between both states and bring about unpredictable consequences', the Ukrainian parliamentary resolution stated. President Yeltsin distanced himself from the decision but he could but not have failed to notice that the issue of Sevastopol and the Black Sea Fleet united the entire Russian political spectrum and the military.

---

229    *Vechirnij Kyiv*, 24-27 and 30 March 1993.
230    *Pravda Ukrayiny*, 23 January and *Holos Ukrayiny*, 4 March 1993.
231    *Rosiyskaya Gazeta*, 13 July 1993. See also Suzanne Crow, 'Russian Parliament Asserts Control over Sevastopol', *RFE/RL Research Report*, vol.2, no.31 (30 July 1993).

The Ukrainian Ministry of Defence sent reinforcements to the Crimea and, 'elaborated recommendations to the government to use in specific conditions that are likely to develop in the Crimea' (see Chapter 7).[232] Similar steps were undertaken by Ukraine in response to Russian threats over the island of Tuzla in autumn 2003. Some Ukrainian parliamentary deputies demanded that Ukraine not only keep its nuclear weapons but also seek operational control over them. Others called it simply a 'declaration of war', but warned that Ukraine would 'defend itself with an appropriate response'. Ukraine appealed to the UN Security Council, which confirmed its territorial integrity, stating that the decision was 'illegal' because it contradicted Ukrainian-Russian treaties and the aims and principles of the UN.

## Conclusions

The Crimea is a far more complex problem than most Western accounts gave it credit that often described it as a 'Russian enclave' fighting for separation from Ukraine. The Crimea is regionally diverse, with a predominantly Ukrainian northern region and a vocal Tatar minority. A 'clean break', if such a possibility existed, of the Crimea from Ukraine would be therefore impossible to undertake as it would be opposed by the northern *rayons*, the Tatars and a sizable proportion of the Slavic population who did not want their territory to become another 'Abkhazia'.

The Ukrainian authorities displayed a very tolerant attitude towards the Crimea, in contrast to other newly independent states of the former USSR towards their national minorities or Russian populations. But, the toleration of the current leadership would have changed if the Crimea threatened secession; it would have then been faced with no choice but to have used non-peaceful means to prevent this happening (as it came close to undertaking in May 1992). Relations with Russia remained strained throughout the 1990s because it was unable to come to terms with Ukrainian sovereignty over the Crimea. This stemmed from Russia's imperial view of Sevastopol and the Crimea as part of 'Russian' history. In reality, the Crimea and Sevastopol

---

232    *Demokratychna Ukrayina*, 12 July 1993.

could only be seen in such a manner if one looked to imperial history as the historical basis for the post-Soviet (non-imperial) Russian state. Such an imperial view of Sevastopol and the Crimea clashes with both the Tatar and Ukrainian viewpoints. The dispute over the island of Tuzla in 2003 shows the degree to which the larger issue of Russia being unable to come to terms with Ukraine's sovereignty over the Crimea continues to remain a thorn in Ukrainian-Russian relations. Russia's massive intervention in the 2004 Ukrainian elections is also a reflection of a continued lack of respect for Ukrainian sovereignty.[233]

---

233    See Taras Kuzio, 'Russian Policy to Ukraine During Elections', *Demokratizatsiya*, vol.13, no.4 (Fall 2005), pp.491-517.

# 5    Ukrainian Policies to the Crimea in the 1990s

Russian-Ukrainian relations are strained but do not suffer from the same degree of historical enmity as the Serbian-Croatian relationship. These strains are mitigated by the lack of ethnic or religious cleavages in Ukraine between ethnic Russians and ethnic Ukrainians, a large number of whom are Russophone. A deep level of historical animosity exists between Russians and Tatars, as most visibly demonstrated by Tatar support for Chechnya in its struggle with Russia.[234] President Yury Meshkov refused to attend commemorations of the fiftieth anniversary of Tatar ethnic cleansing saying sarcastically that, 'These people probably feel the same degree of shame as those Tatars who joined the Nazi battalions and took part in the slaughter of innocent people during the war'[235]. Tatars only account for approximately 15 per cent of the Crimea's population and therefore do not constitute a visible or serious threat to the dominant Russian majority in the Crimea. The Russian leadership (in contrast to the Serbian) did not pursue a militant 'Greater Russia' policy in the 1990s.[236] Of course, this could have changed after 1996 if Boris Yeltsin had lost the presidential elections to Communist leader Gennadiy Zyuganov. The Ukrainian leadership (in contrast to former leaders of the Trans-Caucasian republics) would also only have used force against Crimean separatists as a last resort (see Chapter 7).[237] Nevertheless, the Russian-Ukrainian dispute in the Crimea obtained wide coverage in Western

---

234   Interfax, 14 September 1994.
235   AP, 18 May 1994.
236   The current Russian leadership began following a policy of reestablishing its influence and control over the CIS by non-military means and support for secessionist movements. On this see Fiona Hill and Pamela Jewett, *Back in the USSR. Russia's Intervention in the Internal Affairs of the Former Soviet Republics and the Implications for United States Policy Toward Russia*. Strengthening Democratic Institutions Project (Cambridge, MA: John F. Kennedy School of Government, Harvard University, January 1994).
237   See Suzanne Crow, 'Russia Reasserts its Strategic Agenda', *RFE/RL Research Report*, vol.2, no.50 (17 December 1993).

studies at the time.[238]

This chapter is divided into four sections. The first two discuss the elevation of the Crimean oblast to an autonomous republic in 1991 on the eve of the disintegration of the USSR. This provides an overview of Ukrainian policies to the Crimea. The last two sections deal with specific Crimean issues, Nikolai Bagrov and the Crimean 'party of power' and the endemic of organised crime in the Crimea.

### Oblast to Autonomous Republic

In the December 1991 referendum on Ukrainian independence the Crimea gave the lowest vote - 54 per cent - in support of independence. This was higher though, than the predicted 45 per cent for the Crimea.[239] 'People here will vote for whatever promises a good life, and the economy is better in Ukraine than in Russia', one Crimean Supreme Soviet deputy stated.[240] Crimean support for independence came as a surprise.

Certainly, public opinion in the Crimea has never been unanimous on its future status. Those in favour of the Crimea's separation from Ukraine have tended to be in a minority as have those in favour of an independent republic. The two largest groups in opinion polls in the 1990s tended to be those in favour of remaining within Ukraine (35-45 per cent) and as an independent member of the CIS (20-30 per cent), although this last possibility was rather ill defined.[241] These figures changed after 1993 with the economic crisis in

---

238   See Roman Solchanyk, 'Ukrainian-Russian Confrontation Over the Crimea', *RFE/RL Research Report*, vol.1, no.7 (21 February 1992), R. Solchanyk, 'The Crimean Imbroglio: Kyiv and Simferopol', *RFE/RL Research Report*, vol.1, no.33 (21 August 1992), R. Solchanyk, 'The Crimean Imbroglio: Kyiv and Moscow', *RFE/RL Research Report*, vol.1, no.40 (9 October 1992), Ian Bremmer, 'Ethnic Issues in Crimea', *RFE/RL Research Report*, vol.2, no.18 (30 April 1993), S. Crow, 'Russian Parliament Asserts Control Over Sevastopol', *RFE/RL Research Report*, vol.2, no.31 (30 July 1993), Andrew Wilson, 'Crimea's Political Cauldron', *RFE/RL Research Report*, vol.2, no.45 (12 November 1993) and 'The Elections in Crimea', *RFE/RL Research Report*, vol.3, no.25 (24 June 1994).

239   *The Independent*, 29 November 1991.
240   *The Independent*, 7 September 1993.
241   See Russia's Radio, 6 January, Radio Kyiv, 6 and 8 March and *Moloda Hvardiya*, 20 March 1992.

Ukraine making staying with Ukraine a less attractive option. Nevertheless, this division of views still reflects the serious divisions within the Crimean population over their future status.

Until January 1991 the Crimea was an *oblast* like any other in Ukraine. The growing Ukrainian nationalist movement in 1989-1990, coupled with the passage of a relatively moderate language law in 1989, led to a drive for separatism in the Crimea spearheaded by local communists. This repeated a pattern which took place elsewhere in the former USSR (e.g. the three Baltic republics, Moldova). The movement for separatism as a reaction to Ukrainian nationalism was led by the then chairman of the Crimean Supreme Soviet, Nikolai Bagrov (earlier chairman of the Crimean *oblast* council and first secretary of the Crimean *oblast* Communist Party). An associate of Bagrov, Leonid Grach, headed the extremist Russian Language Society and went on to head the re-registered Crimean branch of the Communist Party Ukraine. Bagrov and Grach forced a public debate on future alternatives for the Crimea which grew after Ukraine declared sovereignty on 16 July 1990.

Fears of a Rukh-Tatar alliance in the aftermath of Ukraine's secession from the USSR was a major driving force behind calls to upgrade the *oblast* to an autonomous republic. 'Rukh is actively supporting the OKND (Organisation of the Crimean Tatar Movement) and calling for Crimea to remain in Ukraine. Then...together we'll kick out the Union, and, to settle accounts, we, Rukh, will give Crimea back to you as a national republic', Crimean Russian nationalists claimed.[242] This reflected the highly exaggerated and misleading arguments made by Russian nationalist-separatists about the threats that allegedly existed against them upon Ukraine becoming an independent state. In late 1990 local Crimean branches of the Communist Party gave their approval to hold a referendum to resurrect the Crimean Autonomous Soviet Socialist Republic which had been abolished in 1945 (although with the conspicuous absence of any consultations with the Tatars). Leonid Kravchuk, then chairman of the Ukrainian parliament, stated his support for a referendum to decide the Crimean *oblast's* fate. He did not oppose autonomous status but refused to accept its separation from Ukraine. Kravchuk feared that if he opposed the elevation of the Crimea from *oblast* to autonomous republic

---

242    *Komsomolskaya Gazeta*, 21 November 1990.

it would petition the USSR Supreme Soviet to revoke the 1954 decision to transfer the Crimea from the Russian SFSR to Ukraine. Ukraine would have then become an independent state in January 1992 without the Crimea. As Kravchuk explained, in January 1991 the referendum could have used one of two bulletins, one upgrading the Crimea *oblast* to autonomous republic and another petitioning the USSR Supreme Soviet to annul the 1954 transfer to Ukraine:

> If we then did not go for autonomy it could be very simple; the Supreme Soviet of the USSR would have adopted a decision to cancel the act of 1954 on the basis of appeals from the inhabitants of Crimea *oblast* and we'd have lost the Crimea completely. That is why I believe that this decision was correct. But, if this decision were to have been transferred to 1992 then there'd have been no question .[243]

It is not surprising that President Kravchuk did not challenge the unconstitutionality of the Crimean referendum. Prior to the August 1991 putsch he never supported Ukrainian independence and also remained a member of the Communist Party. Indeed, the Communist Party throughout Ukraine prior to August 1991, in cohorts with the KGB, attempted to hold back the nationalist tide by supporting separatism in Trans-Carpathia, Donbas, Odesa and the Crimea. Kravchuk must have been aware of these policies but showed little interest in halting them.

The Crimean referendum was held on 20 January 1991. Of the 81 per cent who participated in the referendum, 93.26 per cent voted to revive the Crimean ASSR within Ukraine, as long as Ukraine remained within the USSR.[244] The former Crimean *oblast* was upgraded to the status of autonomous republic and its *oblast* council to that of a Supreme Soviet. In essence, the local Communist Party stayed in control. There was little to differentiate

---

243　Interview with L.Kravchuk, Kyiv, 28 November 1995.
244　The central committee of the Communist Party Ukraine stated that if Ukraine seceded from the USSR the Crimean ASSR had, 'the right to independently decide its fate beyond the confines of Ukraine' (*Molod Ukrayiny*, 23 May 1991). The law 'On the Revival of the Crimean Autonomous Soviet Socialist Republic' was signed by Leonid Kravchuk as parliamentary chairman (*Radianska Ukrayina*, 14 February 1991).

the former *oblast* council from the Crimean branch of the Communist Party. The Tatars boycotted the referendum because it failed to create a Crimean Tatar autonomous republic that they still pressed for. Ukrainian nationalist groups saw the vote as an assault on Ukraine's territorial integrity.[245] The referendum was accompanied by Ukrainophobe hysteria in the Crimean media.[246] National democratic parties, the Ukrainian Autocephalous Orthodox Church and the *Prosvita* Ukrainian Language Society were all denied registration in the Crimea.[247]

As in most ethnic Russian enclaves in the former USSR the local leadership supported the hard-line putchists in August 1991. But the Crimean leadership managed to remain in power despite this black mark because, unlike in Russia, nobody was victimised in Ukraine for supporting the short lived junta. A month after the Ukrainian declaration of independence in September 1991 the Crimean Supreme Soviet adopted its own declaration of sovereignty.

After the disintegration of the USSR in December 1991 the momentum for Crimea's separation from Ukraine gathered pace. In February 1992 the Republican Movement of the Crimea (RDK) began a campaign to collect 180,000 signatures within two months to hold a referendum on the peninsula's fate in accordance with a newly adopted Crimean referendum law. The RDK posed the question in the campaign: 'Are you in favour of an independent Crimean republic in union with other republics?' The contradictions inherent in this double edged question were pointed out in Kyiv - what kind of independent state is it that can only exist in union with others?

The referendum campaign immediately soured relations with the Ukrainian leadership. Nationalist groups in Kyiv demanded tough action against the RDK. The northern *rayons* of the Crimea threatened to hold their own referendum on unification with Ukrainian *oblasts* to the north.[248] The RDK, supported by the then commander of the Black Sea Fleet, Igor Kasatonov, threatened to expel Ukrainian military delegations from Sevastopol and

---

245   *The Independent*, 22 January 1991. See also *Radianska Ukrayina*, 19 January, *Molod Ukrayiny*, 17 and 26 January, 1991.

246   See *Za Vilnu Ukrayinu*, 29 November 1990.

247   *Sobornist*, vol.1, no.11 (January 1991).

248   See the meeting in Krasnoperekopskyi which threatened to secede from the Crimea if the peninsula seceded from Ukraine (*Kyivska Pravda*, 7 April 1992).

to raise funds to support officers who had refused to take the Ukrainian oath of loyalty.[249]

Relations between the Crimea and Kyiv sharply deteriorated between February-May 1992. On 26 February the Crimean Supreme Soviet voted to change its name to the Crimean Republic (from Crimean ASSR) as a further step towards full sovereignty. In the debate over the Crimean constitution a majority voted to remove the words 'within the confines of Ukraine' from the opening line: 'The Crimean republic is a democratic state...'[250] In Sevastopol and Simferopol, particularly, relations between Russian separatists, Ukrainian nationalists and the Ukrainian authorities sharply deteriorated.

Rumours persisted that the National Guard was dispatched from Kyiv, local 'combat units' were being formed from Afghan veterans and demobilised airborne and marine troops. Pro-Ukrainian demonstrators were often attacked and beaten up. Only a minority of officers in the Black Sea Fleet meanwhile, agreed to take the Ukrainian oath of loyalty.[251] The visit to the Crimea by a large group of Ukrainian nationalist paramilitaries also inflamed passions.[252] President Kravchuk sent a strongly worded open letter in April 1992 to the Crimean population condemning the referendum campaign, warning that Kyiv would not tolerate any border changes.

Negotiations between Kyiv and the Crimea did finally produce the legislative basis for the division of powers and responsibilities between them. The Crimean Republic won far reaching powers which covered most spheres, apart from security and foreign affairs. In return, the Crimean Republic was recognised as an inseparable region of Ukraine whose laws would not violate the Ukrainian constitution.[253] The Crimea established 17 ministries, adopted laws on elections which envisaged a presidency, created its own flag and state emblem and a presidential decree allowed the creation of a free economic zone.[254] The Crimean Republic was also given the right to, 'enter in-

---

249    *Visti z Ukrayiny*, no.8, 1993.
250    *Holos Ukrayiny*, 27 February 1992.
251    *Nezavisimost*, 31 October and *News From Ukraine*, no.6, 1992.
252    See Taras Kuzio, 'Ukrainian Paramilitaries', *Jane's Intelligence Review*, December 1992.
253    The law was published in *Holos Ukrayiny*, 5 May 1993.
254    See *Robitnycha Hazeta*, 23 June and *Holos Ukrayiny*, 18 and 25 September 1993. The decree was published in *Holos Ukrayiny*, 25 June 1993.

dependently into social, economic and cultural relations with other states'. In January 1993, the Crimean authorities agreed to the establishment of the mission of the President of Ukraine (in contrast to Presidential prefect, as in the remainder of Ukraine), which was established in the Crimea to safeguard the Ukrainian constitution.[255]

Tensions worsened on 5 May 1992 when the Crimean Supreme Soviet declared 'independence', which was to have been confirmed in a referendum. The Crimean leadership argued that the RDK collection of over 240,000 signatures required them to formally declare independence prior to holding a referendum. In reality, the main objective was to put pressure on Kyiv to redress the law dividing responsibilities between Kyiv and the Crimea, the final draft of which had been changed to the latters disadvantage. Evidence for this is to be found in the vote to include the Crimea within Ukraine in its constitution made on the following day. After the law was modified on 30 June 1992 to suit Crimean objections a decision to 'suspend', not drop, the referendum was made. When it was finally adopted the law did not provide for territorial citizenship but did give the Crimea rights to property and natural resources in the Crimea. This was far more important to the post-communist Crimean 'party of power' than citizenship, as it – like its counterparts elsewhere in Ukraine – saw it as a step to enriching themselves.

The declaration of 'independence' produced a crisis that could have spun out of control. Ukrainian national democratic groups demanded the introduction of presidential rule, the dissolution of the Crimean Supreme Soviet and arrest of Bagrov on charges of 'treason'.[256] Rukh blamed the conservative majority 'party of power' within the Ukrainian Supreme Soviet and government for failing to halt Crimea's slide towards independence. Rukh also demanded that the Kyiv authorities, 'firmly support the return of the Crimean Tatars and other deported peoples to their Motherland, to support their right to self determination'. The statement also demanded a strongly worded protest to Russia over its interference in Ukrainian internal affairs and the prohi-

---

255   The law on 'Presidential Representation in the Crimean Republic' was published in *Holos Ukrayiny*, 27 January 1993. Sevastopol does not come under Crimean jurisdiction, but has an all- Ukrainian status, and therefore its Presidential prefect was already in place.

256   *Moscow News*, no.20, 1992 and *The Independent*, 6 May 1992.

bition of organisations that threaten Ukraine's territorial integrity.

In this statement Rukh revealed its consistent stand in support of Tatar rights and its hostility to Russian designs on the Crimea. This was in contrast to post-communist centrists who have been disinterested in Tatar rights and were more willing to accommodate Russian interests in the Crimea and elsewhere. On the occasion of the 59th anniversary of the 1944 ethnic cleansing of Tatars, Rukh issued a statement that condemned such 'inhuman' policies.[257]

President Kravchuk and Crimean Supreme Soviet chairman Bagrov negotiated a compromise. Kravchuk described the 'independence' decision (made when he was away on a visit to the USA) as 'unconstitutional'. The compromise included the demand that within 2 weeks the Crimean Supreme Soviet rescind its declaration and referendum, which it eventually fulfilled.[258] This prevented the crisis escalating into an 'Abkhazian' scenario where a declaration of independence led to a Georgian military response that was defeated by Russian-backed separatists.

### Ukrainian Policies towards the Crimea

Ukrainian policies towards the Crimea have been cautious which have reflected its overall positive approach towards national minority questions.[259] The Ukrainian Communist leadership, led by then chairman of the Ukrainian parliament, Kravchuk, supported the drive towards restoring the Crimea's autonomy. At the time, national democratic groups protested against the revival of an autonomous republic analogous to that which existed prior to 1944. Ukrainian democratic groups, in contrast to former President Kravchuk,

---

257    www.razom.org.ua (web site of the Our Ukraine bloc).

258    The resolution of the Ukrainian parliament was published in *Holos Ukrayiny*, 15 May 1993.

259    See Susan Stewart, 'Ukraine's Policy toward its Ethnic Minorities', *RFE/RL Research Report*, vol.2, no.36 (10 September 1993). The CSCE has often commended Ukraine for its positive ethnic minority polices. The CSCE (now OSCE) High Commissioner for National Minorities told his Ukrainian hosts that their policy should serve as the standard for other countries to follow (*Holos Ukrayiny*, 7 June 1994).

always voiced their support for the Crimea to be transformed into a Tatar homeland within the confines of Ukraine.

After Ukraine's independence from the USSR in December 1991 the Ukrainian authorities continued their positive policies towards national minorities and Ukraine remained free of the ethnic violence which many other former Soviet republics suffered from. A major plank in former President Kravchuk's appeasement of regional elites who could potentially be a threat to Ukraine's territorial integrity was to co-opt them by striking deals. This exchanged their neutrality vis-a-vis independence with patronage. These policies assisted in maintaining an artificial stability in Ukraine throughout 1992 but the consensus began to brake down in 1993-1994. First, the agreement led to stagnation of the newly independent state with little forward momentum in reform. Second, maintaining former Soviet elites at the local level in the Crimea and Donbas tied former President Kravchuk's hands vis-a-vis economic reform which was largely absent from his own policies.

As the economy improved in Russia under the impact of economic reforms the local population in the Donbas and Crimea began to compare their living standards in Ukraine to Russia in an unfavourable manner. Their revenge came in the January Crimean presidential and March 1994 Ukrainian parliamentary elections and referenda where they voted for leaders and political groups that advocated separation from Ukraine and reintegration with Russia.[260]

Ukraine's plans were severely upset by the election of President Meshkov in January 1994. Kyiv only allowed the presidential elections in the Crimea to take place because it expected that 'its favourite', Bagrov, would win. Bagrov has a similar pedigree to former President Kravchuk; both of them are former leading functionaries in the Communist Party of Ukraine. Bagrov was expected to follow the Kravchuk path; from chairman of parliament to president. Kyiv had counted on Bagrov to keep the lid on the Crimean cauldron by granting him a wide array of powers and rights. In return Bagrov, as former chairman of the Crimean Supreme Soviet, would not seek to harm Ukrainian

---

260    See Taras Kuzio, 'Ukrainian Election Results Point to Growing Regionalism', *Jane's Intelligence Review Pointer*, no.6 (April 1994); R. Solchanyk, 'Crimea's Presidential Election' and Ustina Markus, 'Crimea Restores 1992 Constitution', *RFE/RL Research Report*, vol.3, nos.11 and 23 (18 March and 10 June 1994).

territorial integrity or its security interests. But in assuming that Bagrov would follow the Kravchuk path from parliamentary chairman to president, Kyiv did not take into consideration one vital factor. The Crimea, in terms of a high degree of ethnic awareness and political activism, is more akin to Western Ukraine, the only region where Kravchuk came second to his national-democrat rival, Viacheslav Chornovil, in the December 1991 presidential elections.[261] There were no national-democratic candidates in the June-July 1994 presidential elections in Ukraine, unlike in the Crimea. Of the seven candidates only one, Volodymyr Lanavoi, was from the democratic camp (in contrast to four in the December 1991 elections). Nationalist hopes were pinned instead on Kravchuk as the 'lesser of two evils' against the other frontrunner, Leonid Kuchma. Kuchma stood for, 'a rejection of self isolation, and a restoration of all mutually advantageous economic, spiritual and cultural links with the former republics of the Soviet Union, above all with Russia'. Meanwhile, Ukrainian authors accused the Kuchma government of helping to fan the flames of 'anti-Ukrainian tendencies' in the Crimea.[262]

Could former President Kravchuk have relied on anybody else in the Crimea to maintain Ukrainian sovereignty other than post communists, such as Bagrov? This is unlikely because there were only two serious power brokers in the Crimea: the former Communist *nomenklatura*, grouped around Bagrov and initially the Party of Economic Revival of the Crimea, and the Russian nationalist camp grouped around the Russia Bloc. After the marginalisation of Russian nationalists, Crimean Communists filled the political void as the second power broker in the peninsula.

The Ukrainians numbered, according to the last Soviet census of 1989,

---

261   The Galician region of Western Ukraine and the Crimea gave the highest and lowest support respectively for Ukrainian independence in the December 1991 referendum (nearly 100 percent and 54 percent respectively). They therefore represent the two polar extremes in Ukraine that were reflected in the June-July 1994 Ukrainian presidential elections. Whereas Kuchma obtained 82.5 percent Kravchuk obtained only 7 percent in the Crimea. In Western Ukraine, on the other hand, the voting pattern was reversed and Kravchuk polled 70-90 percent of the vote (*UPI*, 27 June 1994). In the city of Sambir, Lviv *oblast*, Kravchuk obtained an astounding 99 percent of the vote.

262   UNIAR, 20 June 1994. Ukrainian authors accused the Kuchma government of helping to fan the flames of 'anti-Ukrainian tendencies' in the Crimea (*Vechirnij Kyiv*, 9 February 1994).

25.75 per cent of the Crimean population. Together with the Tatar population they therefore made up over a third of the peninsula's population. Theoretically therefore, they could pose a potential danger to the Russian majority. But this was severely hampered by the russification of the Ukrainian population and their political apathy on behalf of their ethnic rights. In the referendum that accompanied the March 1994 parliamentary elections in the Crimea, 78.4 per cent voted for greater autonomy and 82.8 per cent for dual Russian-Ukrainian citizenship (figures higher than the Russian ethnic population of the Crimea).

The Kyiv authorities therefore were left with little choice but to cooperate with the former Communist *nomenklatura* in the Crimea who, after all, were long time acquaintances of the then Ukrainian president. Bagrov had distanced himself from the Republican Movement of the Crimea (RDK), led by Meshkov, after he had obtained what he perceived to be the maximum he could obtain from Kyiv, short of full 'independence'.[263] The May 1992 vote by the Crimean parliament for secession was merely an attempt at pressuring Kyiv to grant greater concessions to the Crimea in the negotiations then taking place over the division of powers between them.

Former President Kravchuk always respected power and influence, moving in that direction in order to be associated with the dominant trend. This was acutely seen during 1990-1991 when he gradually moved towards the nationalist camp as the USSR was disintegrating. In the Crimea he never supported the Tatars because they were insufficiently large or an influential group, such a step would have anyway antagonised the then Bagrov leadership. In a manner similar to Ukrainian nationalist groups, Tatars backed Bagrov and Kravchuk in the Crimean and Ukrainian presidential elections respectively as the 'lesser of two evils'.[264]

---

263    During the Crimean presidential elections Bagrov stated that, 'Crimea's secession from Ukraine is out of the question, Meshkov's policy of promising people to take them into Russia's arms is a road to nowhere'. He referred to the Helsinki agreement, Russian-Ukrainian agreement and the Trilateral Agreement on nuclear weapons as three documents which ruled out border changes (Radio Ukraine, 23 January 1994).

264    The Tatars preferred Bagrov and Kravchuk in a choice pitting them against Meshkov and Kuchma respectively, who were both pro-Russian in their strategic orientations. The leader of the Tatar 'parliament' (Medzhilis), Mustafa Dzhemilev, said that

But, after the election of Meshkov as Crimean president in 1994, and the escalation of the crisis between Crimea and Kyiv, former President Kravchuk dropped any earlier reservations he held against openly supporting the Tatars.[265] Former President Kravchuk stated for the first time on the fiftieth anniversary of the Tatar ethnic cleansing from the Crimea that they were entitled to strive for 'statehood'.[266] Typically for Kravchuk, he never defined what he meant by 'statehood'.

Whereas Tatar groups were already well organised and have remained highly politicised the Ukrainian minority, with a lot of prodding from unofficial and official quarters in Kyiv, only began to politically organise in 1993. Ukrainian national democratic political parties were – and remain - relatively weak in the Crimea, as they are throughout Eastern and Southern Ukraine. The weakness of national democratic and Orange forces in this region could be seen in the 2004 and 2006 elections. Newly organised Ukrainian civic groups and political parties, especially after the election of President Meshkov, made a conscious effort to align the Ukrainian ethnic minority in an alliance with the Tatars. This was an attempt to prevent Russian-speaking Ukrainians from giving their support to Russian nationalists. In March 1994, Ukrainian and Tatar civic organisations issued joint statements calling for cooperation and opposition against President Meshkov who was widely quoted as saying Russian extremist Vladimir Zhirinovsky 'was a highly talented man'.[267] Ukrainian civic groups in Kyiv and their deputies in parliament would, 'be even more uncompromising in defending the interests of the Crimean Tatars'. Meanwhile, the Tatars 'will support Ukrainian organisations on the issues of preserving Ukraine's territorial integrity and consolidating Ukrainian statehood on the territory of the Crimea'[268] .

On 28 November 1993, Ukrainian civic groups and political parties

---

the Crimean Tatars would, 'definetly be against Leonid Kuchma' because they viewed the Tatar question as purely a 'Crimean ethnic minority' question (UNIAN, 29 April 1994). On Tatar support for Kravchuk see *Molod Ukrayiny*, 17 June 1994.

265    See the commemorations of the fiftieth anniversary of the deportation of the Crimean Tatars attended by former President Kravchuk (*Holos Ukrayiny*, 21 April, 17 May 1994 and ITAR-TASS,18 May 1994).

266    *Holos Ukrayiny*, 18 May 1994.

267    *Kurier*, 22 March 1994.

268    Radio Ukraine, 29 March 1994.

throughout the Crimea gathered to establish the Civic Congress of the Crimea.[269] One of the first statements of the Civic Congress was a call to boycott the Crimean presidential elections which would be the, 'last step on the way towards tearing Crimea away from Ukraine'. From the outset therefore, the Ukrainian Civic Congress, the only all-Crimean representative Ukrainian body, came out (like the Tatars) against a presidential institution in the Crimea.[270] The Ukrainian Civic Congress described itself as a 'shadow parliament' in opposition to the then Crimean leadership. In late May 1994, after the re-adoption of the 1992 separatist constitution by the Crimean parliament, it issued an appeal stating that, 'A totalitarian dictatorship is emerging in the Crimea, built on the basis of open Russian chauvinism'. The Civic Congress went on to state that,

The pro-Russian chauvinists and their media are trying to convince people that Kyiv is responsible for all of Crimea's troubles...This campaign has already reached its goal: fear is common among Crimean residents and households are becoming involved in interethnic clashes.

The demands of the Ukrainian Civic Congress were echoed by democratic and national democratic groups in Kyiv. These demands included:[271]

- Dissolve the Crimean Supreme Soviet;
- Abolish the Crimean presidency;
- Impose direct presidential rule by Kyiv over the Crimea;
- That any settlement of the Black Sea Fleet should include withdrawal of Russian ships from Ukrainian territory;
- No leases of Ukrainian territory should be granted to foreign mili-

---

269    On the congress see *Post Postup*, no.44 (2-8 December 1993). On the extraordinary congress of the Civic Congress see *Holos Ukrayiny*, 25 January 1994.

270    The law 'On the President of the Crimean Republic' was adopted by the Crimean Supreme Soviet in 1993 under Bagrov in the hope that he would be its first beneficiary. While former President Kravchuk believed this to be the case and he did not oppose the institution of presidency in the Crimea. The appeal by the Civic Congress demanded that former President Kravchuk condemn the attempt of the 'communist party *nomenklatura*' (i.e. Bagrov) to install a presidency in the Crimea (*Narodna Hazeta*, no.50, December 1993).

271    See the statement on obtaining international diplomatic support to solve the Crimean crisis by the Christian Democratic Party of Ukraine (*Vechirnij Kyiv*, 2 June 1994).

tary bases;

- Recognition of the *Majlis* as the official representative of the Crimean Tatars; [272]
- Abolish Crimean autonomous status.[273]

The only demand which was acted upon by the Ukrainian leadership was that of introducing a presidential representative, Valery Horbatov, in the Crimea in April 1994.[274] Even then the position only remained until June 1994 when the newly elected local councils abolished Presidential prefects throughout Ukraine.

After the election of Meshkov as President of the Crimea relations between Ukraine and the Crimea steadily deteriorated. Meshkov and his allies in the newly elected Crimean Supreme Soviet clouded their strategic aims by advocating at different times to remain within Ukraine, create a Crimean independent state or union with Russia. Their clear aim was to remain in Ukraine only on the basis of a treaty between the Crimea and Kyiv, similar to federal republics in the Russian Federation. Such a step would have led to the federalisation of Ukraine.

To the Ukrainian authorities these steps were anathema and they followed a three pronged responce - legal, economic and military - to attempt to forestall President Meshkov's aims in the Crimea and the city of Sevastopol. First, they annulled numerous decrees by President Meshkov and laws adopted by the Crimean Supreme Soviet by asserting the supremacy of Ukrainian over Crimean legislation. Second, economic sanctions were threat-

---

272    Radio Ukraine, 31 May 1994. The deputy chairman of the Crimean Supreme Soviet, Viktor Mezhak, ridiculed the shadow parliament as not possessing the authority to speak on behalf of Crimeans (ITAR-TASS, 1 June 1994).

273    *Samostiyna Ukrayina*, no.18 (15-18 May). See also the statement of the Democratic Coalition Ukraine electoral bloc (*Holos Ukrayiny*, 9 February) and by Rukh chairman, Chornovil (*Vechirnij Kyiv*, 18 May). Chornovil demanded that steps be taken, 'to rebuff foreign intervention into the affairs of our state, to prevent armed conflct in the centre of Europe...' The Ukrainian National Assembly added stronger demands such as the introduction of martial law in the Crimea, arrest of Crimean leaders, introduction of further security forces and its administration by the Ukrainian Ministry of Defence (UNIAR, 20 May 1994).

274    Reuters, 2 April 1994. See the hostile Crimean response and Ukrainian reply in *Holos Ukrayiny*, 12 April 1994.

ened against the Crimea. The Crimea had a budget deficit and relied on Ukraine for fresh water, energy and foodstuffs. The northern Crimean canal, which took its water from the Dnipro river, was built at a cost of $2 billion while the Crimea was part of Soviet Ukraine. The Crimea receives 75 per cent of its industrial products and 85 per cent of its electricity from Ukraine. Then President Kravchuk warned, 'The economic consequences of Crimea's separation from Ukraine would be catastrophic'.[275] Third, while openly declaring the inadmissibility of the use of force Ukraine's security presence in the Crimea, which was already more than double that in the Soviet era, was increased. Personnel, equipment and bases were strengthened in the Crimea (see Chapter 7).

In February 1994, the Ukrainian parliament adopted the first in a number of legal resolutions dealing with the Crimea. The resolution rejected separate Crimean citizenship or dual citizenship. This Russian policy was promoted throughout the CIS but only introduced by Turkmenistan and Moldova (Turkmenistan abrogated it in 2003). The resolution also called for the introduction of a presidential prefect in the Crimea (which was later undertaken). It also ruled out any changes in Ukraine's borders which were 'unitary, indivisible, inviolable and integral'. The resolution demanded that the Crimea should bring the constitution and other legislative acts of the Crimean republic into conformity with Ukraine's constitution and legislation.[276]

Then Ukrainian parliamentary chairman Ivan Pliushch said that '[w]e can no longer tolerate violations of the constitution by the Crimean authorities.'[277] But, the deadline passed and it was ignored by the Crimean authorities. Pluishch complained: '[T]his is a planned, coordination of great power, chauvinistic politicians from separate political forces in Russia, who inherited their traits from the former USSR.'[278]

As soon as Meshkov was elected president he declared his support for a referendum on the future of the Crimea. The referendum, which asked Crimean citizens three questions on greater autonomy, dual citizenship and to

---

275  Mykola Shpakovaty (ed.), *Leonid Kravchuk. Our Goal - A Free Ukraine* (Kyiv: Globus, 1993), p.45.
276  *Holos Ukrayiny*, 1 March 1994. The Crimean Supreme Soviet voted in favour of dual citizenship in July 1994.
277  AP, 25 February 1994.
278  *Holos Ukrayiny*, 20 April 1994.

give the Crimean president greater powers to rule by decree, was annulled by President Kravchuk but went ahead as a poll. He also called for a boycott of the Ukrainian parliamentary elections by taking away the ballot papers (the call was largely ignored with an average turnout of nearly 61 per cent). Three legally non-binding opinion polls went ahead simultaneously with the Crimean and Ukrainian parliamentary elections in March 1994. After threats from Kyiv, Meshkov's aides admitted they were not legally binding and only 'consultations'. They therefore were not a threat to Ukraine's territorial integrity[279] and as 'consultative opinion polls' their results were ignored. The issue was later further clouded by the claim that the results would determine Meshkov's policies. The Crimean poll asked Crimean residents if they supported the right to dual citizenship, Crimean presidential decrees having the force of law and relations between the Crimea and Ukraine regulated by a treaty and agreement. On a 67.2 per cent average turnout the following support was given to the four questions included in the opinion poll held simultaneously with the Crimean and Ukrainian elections, as seen in Table 5.1:[280]

Table 5.1 1994 Crimean Opinion Poll (Referendum) in Percent

| Question | Crimea | Sevastopol |
|---|---|---|
| Restoration of the May 1992 constitution | 78.4 | 83.3 |
| Dual citizenship | 82.8 | 87.8 |
| Presidential power | 77.9 | 82.3 |

Source: Central Election Commission, www.cvk.gov.ua.

Despite tough rhetoric from Kyiv the Ukrainian authorities continued to make concessions and extend deadlines. In the words of Serhei Holovatyy, a leading deputy from the Reforms parliamentary faction and president of the Ukrainian Legal Foundation, 'the President of Ukraine has shown indecision with regard to the leadership of the autonomous republic. We are now in a state where Leonid Kravchuk is no longer able to do anything because he is

---

279    UNIAN, 17 January 1994.
280    *Krymskie izvestiya*, 25 March 1994.

three years late.'[281]

Few of Meshkov's policies were remotely connected to economic policy, over which Kyiv gave full control to the Crimea. They were even beyond the prerogative of the Tatar autonomous republic in the Russian Federation which President Meshkov often liked to point to as an example of how Crimea's relations should be established with Kyiv.

Despite rumours of impending presidential rule[282] the Ukrainian authorities only issued another ten day ultimatum after the Crimean parliament voted on 19 May to reintroduce the May 1992 constitution which had been adopted when the Crimea declared independence. Again, former President Kravchuk threatened dire consequences if the Crimean Supreme Soviet did not rescind its decision and return to the September 1992 Crimean constitution.[283] 'If the Crimean authorities violate the Ukrainian constitution, we have enough power to force respect', President Kravchuk warned.[284] The Ukrainian parliamentary resolution (see Table 5.2) described the return to the May 1992 constitution as, 'a step towards Crimea leaving the composition of Ukraine'. It gave an ultimatum, which, like previous ultimatum's, was allowed to pass and then was extended to allow time for negotiations.[285] This tactic had worked well in summer 1992 when Bagrov backed down and 'suspended' the declaration of 'sovereignty' (independence). But, Meshkov was of a different political breed to Bagrov.

---

281  ITAR-TASS, 23 May 1994.See also Holovatyy's appeal to the CSCE (*Vechirniy Kyiv*, 25 May 1994). Holovatyy was referring to Kravchuk's initial support for Crimean autonomy in 1990-1993 when his ally, Bagrov, was in charge of the peninsula. See aslo S. Holovatiy, 'Sevstopolska Ahresiya', *Narodna Armiya*, 26 December 1996 and Ambassador Yuriy Shcherbak's speech to the Washington-based Center for Strategic and International Studies, *The Ukrainian Weekly*, 22 December 1996.

282  AP, 24 May 1994. This was also reported on Russian television five days earlier.

283  See former President Kravchuk's appeal to the Crimean Supreme Soviet (*Uriadovyj Kurier*, no.18 [21 May 1994]) and the joint appeal by Ukrainian president and government (*Holos Ukrayiny*, 19 May 1994). On Ukrainian television (19 May) Kravchuk drew a line in the sand, 'Everybody must understand that there is a limit for any society, for any state which no one is allowed to exceed. This limit is the territorial integrity of the state'.

284  *AFP*, 19 May 1994.

285  *Holos Ukrayiny*, 24 May 1994.

Table 5.2 Votes in Ukrainian Parliament on Rejecting Legislation Upgrading Crimean Autonomy to Statehood (20 May 1994)

| Faction | Yes | No | Ab-stain-ed | Not voting | Ab-sent | Per cent in favour |
|---|---|---|---|---|---|---|
| Communist | 31 | 23 | 7 | 1 | 22 | 37 |
| Socialist | 16 | 1 | 6 | - | 2 | 64 |
| Agrarians | 22 | 1 | 3 | 2 | 8 | 78 |
| Inter-Regional Reforms | 15 | 1 | 1 | - | 4 | 71 |
| Unity | 18 | 4 | 2 | 1 | 1 | 69 |
| Centre | 22 | - | 1 | 1 | 11 | 79 |
| Reform | 23 | - | - | 1 | 5 | 96 |
| Statehood | 24 | - | - | - | 1 | 93 |
| Rukh | 25 | - | - | - | 2 | 62 |
| Independent | 15 | 1 | 1 | - | 4 | 71 |
| Total | 211 | 31 | 21 | 6 | 60 | 62 |

Source: O.M. Haran and O. Mayboroda, *Ukrayinski Livi: Mizh Leninizmom i Sotsial Demokratieiu* (Kyiv: KM Akademia, 2000), p.96.

The Ukrainian parliamentary resolutions were usually adopted by two thirds of the newly elected deputies. Although the 1994-1998 Parliament had a large left-wing caucus many from this camp also adopted a tough line on the Crimea. President Meshkov's anti-communism allowed Communists and Socialists in both Ukraine and the Crimea to distance themselve from him. A leading member of the Socialist Party of Ukraine, Volodymyr Marchenko, stated that,

Socialists will not agree to Crimea's secession from Ukraine. The territorial integrity of the state envisages Crimea within the composition of Ukraine. This is unequivocal.[286]

---

286   UNIAN, 20 May. Grach, leader of the Communist Party of the Crimea, issued a statement denouncing the return to the May 1992 constitution which 'allows dishon-

Former President Kravchuk condemned the policies of the Crimean leadership which aimed to separate the Crimea from Ukraine and return it to Russia. The second plank of this 'strategic course' was the 'restoration of the former Soviet Union', he claimed.[287] He dismissed any notion of a relationship between the Crimea and Ukraine based on a treaty along the lines of Tatarstan and Russia because Ukraine was not a federal state. The Tatar-Russian Federation Treaty delegated the military, Ministry of Internal Affairs and security spheres to the central Russian authorities.[288]

The Ukrainian authorities opted to ignore their own deadline after extending it for three days to allow for negotiations to continue. Meanwhile, the Ukrainian authorities began to implement the second plank of their policy towards the Crimea; namely, to threaten and implement economic sanctions as an additional form of pressure.[289] Former President Kravchuk threatened to cut off electricity and water and added,

Let's speak frankly, Crimea today is a region which is subsidised by Ukraine. We don't have to go into all the figures; there's energy, water, etc. As the Russian saying goes, don't try to wear clothes that don't fit.

A similar policy had been applied in 1918 by the Ukrainian Hetmanate state against the Crimea which brought it to heel within three days. The Crimea draws only 20 per cent of its water from within its territory; the remainder is taken from the Dnipro river in Ukraine via a canal that could be easily closed by the Ukrainian authorities.

Then acting Prime Minister Yukhym Zvyahilskyy, himself from the Donbas, added his support to the idea of economic sanctions. The Crimea, he claimed, was in debt to Ukraine to the tune of 1,500 billion *karbovanets*. 'We must turn to sanctions like those used by Russia against Ukraine. We have

---

ourable leaders in Ukraine, Crimea and Russia to inflame interethnc hostility and a bloody conflict' (UNIAR, 22 May 1994).

287 Kravchuk has often repeated that there are political forces in Ukraine and Russia who seek the restoration of the former USSR but he warned that it would lead to civil war and bloodshed (Reuters, 3 June 1994).

288 See Kravchuk's speech to the Ukrainian parliament after the end of the ten day deadline (*Holos Ukrayiny*, 4 June 1994). See also *The Wall Street Journal* and *Financial Times*, 2 June 1994. A resolution of the Ukrainian parliament on action to be taken followed Kravchuk's speech was published in *Holos Ukrayiny*, 3 June 1994.

289 Matthew Kaminski, 'Clouds gather over Crimea as Russian tourists stay away', *Financial Times*, 16 August 1995.

enough levers such as the supply of water and electricity'. He refused to call it an 'ultimatum', 'This is a tougher approach to our relations'.[290] Then Crimean Prime Minister, Yevgeniy Saburov, later accused Kyiv of having imposed economic sanctions by scaring away tourists, who are a major source of income in the Crimea. He also condemned the curtailment of financial credits and halting of the construction of a water pipe to Sevastopol.

### Bagrov and the Crimean 'Party of Power'

The former Crimean *oblast* (until 1990) Communist Party branch divided into two groups. One group were the post-Communists who created, as in the remainder of Ukraine, centrist parties of power, such as the Party of Economic Revival of the Crimea (PEVK). The second group were hard line Communists grouped around Grach who were allowed to re-legalise the Communist Party throughout Ukraine in October 1993 after it had been banned in August 1991. Although both were hostile to one another on issues such as economic reform, they both were opposed to Russian nationalists.

Between summer 1992 to the winter of 1993 Bagrov came under attack from two camps. On the one hand, Russian nationalists accused him of having 'sold out' to Kyiv as he stepped back from Crimean independence. On the other hand, his former Communist colleagues reestablished the Communist Party in the Crimea and attacked him for having 'betrayed' Communist ideals and the aim of reconstituting the former USSR. The two camps, Bagrov's 'party of power' and Grach's Communists, became the only serious political forces in the Crimea after Meshkov's ouster as President in March 1995. In the 1998-2002 and 2002-2006 Crimean Supreme Soviets, Grach's Communists faced the new 'party of power', the People's Democratic Party (NDP), after the PEVK went into decline. The NDP went into decline after Kuchma left office and was replaced by the Party of Regions in the 2006 elections (see Chapter 6). Essentially, Crimean politics have been dominated by the Communists and a pro-Kyiv 'party of power', which at first was local (PEVK) and then a regional branch of an all-Ukrainian centrist political force (NDP, Party of Regions). Russian ethnic nationalists, such as Meshkov, were there-

---

290    UNIAN, 20 May 1994.

fore a blip in the Crimea's politics as pure ethnic Russian nationalism has always been unpopular throughout Ukraine. In the Crimea, the Soviet nationalism and pan-Slavism of the Communists competed with the pro-Russian orientation of centrist 'parties of power (PEVK, NDP and Party of Regions), two political constituencies who never supported separatism.

Tatar and national democratic political parties have remained unpopular in the Crimea. Tatars only had guaranteed representation in the 1994-1998 Crimean Supreme Soviet. Since then they have been elected as part of Rukh (1998) or Our Ukraine (2002, 2006) to the Ukrainian parliament. National democratic parties did well in the proportional half of the 2002 elections to the Ukrainian parliament held in the Crimea but fared worse in the 2006 elections. In elections to the Crimean Supreme Soviet, which were held on a majoritarian first past the post system until 2002, national democratic parties did poorly. In the 2006 elections, the first holding fully proportional elections, the Party of Regions swept the Crimean Supreme Soviet where it controls a parliamentary majority.

Political forces and personalities from the Kuchma regime which lost the 2004 elections re-grouped in the Crimean parliament elected in 2006. In 2006, the configuration in the Crimean parliament changed back towards domination by pro-Russian groups who advocated close ties with Russia and the CIS, but not separatism. The Crimean parliament's three largest factions are For Yanukovych (44), Union (11) and Crimea (10). The Union (Soyuz) faction has close links to the Progressive Socialist Party that, in an alliance with the Party for Russian-Ukrainian Union, failed to enter the Ukrainian parliament. Senior former members of the Kuchma regime were elected in the For Yanukovych bloc to the Crimean parliament. Some of these deputies, such as First Deputy Prime Minister Dmytro Tabachnyk (head of Kuchma's administration in the 1990s), returned to government after Viktor Yanukovych became Prime Minister on 4 August 2006.

The Bagrov team organized in the PEVK in the first half of the 1990s was a local 'party of power' that was disinterested in separatism and concerned only for power and self-enrichment. The PEVK disintegrated in the second half of the 1990s after it was increasingly accused of links to organised crime, and replaced first by the NDP and since 2006 by the Party of Regions. Bagrov, as Crimean Supreme Soviet chairman, declared 'sovereignty', *not* independence, on 5 May 5 1992 when 118 out of 176 deputies present voted for it. Sovereignty was understood as control over local resources vis-à-vis Kyiv, in the same manner as Ukraine's declaration of sovereignty in July 1990 vis-à-vis the Soviet centre. It was undertaken in reaction to the 29 April 1992 law 'On the Division of Authority Between Ukraine and the Republic of Crimea'. After the Crimean Supreme Soviet's declaration of sovereignty and threat of a referendum on independence, Bagrov obtained a better draft of this law from Kyiv in October 1992. He therefore used these two steps to extract concessions from Kyiv because he had *never* intended to go for independence and knew the line that he could not cross. Bagrov said:

The Act of Declaration of State Sovereignty – and I am stressing that: state sovereignty, not independence – is not an attempt to violate the integrity of Ukraine's borders. The goal of the act is to emphasise that the Crimea is not an ordinary region, but a republic that should be taken into account.[291]

Two years later the Crimean situation changed as Meshkov and his nationalist allies restored the threat of a referendum on 20 May 1994 (after Meshkov's ouster this was rescinded by presidential decree on 5 July 1995). Meshkov's 27 March 1994 'consultative polls' asked if Crimeans wanted additional autonomy within Ukraine.

Between May-September the Ukrainian parliament and Crimean Supreme Soviet discussed how powers would be delimited between them. The boundaries of this discussion were laid out by Kravchuk (he would not tolerate any threats to Ukraine's territorial integrity) and Bagrov (he would call for a referendum on the Crimea's status if he did not obtain what he wanted). This was a tacit recognition on Kravchuk's part that the Ukrainian state at that time lacked strong state institutions which meant that it had little choice but to delegate the management of the Crimea to Bagrov and the PEVK. The central authorities did control the local security forces (National Guard, Border Troops, armed forces, Security Service, see chapter 7), but national democratic, anti-separatist parties had a small support base in the Crimea which was primarily among Tatar voters.

---

291  *Krymskie Izvestia*, 9 May 1992.

The Black sea Fleet was also a source of instability as its status was that of a former Soviet military unit until agreements were signed in May 1997 that legally codified its 'temporary' (according to the July 1996 constitution) presence for 20 years. Soviet flags were then replaced by Russian flags on the Black Sea Fleet. The 17 December 1992 law on a 'Presidential Representative in the Crimea' was not implemented until *after* Meshkov became president in April 1994. The duties of Ukraine's presidential representative in the Crimea were to ensure the region observed the Ukrainian constitution, implemented presidential decrees and government resolutions.[292]

Meshkov, unlike Bagrov, was seen as a serious threat to *Ukraine's territorial integrity*. Kyiv relied on Bagrov telling him that his 'control' of the Crimean situation meant that it was fine to go ahead with a presidential election because he was certain to win. Yevhen Bersheda, then a member of the National Security Council, said that they had 'messed up' and had only agreed to the holding of elections believing that Bagrov would win.[293] In April 1993 Bagrov sent a request from the Crimean Supreme Soviet presidium for the creation of a new presidential institution. A law to this effect was adopted on 14 October 1993 and elections were held on 16 January 1994. In the second round Meshkov obtained 75 per cent and Bagrov 23 per cent. After Bagrov lost, it is little wonder that Kuchma abolished the Crimean presidency in March 1995. Meshkov appealed to no avail to Russia, 'not to allow arbitrariness and to protect the universally recognized, inalienable civil, political, ethnic, religious and linguistic rights of the inhabitants of the Crimea'.[294]

Meshkov's appeal was followed by an attempt to hold a referendum on joining the Russian-Belarusian union which was blocked by Kyiv. President Kuchma took control of the Crimean government and only rescinded this after it agreed not to finance the referendum. Ukraine also demanded that Russia close its Crimean Consulate which it accused of illegally giving Russian citi-

---

292    Interview with presidential representative Anatoliy Komiychuk, *Ukrayina moloda,* 12 August 1989.

293    Interview with Yevhen Bersheda, National Security and Defence Council, Kyiv, 20 February 1994.

294    See the appeal of Crimean President Meshkov to President Yeltsin, the State Duma and the 'people of Russia' in *Krymskiye Izvestiya,* 23 March 1995 which was reprinted with a critical commentary in *Vechirniy Kyiv,* 28 March 1995. The Ukrainian parliament responded with its own appeal (*Holos Ukrayiny,* 14 April 1995).

zenship to residents of Ukraine. First Deputy Foreign Minister Borys Tarasiuk said, 'According to the Vienna convention (on diplomatic activity) consulates should provide services to citizens of the country which they represent'.[295] The Consulate was allowed to re-open in 1999.[296]

Ukraine did not feel threatened by a Crimean President committed to 'sovereignty' (Bagrov) but this was different with a President committed to 'independence' (Meshkov). After Meshkov and Sergey Tsekov were removed from the presidency and Crimean Supreme Soviet respectively in spring 1995, the region returned to being controlled by pro-Ukrainian centrist loyalists (a situation that had existed between 1991-1993). This configuration has continued until  the 2006 elections. During the 1990s the Crimea was only ruled by nationalists for less than 2 years (1994-1995) when Meshkov and his allies were in power.

Although the ouster of Meshkov removed the threat of separatism and marginalised Russian nationalism in the Crimea it also gave Russia an additional excuse to delay the signing of the treaty with Ukraine.[297] Between 1994-1997 there were nine postponements of Yeltsin's visit to Ukraine. The Crimean question and Russia's unwillingness to recognise Ukraine as an independent state – were the two major reasons for his postponed visits.

In October 1992 a compromise led to the Crimea agreeing not to be a subject of international law, its status could not be changed without Ukraine's agreement and – importantly – Ukraine recognised Crimea's right to ownership over its land and resources. The local former Communist *nomenklatura* (Bagrov and PEVK) received what they wanted from this compromise, and so did Kyiv. Kyiv turned a blind eye to Bagrov's transformation of the Crimea into his and the PEVK's personal fiefdom in 1992-1994. Russian nationalists in the Crimea saw this compromise as a 'sell out' because they then understood that Bagrov's declaration of sovereignty in May 1992 was never understood to mean independence from Ukraine.

---

295   AP, 28 March 1995.
296   ITAR-TASS, 18 March 1999.
297   James Rupert, 'Yeltsin Delays Signing Kiev Accord', *International Herald Tribune*, 17 April 1995. For a lengthier analysis see David R. Marples and David F. Duke, 'Ukraine, Russia, and the Question of Crimea', *Nationalities Papers*, vol.23, no.2 (June 1995), pp.261-289. For a Ukrainian viewpoint see Volodymyr Skachko, 'Krymska karta u Rosiyskomu pasiaynsi', *Holos Ukrayiny*, 7 April 1995.

## Organised Crime and Corruption

The Crimea became one of the most corrupt regions in Ukraine during the 1990s. Organised crime and politics entered into a close marriage. Other Ukrainian regions with high levels of organised crime included Odesa and the Donbas. As the Crimean former *nomenklatura* divided up local spoils through *prykhvatiziya* ('grabisation') organised crime increasingly became a threat. By the mid 1990s the presidential think tank, the National Institute Strategic Studies, believed organised crime was a bigger threat than separatism (i.e. in terms of Kyiv losing control over the Crimea).[298] The head of the Crimean Security Service (SBU), Major-General Oleksandr Kosyanenko, said the Crimea was the most criminalised region of Ukraine.[299]

The Crimea was economically important for its military-industrial complex, space industry, energy and tourism. Anatoly Franchuk, a Kyiv loyalist with personal links to Kuchma, was Bagrov's first deputy who went on to become Crimean Prime Minister. This reflected the close ties of the Crimean 'old boy' former *nomenklatura* network to Kyiv.

A great deal of the violence that took place during the election campaign in 1993-1994 was political only in so far as organised crime used politics to protect and promote its interests. For example, the Crimean Christian Liberal Party was wiped out literally as a local political force at this time. The Christian Liberal Party controlled the petrol and metals market in the Crimea and had, 'united the Crimean criminal-economic world into a single attack force'.[300] A portion of the violence suffered by the Tatars during this period (arsons and pogroms took place in Feodosiya, Sudak) was related to organised crime because they often had to work in the shadow economy where they clashed with criminal elements. The Tatars also clashed with local organised crime because some were involved in the narcotics trade between Uzbekistan-Crimea-Ukraine-Russia. Tatar nationalism was a convenient cover for this trade.

---

298   Interview with Oleksandr Moskalets, National Institute Strategic Studies, Kyiv, 29 November 1995.
299   *Krymskiye Izvestiya*, 25 March 1997.
300   *Izvestiya*, 5 July 1995.

By the mid 1990s during Meshkov's presidency, 'the line between crime, politics and economics has turned out to be fine'.[301] President Meshkov was, according to some reports, himself linked to organised crime through the shadow economy company IMPEKS-55 which bankrolled his party in 1992-1995. This uncontrolled situation led to a presidential decree that condemned the local Crimean authorities and law enforcement who, 'have failed to react to them and equally, with the perpetrators getting off scot-free in most cases, and preventive measures remain scarce and ineffective'.[302] This came three months after Kuchma abolished the Crimean presidency in March 1995.

Then Deputy Prime Minister for national security, and former Security Service (SBU) chairman Yevhen Marchuk, was tasked with coordinating with the local authorities measures to 'stabilise' the situation using the Ministry of Interior (MVS), SBU and the National Guard. The Ukrainian and Crimean governments were ordered to provide personnel, finance and technical equipment for the local security forces. The National Guard were instructed to follow orders from the MVS, 'to ensure the urgent participation of National Guard units in protecting public order'.

There were also two other alarming trends. First, co-operation between the MVS and organised crime,that had also become prevalent in Kyiv and Donetsk. This concern led to the creation of a counter-intelligence unit within the Crimean MVS directly subordinated to Kyiv. Second, the influx of large numbers of weapons from the separatist regions of Trans-Dniestr and Chechnya.[303]

Real power in the Crimea in the 1990s was held by two groups; that of Ukraine's then permanent Presidential representative, Dmytro Stepaniuk, and organised crime (which in the Crimea was always closely tied to local politics). Few arrests were made for the 100 average annual contract killings undertaken in the mid 1990s during the peak of organised crime activity in the Crimea. At stake was privatisation of assets once held by the Communist Party or its affiliated institutions. 'People enter politics now merely to line their

---

301    *Izvestiya*, 5 July 1995.
302    *Uriadovyi Kurier*, 29 June 1995.
303    See Taras Kuzio, 'Why are Ukraine and Moldova unable to resolve their border dispute?', *RFERL Newsline*, 28 January 2003.

pockets', Crimean Communist Party leader and former Crimean Supreme Soviet Chairman Grach, freely admitted. He pointed to the close ties between the peninsula's political, business and organised crime world's. Such a symbios also existed in Donetsk.[304] Russian nationalist-separatist factions within the Crimean Supreme Soviet had close ties to Russian organised crime in the 1990s. They often used the peninsula as a staging off area to the offshore island of Cyprus, which was then Ukraine's third largest foreign investor.

120 active criminal gangs existed in the 1990s in the Crimea of which 52 were organised into mafia-style families. Three of these extended their influence throughout the peninsula and beyond into Ukraine, Russia and even Western Europe. The accumulated capital of these three mafia groups ('Seylem', the 'Sheviov' group and the 'Bashmaki') reportedly exceeded that of the entire Crimean annual budget. 'Seylem' and the 'Bashmaki' controlled imports of metal and oil into the Crimea and their export and acted as patrons to local banks and commercial firms involved in tourism and transportation. The 'Sheviov' group was led by Vladimir Sheviov, an Armenian born in Russia who moved to the Crimea in 1985 and was reportedly one of the richest individuals on the peninsula. The 'Seylem' were a Tatar and Armenian organised crime group who were closely tied to the PEVK. Violence in summer 1995 in the Crimea which led to riots and the deaths of two Tatars was due to conflict between the 'Seylem' and 'Bashmaki' organised crime families. The 'Bashmaki' were a Crimean organised crime group who also had close ties to the PEVK. The deposed Crimean Supreme Soviet chairman, Supruniuk, was supported by the PEVK which was then led by Vladimir Sheviov, a deputy of the Crimean Supreme Soviet.

---

304   See Kerstin Zimmer, 'The Comparative Failure of Machine Politics: Administrative Resources and Fraud', *Canadian Slavonic Papers*, vol.47, nos.3-4 (September-December 2005), pp.361-384.

## Conclusions

Ukrainian policies towards the Crimea were a mixture of appeasement and rejection of the demands of the Crimean leadership. They drew the line at secession through legal means and military and economic pressure. At least two thirds of the Ukrainian parliament's deputies would always vote to annul any threats to its territorial integrity regardless of their disagreements about domestic political and economic questions. If economic and legal means did not work the Ukrainian authorities had the ultimate threat of using the security forces. President Kuchma was unlikely to have used the security force option except as a last resort because it had failed in Moldova and Georgia. There was also the presence of a large number of Russian troops in the Black Sea Fleet in the Crimea.

The 'normalisation' of Ukrainian-Russian relations after Kuchma's election in 1994 rested on an agreement being reached over the Black Sea Fleet coupled with the signing of an inter-state Russian-Ukrainian treaty. Both of these had eluded his predecessor, Kravchuk. Success in these two areas also led to the 'normalisation' of relations between Ukraine and the Crimea. This was clearly seen in 1997-1998 when Russia and Ukraine signed a treaty and Black Sea Fleet agreement and the Crimea adopted its constitution.

The elevation of the Crimea in 1991 from *oblast* to autonomous status returned it to that of the 1922-1945 era when it was an autonomous republic within the Russian SFSR. Both then, and since 1991, the Crimea was not, and continues to not be, a Tatar 'homeland'. If anything the situation is far worse today as the 1944 ethnic cleansing of Tatars and post war influx of ethnic Russians radically changed the ethnic composition of the Crimea.

Ukrainian policies towards the Crimea in the 1990s can be described as firm and non-violent. As this chapter demonstrates, the Ukrainian authorities adopted a successful mix of policies to contain the threat of Crimean separatism. At the same time, the threat was in many exaggerated. Russian nationalist-separatism was only a mass movement for a short period of time in 1994-1995 when the local 'party of power' lost control of the peninsula. In 1990-1992 the 'party of power' cooperated with Russian nationalists but determined the maximum parameters of their possible actions (i.e. sovereignty, not independence). Kyiv was forced to rely on Bagrov and the Crimean 'party of power' to contain Russian nationalists. The down side to this was the growth of high levels of organised crime in the Crimea that Kyiv tolerated in exchange for political and territorial loyalty. National democrats have always been weak in the Crimea to become a political force that Kyiv could rely upon. The Communists only became a reliable ally in 1998 when they proved useful in adopting a Crimean constitution acceptable to Kyiv. Since 1995 Russian nationalists have been marginalised and the two dominant political forces have remained Communists and centrists.

# 6    Elections and Constitution Making in the Crimea

This chapter is divided into six sections. The first two deal with the 1994 Ukrainian presidential and parliamentary elections in the Crimea. The third and fourth sections survey the rise and fall of President Yuriy Meshkov, head of the Russian nationalist-separatist movement, and the subsequent marginalisation of separatism in the Crimea. The last two sections provide an overview of the constitution making process in the Crimea and elections in the Crimea from 1998-2006.

## 1994 Crimean and Ukrainian Presidential Elections

During the 1994 Ukrainian presidential elections Supreme Soviet chairman Nikolai Bagrov did not back privatisation or radical economic reform (just like his centrist allies in Kyiv, such as President Leonid Kravchuk). In Bagrov's view, foreign investment could not be allowed into the Crimea because, 'Morgans, Rockefeller's and other big capitalists from the West will buy up the whole of the Crimea'.[305] Bagrov was also cautious about private property, especially on land, because, 'We are unsure yet just how much Crimean land is worth'.[306] This cautious approach to economic reform was true in 1994 of the post-Communist 'party of power' throughout Ukraine. Only after Leonid Kuchma was elected in 1994 did it switch to supporting economic reform provided they became its main beneficiaries.[307]

One of Bagrov's main backers was the Party of Economic Revival of the Crimea (PEVK), the party of the 'fat cats'[308], which linked together the clannish interests of the post-communist Crimean *nomenklatura* 'party of

---

305    *Economist*, 8 January 1994.
306    Intelnews, 15 January 1994.
307    See Rosaria Puglisi, 'The Rise of the Ukrainian Oligarchs', *Democratization*, vol.10, no.3 (Autumn 2003), pp.99-123; Taras Kuzio, 'Oligarchs, Tapes and Oranges: Kuchmagate to the Orange Revolution', *Journal of Communist Studies and Transition Politics*, vol.23, no.1 (March 2007), pp.5-31.
308    *Post Postup*, no.39 (28 October-3 November 1993).

power'.[309] The PEVK stood firmly opposed to both the nationalist Russia bloc and the Communists. Ironically, the backing that Bagrov received as presidential candidate from the December 1993 PEVK congress transformed him into a, 'great Ukrainian patriot'[310]. This was the very same individual who, as Crimean Supreme Soviet chairman, had orchestrated the May 1992 declaration of independence (sovereignty). Although he later claimed that this was in support of sovereignty, not independence.

Other pro-Russian candidate's from the Russian Society and the Movement of Voter's for the Crimean Republic supported Meshkov's Russian nationalist separatism. Meshkov, presidential candidate of the Russia bloc, was also leader of the Republican Movement of the Crimea (RDK), the main body which had campaigned for Crimean separatism in 1991-1993. He aimed to unite all patriotic forces into one, 'great anti-Bagrov bloc' who, 'stand for Crimea within Russia and for the independent development of the Crimean Republic...'. He was especially critical of Bagrov for having used the RDK to exert pressure upon Kyiv to extract a large degree of autonomy. The RDK therefore backed calls for a return to the May 1992 proposal to hold a referendum on 'independence' (*nezalezhnist/nezavisimost'*). He also backed a return to the 6 May 1992 constitution, both of which had been 'suspended' by Bagrov when he was Supreme Soviet chairman, in return for concessions by Kyiv.[311]

Meshkov's policies combined a mixture of local Crimean nationalism coupled with pro-Russian separatism. He backed the Crimea's 'orientation towards union with Russia' and a relationship to Ukraine only on the basis of a federal treaty. On the whole his policies remained vague. Meshkov admitted he favoured Crimean independence, 'but not in the sense of independence like Ukraine, but rather an independent republic that has the right to return to that single economic, political and cultural space from which it was forcibly torn.'[312]

---

309   The PEVK used left-wing slogans which had little connection to the interests of former high ranking Communists. See *Kyivska Pravda*, 15 September 1992.
310   *Post Postup*, no.47 (23-29 December 1993)
311   *Holos Ukrayiny*, 11 November 1993.
312   *Krymskaya Izvestiya* and *Krymskaya pravda*, 22 and 25 December 1993.

Meshkov argued that, 'the republic itself should have the rights of an independent state and act as a subject of inter-state relations'.[313] In other words, there should be a confederation between two equal entities (Crimea-Ukraine). This was similar to the demands made by Trans-Dniestr and Abkhazia towards Moldova and Georgia respectively. After coming to power in 2000, the Moldovan Communist Party initially supported such policies, but backed away from these steps in the face of strong domestic opposition and Russian policies that refused to give up the Trans-Dniestr.[314]

Bagrov backed the continuation of the status quo and believed that the Crimean President, 'should be neither pro-Ukrainian nor pro-Russian, but pro-Crimean'.[315] All candidates called for the 'demilitarisation' of the Crimea and all of them, except Bagrov, supported the Black Sea Fleet completely placed under Russian control and based in Sevastopol.[316] The Crimean Communists were opposed to the anti-communism of Meshkov and his overt Russian nationalism. Nevertheless, they agreed with Meshkov's nationalists that the Crimea was alleged threatened by Tatar Islamic fundamentalism. They also supported Moscow's call for the region to join the CIS as a separate entity to Ukraine and to re-join the rouble zone.

Bagrov lost the elections, like Kravchuk in Ukraine seven months later, due to the voter's association of him with the 'party of power'. The authorities were blamed for the economic crisis.[317] Bagrov correctly predicted, '[d]iscontent is the only answer in this election. People don't vote for a programme and this is our tragedy. They want to live better but I can't make promises. They will be disappointed very soon.'[318]

The Tatars had backed Bagrov as the 'lesser of two evils' in comparison to Meshkov. They refused to recognise Meshkov as President of the Crimean Tatar people[319] and were highly disappointed in Kyiv's mild approach to the

---

313    UNIAN, 2 December 1993.
314    See Taras Kuzio, 'Is Federalization the Right Option for Moldova?', *RFERL Newsline*, 10 March 2003.
315    *Visti z Ukrayiny*, 28 October-3 November 1993.
316    *Narodna Armiya*, 13 January 1994.
317    *Post Postup*, no.1 (3-9 February 1994).
318    *The Independent*, 3 January 1994.
319    *Nezavisimaya Gazeta*, 4 February 1994.

victory of Meshkov.[320] Kyiv had failed, in the view of the Tatars, to protect Ukraine's national interests in the Crimea. The Ukrainian Civic Congress of the Crimea held its inaugural congress on 28 November 1993 and was officially registered on 8 February 1994.[321] It called for a boycott of the Crimean presidential elections believing that the post of Crimean Presidency should be abolished. Although many Ukrainians voted for Grach and Bagrov, some must have also voted for Meshkov as Crimean President and for his Russia bloc in Crimean Supreme Soviet elections.[322] In other words, Meshkov's Russian nationalism also attracted Russophone Ukrainian voters in the Crimea.

The main contest in the Crimea's only presidential election was between Meshkov and Bagrov, with the latter backed by Kyiv, the Tatars and ethnic Ukrainians with a national democratic orientation. In the first round on 16 January 1994, Meshkov and Bagrov obtained 38.49 and 17.55 per cent respectively of the vote. The remaining candidate's obtained less than 15 per cent. Sergei Shuvainikov, leader of the Russian Party of Crimea (backed by Vladimr Zhirinovsky's extremist Liberal Democratic Party) and Leonid Grach, leader of the Crimean branch of the Communist Party of Ukraine, also obtained respectable 13.65 and 12.18 per cent votes, as seen in Table 6.1:[323]

---

320   See the comments by Mustafa Dzhemiliyev, leader of the Tatars, in *Post Postup*, 3-9 February 1994. On Tatar backing for Bagrov see Intelnews, 15 January 1994.

321   *Post Postup*, 28 October-3 November 1993.

322   Andrew Wilson, 'The Elections in Crimea', *RFERL Research Report*, vol.3, no.25 (24 June 1994), p.15.

323   See Roman Solchanyk, 'Crimea's Presidential Elections', *RFE/RL Research Report*, vol.3, no.11 (18 March 1994).

Table 6.1 Round One of Crimean Elections: 16 January 1994[324]

| Candidate | Vote | Per cent |
|---|---|---|
| Yury Meshkov | 557,225 | 38.5 |
| Nikolai Bagrov | 245,042 | 16.9 |
| Sergei Shuvaynikov | 196,342 | 13.6 |
| Leonid Grach | 176,330 | 12.2 |
| Ivan Yermakov | 90,347 | 6.2 |
| Vladimir Verkoshansky | 14,205 | 0.1 |

Source: Central Election Commission, www.cvk.gov.ua.

The votes for Shuvainikov and Grach went to Meshkov in the second round two weeks later on 30 January when Meshkov and Bagrov obtained 72.9 and 23 per cent respectively, as seen in Table 6.2:[325]

Table 6.2 Round Two of Crimean Elections: 30 January 1994

| Candidate | Vote | Per Cent |
|---|---|---|
| Yury Meshkov | 1,040,888 | 72.9 |
| Nikolai Bagrov | 333,243 | 23.4 |

Source: Central Election Commission, www.cvk.gov.ua.

The 1994 presidential election campaign was conducted under allegations of a 'threat' from Ukrainian nationalism to the Crimea. 'All of Ukraine's and the Crimea's woes are due to west Ukrainian nationalism', the leader of the People's Party of the Crimea claimed.[326] Predictably, national democratic and nationalist parties and civic organisations in Kyiv vehemently protested at Meshkov's election. 'They (the elections) were held in an atmosphere of blatant Ukrainophobia, with overt financial support from benefactors from the rouble zone', the Congress of National Democratic Forces (KNDS), complained.[327] The reference to the 'rouble zone' was to Russia. The 1994 national-democratic Democratic Coalition 'Ukraine' electoral bloc demanded the

---

324   Andrew Wilson, 'Parties and Presidents in Ukraine and Crimea, 1994', *The Journal of Communist Studies and Transition Politics*, vol.11, no.4 (December 1995), p.370.
325   *Ibid.,* pp.370-371.
326   *Kyivski vidomosti*, 10 February 1994.
327   Radio Ukraine World Service, 31 January 1994.

establishment of law and order by bringing the Crimea to heel in a more forceful manner.[328] Their colleagues in the KNDS complained that former President Kravchuk, 'keeps resorting to defensive statements as he watches it happen'.[329] The radical right protested in even more stronger terms. The most notorious comment was by the Ukrainian National Assembly who threatened that, 'Crimea will be Ukrainian or depopulated!'[330]

A Ukrainian parliamentary resolution after Meshkov's victory entitled 'The Status of the Autonomous Republic of the Crimea in Conformity with the Existing Constitution and Legislation of Ukraine' outlined the following position of the Crimea before a constitution had been adopted:[331]

-     The Crimea has no state sovereignty;
-     The Crimea cannot conduct foreign policy;
-     The Crimean constitution cannot infringe the Ukrainian constitution;
-     The Crimea is an integral component of Ukraine whose borders could not be altered;
-     The Crimea does not possess its separate citizenship, security forces or monetary-financial system;
-     The Crimea was given one month to bring its constitution and legislation into conformity with Ukraine's.

Meshkov's Russia Bloc followed his success in the Crimean presidential elections when it obtained 57 out of 98 seats in Crimean parliamentary elections. The Russia Party of Crimea obtained one seat giving Russian nationalists a total of 58. The Communists failed badly and only obtained 2 seats, with many of its votes going to Russian nationalists. This trend re-appeared in the 2004 and 2006 elections when Communist voters in the Crimea, and in Eastern Ukraine, migrated to Yanukovych and to the Party of Regions. In the 1994 elections to the Crimean Supreme Soviet, pro-Ukrainian centrists took only 19

---

328    *Holos Ukrayiny*, 26 January and 9 February 1994.
329    Radio Ukraine World Service, 31 January 1994.
330    See Taras Kuzio, 'Paramilitaries in Ukraine', *Jane's Intelligence Review*, vol.6, no.3 (March 1994).
331    *Uriadovyi Kurier*, 3 March 1994.

seats, 6 of which were for the PEVK. The Tatar *Kurultai* obtained its quota of 14 seats and cooperated with pro-Ukrainian centrists.[332] The 1994-1998 parliament was the only post-Soviet Crimean Supreme Soviet where Tatars were allocated a quota of seats. As the leaders of the Tatars pointed out, '...we again appear to be better defender of the interests of the Ukrainian state than the Ukrainians themselves'. In the 1998, 2002 and 2006 elections, Tatars were not allocated seats in the Crimean Supreme Soviet. Crimean Tatars have always been close allies of national democratic forces in Kyiv. In the 2004 presidential elections, Viktor Yushchenko obtained 15.41 percent support in the Crimea of which it is estimated that Tatar voters contributed 10-11 percent. Without Tatar votes, Yushchenko's ratings would have been similar to the 4.21 percent he obtained in Donetsk oblast.Tatars delegated senior representatives to Rukh in the 1998-2002 and to Our Ukraine in the 2002-2006 and current Ukrainian parliaments. Mustafa Dzhemilev, head of the unofficial Crimean Tatar parliament, is a parliamentary deputy within President Yushchenko's Our Ukraine faction.

### 1994 Ukrainian Parliamentary Elections

The Crimea sends 23 deputies to the Ukrainian parliament. Despite a widespread indirect call (it is illegal to call for a boycott of elections) by Meshkov's Russia bloc to boycott the 1994 Ukrainian parliamentary elections all of the seats were taken up, the remainder being voted on in the December 1995 by-elections. Crimean's therefore ignored the call for a boycott and they voted in the Ukrainian elections.[333] Only the Russia bloc called for a boycott while other political parties ignored this call: the Communists, centrists (PEVK, Union in Support of the Crimean Republic), national democratic parties and civic groups.

---

332    The *Kurultai* is run by the *Mejlis* (Crimean parliament) between Assemblies.
333    Reuters, 11 April 1994.

After the elections, centrists in the Crimean Supreme Soviet created a bloc consisting of the Union in Support of the Crimean Republic, PEVK, Democratic Party of the Crimea, and Civic Forum of the Crimea.[334] The Agrarian Party of the Crimea, like its equivalent in Ukraine, was also an ally of the centrists.[335] The Communists stood in opposition to the centrists in the PEVK, the local 'party of power', as they had supported the former Crimean speaker Bagrov, Meshkov's main challenger in the Crimea in the 1994 presidential elections. The Communists opposed calls for free economic zones, claiming the only way out of the economic crisis was to revive the former USSR as a voluntary union through republican-wide referendums. The failure of the boycott of the Ukrainian parliamentary elections could be seen in the turnout which was 62.4 and 64.7 per cent in the first and second round's respectively. This turnout was similar to that for elections to the Crimean Supreme Soviet elections.

A boycott by the Russian bloc opened the way forward for its only other strong rival, the Communists, to gain the majority of the Crimean seats allocated to the Ukrainian parliament. In the 1998, 2002 and 2006 elections, Russian nationalists no longer called for boycotts. In these three elections, Crimeans overwhelmingly endorsed pro-Russian centrist political forces. The Crimea voted overwhelmingly for Kuchma in the 1994 Ukrainian presidential elections. On numerous occasions Meshkov had backed Kuchma in the presidential elections and congratulated him on his victory. The total number of votes in the Crimea for the seven presidential candidates was outlined in Table 6.3:[336]

---

334   UNIAN, 3 February 1994.
335   UNIAR, 7 February 1994.
336   The figures were taken from Yaropolk Kulchyckyj (ed.), *Repeat Voting Presidential Election Guide Book* (Kyiv: International Foundation for Electoral Systems, 1994).

Table 6.3 First Round of 1994 Ukrainian Presidential Elections in the Crimea

| % | Leonid Kravchuk | Leonid Kuchma | Volody-myr La-novyi | Olek-sandr Moroz | Valerii Babych | Petro Talanchuk | Ivan Pliushch |
|---|---|---|---|---|---|---|---|
| Cri-mea | 7.43 | 82.58 | 3.36 | 1.26 | 1.93 | 0.22 | 0.30 |
| Se-vas-topol | 5.55 | 82.11 | 3.97 | 2.42 | 1.05 | 0.30 | 0.44 |

Source: Central Election Commission, www.cvk.gov.ua

During the second round of the Ukrainian presidential elections, Ku-chma and Kravchuk obtained the following results in the Crimea and the city of Sevastopol that are outlined in Table 6.4:[337]

Table 6.4 Second Round of 1994 Ukrainian Presidential Elections in the Cri-mea

| % | Kravchuk | Kuchma |
|---|---|---|
| Crimea | 8.88 | 89.70 |
| Sevastopol | 6.54 | 91.98 |

Source: Central Election Commission, www.cvk.gov.ua.

Despite a very high popular mandate in the Crimea for Kuchma he went about subduing separatism in a more radical manner than his 'nationalist' predecessor, Kravchuk. This was largely accomplished with the help of Dep-uty Prime Minister for national security Yevhen Marchuk, the former chairman of the Security Service of Ukraine (SBU) under Kravchuk. Between 1994-1995, Marchuk was successful in undermining the separatist movement from within by using his SBU background and network. Kuchma's popular mandate also allowed Marchuk to adopt a tougher line on the lease of Sevastopol to the Black Sea Fleet (Russia had demanded 99 years but in the end only ob-tained 20).

---

337   *Vechirnij Kyiv*, 15 July 1994.

### Rise and Fall of Meshkov

Meshkov came to power in the Crimea as it's first and last President on a rabidly anti-Ukrainian platform that could have led to more dramatic conflict with Kyiv. One of his first acts was to symbolically change Crimea to Russian time, making it an hour behind Ukraine's, although this was largely ignored in the Crimea. His demand that the security forces in the Crimea be subordinated to the Crimean republic and that Crimean conscripts only serve in the peninsula were potentially dangerous and never implemented (see chapter 7). Prior to being elected Meshkov had regularly called Kravchuk a 'nazi' or a 'fascist'. In Meshkov's eyes, 'The situation is that we are trying to rescue ourselves from a nationalistic Ukraine with the help of a democratic Russia'.[338] By seceding from Ukraine, the Crimea could become a 'showcase' for economic reform. 'We have one goal: to split from Kyiv's silly economic and political policies', Meshkov declared.[339]

Meshkov came to power with 'a ragbag of promises'[340] which would have been impossible for any politician to implement (e.g. re-join the rouble zone, peace, unity, stable incomes, independence, union with Russia, etc.,). This was compounded by the fact that his plans as to how to implement his policies were vague and his priorities were constantly changing. Meshkov's campaign demand for Crimea's separation from Ukraine changed after his election to a policy of joint Ukrainian-Russian ownership. The Crimea would undertake this by becoming a separate member of the CIS as, 'a subject of the union treaty'[341]. The Crimea formed part of the Russian people, Meshkov believed. Therefore, 'The restoration of unity is, I hope, a question of the very near future'.[342] More radical elements in the Russia bloc demanded a confederal East Slavic Union rather than unification of the Crimea with Russia.

Some of Meshkov's election language resembled that of Kuchma's during the Ukrainian presidential elections held in June-July 1994; hence, the Crimea's preference for Kuchma over Kravchuk. Calls by Meshkov for reviv-

---

338    *The Washington Post*, 28 March 1994.
339    *The Economist*, 8 January 1994.
340    *The Independent*, 31 January 1994.
341    *Moskovskiy Komsomolets*, 19 February 1994.
342    ITAR-TASS, 4 February 1994.

ing economic ties to Russia and condemnation of Kravchuk's 'isolationist' policies vis-à-vis Russia and the CIS could have come from Kuchma's election rhetoric.[343] At the same time, Kuchma never backed federalism, Russian as a 'state' language (he only raised the issue of Russian as an 'official language') or any radical expansion of Ukraine's participation in the CIS. Kuchma was also more willing to adopt harsher measures against Crimean separatism. Kravchuk permitted the creation of a Crimean presidency, thinking Bagrov would win the newly created position. In contrast, Kuchma dismantled the position after Bagrov failed to be elected.

The Russia bloc put forward the largest number of its candidates in Sevastopol and Yalta.[344] It was precisely in these regions along the southern Crimean coast where it also received the highest number of votes. This is a region cut off from the more rural northern Crimea and includes many former Soviet retirees (pensioners represent a third of the Crimean electorate[345]), dacha's, sanatorium and former military personnel. The victory of the Russia bloc enabled it to dominate the Crimean Supreme Soviet by ensuring that the chairman and his deputies came from within its ranks.

The Russia bloc consisted of a motley assortment of Russian nationalist parties in the Crimea, such as the Republican Party of the Crimea, the Republic Movement of the Crimea (RDK), the People's Party of the Crimea, the Russian Language Movement of the Crimea, the Afghan Veterans Union, the Russian Society of the Crimea, the Bloc of Leftist and Patriotic Forces (formerly the Sevastopol branch of the 'red-brown' National Salvation Front) and the Union of Soviet Officer's of the Crimea.[346] Many of these politial forces would have been dubbed as the 'red-brown' alliance in Russia.

A factor which undoubtedly contributed to a rapid decline in then President Meshkov's popularity and that of his Russia bloc was the view of many Crimeans that his extreme nationalism had caused a precipitous decline in relations with Kyiv which, in turn, had made the economic situation worse. Tourists began to visit the Crimea in fewer numbers. The new ruling Russia

---

343    *Post Postup*, 3-9 February 1994 and Reuters, 17 January 1994.
344    *Holos Ukrayiny*, 25 February 1994.
345    Reuters, 16 January 1994.
346    For a review of political parties in the Crimea see Andrew Wilson, 'Crimea's Political Cauldron', *RFE/RL Research Report*, vol.2, no.45 (12 November 1993).

bloc lacked political experience and sophistication. It's appointment of outsiders, such as former Crimean Prime Minister Yevgenny Saburov from Moscow, led to resentment from local officials who had expected a greater share of the 'spoils' of office.

## Marginalisation of Russian Separatism, 1995-1998

*Centrists Re-gain Control of Crimean Supreme Soviet*
The use of a variety of non-violent policies by the Ukrainian leadership to bring the Crimea back within its sovereignty were successful by the mid 1990s. Within the space of only one year between spring 1994 spring 1995 support for pro-Russian separatism in the Crimea collapsed. The leadership of the autonomous region was replaced by pro-Ukrainian local leaders from the 'party of power'.[347]

The Russia bloc had always been an artificial entity and therefore began to disintegrate after the 1994 elections. With just five seats clear of a majority (54 out of 98) in the Crimean Supreme Soviet any splits within their ranks proved to be disastrous in limiting their ability to pursue their agenda against the PEVK, Communists and Tatar's. Even at its peak therefore, Russian nationalists could not command the loyalty of the majority of Crimean deputies. The Russia Bloc had always been a compromise of two tendencies. One of these had stood for a 'sovereign democratic (Crimean) state' in union with Ukraine, Belarus and Russia within the CIS. The second more radical strand called for unification of the Crimea with Russia.[348] This strand was too radical for most Crimeans and never received support from Russia (unlike covert Russian support for Abkhaz and Trans-Dniestr separatism in Georgia and Moldova respectively). In the end, the pan Eastern Slavic orientation won out, as seen in the reincarnation of the Russia bloc as the Union (*Soiuz*) party in the second half of the 1990s. Soiuz's allies became the 'red-brown' Progressive Socialist Party.

---

347    See Tor Bukkvoll, 'A Fall From Grace for Crimean Separatists', *Transition*, vol.1, no.21 (17 November 1995).
348    A referendum on such a question was held by the Trans-Dniestr enclave of Moldova on 25 December 1995.

The RDK and *Souiz* had, and continue to have, links to the Bashmaki organised crime group that was funded by businesses such as Impeks-55. In the Crimea they cooperated with a second offshoot of Meshkov's former Russia bloc, the Russian Community of the Crimea led by Vladimir Eterekhov, a member of the State Duma's Council of Compatriots, and former deputy chairman of the Crimean Supreme Soviet, Sergei Tsekov. In Sevastopol their main ally was the extremist Aleksandr Kruglov, head of the local branch of the Russian All-Peoples Union led by State Duma deputy Sergei Baburin.

Support for the Russia bloc disintegrated by the end of 1994 due to infighting between the Crimean Supreme Soviet and Crimean president. They were also unable to deal with the economic crisis or attract foreign investment and tourists, despite populist promises to the contrary during the 1994 elections. In addition, Russia was pre-occupied with a severe separatist conflict in Chechnya, making it unlikely that Russia could intervene as it had done in Georgia and Abkhazia. A Russian commentary in the *Izvestiya* newspaper believed: 'It seems Leonid Kuchma has selected an ideal moment to cut the Crimean knot. Russia is now so tied up with Chechnya that its leaders have neither the strength, the desire or the possibility of playing the Crimean card.'[349]

The presidential campaign in the Crimea had been dominated, 'by illusions of the republics economic potential with Russia's patronage'. In fact, the Crimea is a heavily subsidised region by the central authorities. In addition, Russia and Ukrainian tourists no longer flocked in large numbers to the Crimea, as they had in the former USSR, because they could now travel abroad.

Rapid shift in popular moods in the Crimea were reflected in an opinion poll conducted in Autumn 1995 where then Prime Minister Anatoliy Franchuk, Kuchma's then son-in-law, was voted the most popular politician in the Crimea. Refat Chubarov, leader of the *Kurultai* Tatar faction in the Crimean parliament, and Dhemiliev, leader of the Tatar *Mejilis* 'parliament', came second and fourth respectively. Volodymyr Sheviov, leader of the (pro-Bagrov) PEVK,

---

349    *Izvestiya*, 23 March 1995. Konstantin Zatulin, head of the State Duma's committee for CIS Affairs, linked Kiv's decision to abolish the Crimea's presidency to Russia's pre-occupation with Chechnya (Interfax-Ukraine, 17 March 1995).

came third. Grach, leader of the Crimean branch of the Communist Party of Ukraine came only fifth.[350]

On 9 October 1996, the Crimean Supreme Soviet voted 74:2 to dismiss its speaker, Russian nationalist Yevhen Supruniuk, and then voted 59:26 to replace him with pro-Ukrainian loyalist Vasyl Kyseliov. Supruniuk was in hospital during the vote following a mysterious, and still unresolved, kidnapping. While in hospital his post was temporarily held by Chubarov, leader of the Tatar parliamentary faction. Uncharacteristically for the Tatars, they joined together with other pro-Russian factions to vote out Supruniuk, who was accused by the latter of being too 'pro-Ukrainian'. Kyseliov was born in 1948 in Russia but had worked within the agricultural sector on the Crimean peninsula during the previous 25 years. Between the mid 1980s to mid 1990s he was chairman of the *Druzhba Narodov* (Friendship of Peoples) collective farm. In contrast to the deposed speaker, Kyseliov was more pro-Russian with some views that were reminiscent of former Crimean President Meshkov. Kyseliov denied that he would also promote pro-Russian separatism. 'The renewal of pro-Russian feeling is possible only in the economic sphere and I'll do everything to restore business ties with Russia', Kyseliov cautioned. Such pro-Russian economic views were similar to those espoused by Kuchma himself and other centrists who had strong business and corrupt links to Russia. Kyseliov was bowing to local feelings which quickly turned against separatism in winter 1994-1995. Tsekov, the former Crimean Supreme Soviet chairman and a leading ally of Meshkov's, admitted that, 'Separatism as Ukraine saw it - rejoining Russia - did not have much support (in the Crimea)'. The Crimea had a pro-Russian orientation but this did not ultimately translate into separatism.

Following the ouster of Meshkov in 1995-1998 the Crimean Supreme Soviet was re-configured into three main groups – PEVK and *Souiz* party with 40 deputies each and 14 Tatars. Only after the 1998 elections did the Communists return in large numbers to the Crimean Supreme Soviet as in the 1994 elections, many of their votes had gone to Russian nationalists. After 1998 the Tatars were no longer allocated their quota of 14 seats.

---

350   *Flot Ukrayiny*, 16 September 1995.

The election of the more pro-Russian Kyseliov as Crimea's new Supreme Soviet chairman provded him with limited possibilities to alter Crimea's strategic and geo-political course. Both the Crimean Supreme Soviet and government had (and continue to have) few *real* powers. The Crimean Supreme Soviet or government (the post of President was abolished by Ukrainian presidential decree in March 1995), have no influence over the appointment of the heads of the local branches of the 'power ministries' (SBU, Ministry of Interior, Ministry of Defence, National Guard [until they were abolished in 1999], and Border Troops). Crimean officials can only meet foreign dignitaries after obtaining prior agreement from the Ukrainian Ministry of Foreign Affairs.

On the eve of the 1998 elections pro-Ukrainian centrists united to form the Crimea is Our Home Movement (the name was suspiciously similar to Our Home is Russia, the then 'party of power' in Russia led by former Prime Minister Viktor Chernomyrdin). The new Crimean bloc included the People's Democratic Party (NDP), Inter-Regional Bloc of Reforms (MRBR)[351], Agrarians and the Social Democratic united Party (SDPUo). Ukraine's presidential representative in the Crimea was an Agrarian party member. After 1998, the PEVK was eclipsed by the NDP as the local pro-Ukrainian 'party of power'. The NDP and MRBR merged in 2001. The NDP was itself eclipsed by the Party of Regions in 2006.

### Political Parties

The Communists were illegal in the Crimea, as they were throughout Ukraine, until a new Communist Party of Ukraine was registered in October 1993. Crimea has always represented one of its largest branches with 10,000 out of 150,000 Communist Party members. One factor which permitted the rise of Russian nationalists in 1991-1993 was the lack of a Communist presence in the Crimea as their voters had migrated to Russian nationalists.

After Ukraine adopted its constitution in June 1996 regionally-based parties were banned. In October 1996 the Ukrainian Ministry of Justice therefore revoked the registration of 15 Crimean political parties and groups after they refused to re-register themselves as either all-Ukrainian parties (which

---

351    The MRBR and NDP merged in 2001.

requires them to have branches in two thirds of Ukraine's *oblasts*) or as regional branches of existing Ukrainian parties. Of Crimea's then seventeen political movements only two re-registered with the Ukrainian Ministry of Justice as all-Ukrainian political parties. The Union in Support of the Crimean Republic became the Crimean branch of the NDP, the Crimea's then new 'party of power'. Meshkov's former Republican Party of the Crimea became the *Soiuz* (Union) party while the Russian Party of the Crimea became the Slavic Unity Party.[352] *Soiuz* and the Slavic Unity parties have remained highly marginal political forces.

The PEVK changed its name to the Party of Economic Revival (PEV) as an all-Ukrainian party. In the 1998 elections it cooperated with the Democratic Party, formerly one of Ukraine's first national democratic parties that had been taken over by business interests in the 1990s. After the 1998 elections the PEV slowly lost its influence when Kyiv destroyed one of its main financial benefactors, the 'Seylem' organised crime group for which the party had been a political *'krysha'* (criminal slang for a political roof).[353] 16 out of the 100 deputies in the 1998-2002 Crimean Supreme Soviet had links to organised crime, Yuriy Krawchenko, Minister of Interior alleged.[354] As one commentator wrote:

> The party he created (PEVK/PEV) is a symbiosis of former party *apparatchiks* who support the government and businessmen under the protection of criminal groups. The PEV is very well-placed financially. Its main goals are power, money, property, and the immunity from prosecution that goes with election to parliament.[355]

Other Crimean parties also had links to organised crime. Russian nationalists had long worked together with organised crime through structures such as IMPEKS-55 which channelled funds from nationalist groups in Russia

---

352    Volodymyr Prytula, 'Avtonomiya v ochikuvannia peredvyborchykh bataliy', *Holos Ukrayiny*, 29 May 1997.
353    *Ukrayina moloda*, 13 February 1998.
354    *Uriadovyi Kurier*, 13 October 1998.
355    Vyacheslav Lebedev, 'Crimea: The situation is stable, but the future looks bleak', *Prism, Jamestown Monitor*, vol.4, no.1 (9 January 1998).

and the Russian parliament to Meshkov's party.[356] Ruvi Aronov, deputy head of *Soiuz* (formerly Meshkov's bloc), had links to rival organised crime groups.[357]

The PEVK/PEV's position as the Crimean 'party of power' was taken by the NDP. The NDP was Ukraine's first experiment as a 'party of power' under NDP leader and Prime Minister Valeriy Pustovoitenko in 1997-1999, but ultimately failed to become a well established Ukrainian 'party of power'. Led by Volodymyr Sheviov the PEV continued to exist as one of the many marginal Crimean parties. In 2003 it was threatened with being disbanded by the Ministry of Justice because it did not have regional branches in a minimum of half of Ukraine's *oblasts*.

The Russian Party of the Crimea, one of the largest pro-Russian groups in the Crimea, had, together with 14 other parties, its registration revoked. It protested that, 'a Crimean party with an all-Ukrainian status is a legal nonsense'. Led by Shuvainikov it re-formed under a new name, the Congress of Russian People, with the aim of copying the tactics of the Tatar *Mejlis* as a civic group. The Congress of Russian People, like *Soiuz*, agitated for a new East Slavic union of Belarus, Ukraine and Russia that supported Ukraine's membership of the Belarusian-Russian union. *Soiuz* failed to attract support for the union as it had limited support only on the extreme left. It abrogated to itself the right to use acts of civil disobedience and reserved the right to use arms in the event of genocide or open terror against the Russian people or its representatives, as well as attempts to colonise 'native Russian territories'.

*Soiuz* and other Russian nationalist groups in the Crimea re-formulated themselves into pan Eastern Slavic parties campaigning for Ukraine's membership of the Russian-Belarusian union and in defence of Russian speakers and the Russian language. In these policy objectives their natural allies were equally marginal parties in the Donbas, such as the Slavic Party (formerly the Civic Congress).

---

356    Andrew Wilson, 'The Elections in the Crimea', *RFERL Research Report*, vol.3, no.25 (24 January 1994), p.10.

357    *Nezavisimaya gazeta*, 21 January 2000. These links were confirmed by Grach in a conversation with this author in Brussels, 7 September 1998.

In the Crimea only two political forces have continually dominated politics:

1. 1991-1996: Russian nationalists and the post-Communist 'party of power' (PEVK).
2. 1997-2004: 'party of power' NDP and the Communists.
3. 2006-...: 'party of power' Party of Regions and the Communists.

## Crimean Constitution Making

### The 'Separatist' Constitution

On 20 May 1994 the Crimean parliament, whose leadership was at that time under the control of the Russia bloc and backed by then President Meshkov, reintroduced the 6 May 1992 constitution. The May 1992 constitution had been adopted only days after the Crimean parliament had declared independence from Ukraine. Grach, leader of the Crimean Communists, came out against the adoption of the May 1992 constitution fearing it would lead to conflict with Kyiv. Four years later he promoted a different and therefore less antagonistic constitution which was adopted by the Crimean Supreme Soviet in October 1998. The re-adoption of the May 1992 constitution was accompanied by an appeal by the Crimean Supreme Soviet to the UN, CSCE (now OSCE), Russian President and Federal Assembly as well as to the Ukrainian people.[358] The appeal claimed that the then Ukrainian leadership was, 'aiming to destroy the statehood of the Republic of Crimea. It threatens to use force, including military force'.[359]

---

358 *Krymskiye izvestiya*, 23 March 1995.
359 During May 1994, at the time of the adoption of the May 1992 constitution, then President Meshkov attended a Grand Assembly of Cossack Host Atamans in Krasnodar (UNIAN, 21 May 1994). Meshkov may have been looking for paramilitary allies in the event of a violent crackdown on Crimean separatism by Kyiv. Russian Cossacks had already taken part in supporting separatists in Moldova, Georgia and Bosnia-Herzegovina.

The contentious five articles in the May 1992 constitution were as follows:[360]

- Relations between the Crimea and Ukraine are to be based on a federal treaty;
- The treaty forms the basis for a relationship between two sovereign states;
- The Crimea controls all natural resources located on its territory;
- Crimean's have the right to dual citizenship;
- The Crimean Republic has the right to its own security forces.

All five demands were seen in Kyiv as provocative and therefore rejected by all Ukrainian political groups in Kyiv, regardless of their position on the political spectrum.

### Grach's Crimean Constitution[361]

A new Crimean constitution could only be adopted after the Crimean presidency was abolished in March 1995 and the leadership of the Crimean Supreme Soviet was changed in June of the same year. In addition, the adoption of the Crimean constitution was held up by Ukraine being the slowest CIS country to adopt a post-Soviet constitution.[362] Realistically therefore, no Crimean constitution could have been adopted until after June 1996 when the Ukrainian parliament adopted a Ukrainian constitution. The Ukrainian constitution created a semi-presidential unitary republic with the Crimea the only exception to this rule. All Ukraine's political parties supported the drive to adopt a non-separatist constitution in the Crimea. Only the remnants of the Russian nationalists protested. The *Souiz* party was a major critic of these moves but was itself accused of being 'in reality [...] the locomotive of confu-

---

360   See Ustina Markus, 'Crimea Restores 1992 Constitution', *RFE/RL Research Report*, vol.3, no.23 (10 June 1994).
361   See Vyacheslav Savchenko, 'V Krymu znovu vidkryvsya konstytutsiynyi sezon', *Demos*, no.14, 1995, pp.16-19.
362   See Kataryna Wolczuk, *The Moulding of Ukraine. The Constitutional Politics of State Formation* (Budapest: Central European University Press, 2001), pp.243-244.

sion and contradiction. On paper it supports union, but, in reality, it supports Crimea's isolation and bolsters hostile sentiment inside Crimea.'[363]

Opposition to a Crimean constitution also came from among national democrats who voted against granting the Crimea any autonomous status whatsoever.[364] Many of their objections were shared by the left and centre who were critical of a Crimean presidency, a federal treaty between Crimea and Ukraine, separate security forces, Crimean citizenship and dual citizenship with Russia.[365] Of Ukraine's centrists only the Inter-Regional Bloc of Reforms supported a federal treaty because the party supported a federal territorial arrangement for the whole of Ukraine (see chapter 2). The MRBR merged with the anti-federalist NDP in 2001.

National democrats wanted to go further and deny the Crimea any constitution claiming that, as Ukraine is a unitary state it should not include any autonomous entities. The Crimea should be therefore given a status short of autonomy with no parliament, but merely a regional chamber. National democrats looked to the Tatars as the only indigenous people in the Crimea, not to ethnic Russians for whom they created an autonomous entity.

The centre and left disagreed with the national democrats that granting autonomy to the Crimea would lead to a domino effect in other Ukrainian regions. But, they agreed with them that autonomous status for the Crimea was an exceptional case that should not be repeated elsewhere.[366] Compromise on the Crimea by national democrats was traded for compromise by the left on Ukraine's national symbols.[367] This showed how the adoption of the Ukrainian and Crimean constitutions in 1996 and 1998 respectively were closely inter-connected.

Public support for granting Crimea autonomous status was never high. If Ukraine's political elite had followed public opinion they would have rejected any autonomous status for the Crimea all together. In one poll conducted by the Russophile Ukrainian Centre for Political and Conflict Studies they found that 53.11 per cent of Ukrainians believed that the Crimea should be given

---

363   *Dzerkalo tyzhnya*, 17-23 October 1998.
364   K. Wolczuk, *The Moulding of Ukraine*, p.215.
365   K. Wolczuk, *The Moulding of Ukraine*, p.159.
366   *Ibid.*
367   K. Wolczuk, *The Moulding of Ukraine*, p.243.

the same status as any Ukrainian *oblast*. 44.02 per cent of Ukrainians backed an autonomous status while a miniscule 0.96 per cent supported its transfer to Russia.[368]

These poll results were confirmed by others conducted by different organisations at the same time, as outlined in Tables 6.5 and 6.6:

Table 6.5 Do You Support Autonomous Status for the Crimea?

| Answer | Ukraine | Kyiv | Crimea |
|---|---|---|---|
| Yes | 18 | 20 | 36 |
| Yes, somewhat | 17 | 28 | 24 |
| No, somewhat | 16 | 9 | 11 |
| No | 15 | 23 | 2 |
| Not enough information | 18 | 16 | 19 |
| Don't know | 15 | 4 | 8 |

Source: Elihie N. Skoczylas, *Ukraine 1996. Public Opinion on Key Issues* (Washington, DC: International Foundation Electoral Systems, 1997), p.81.

Table 6.6 Should Crimea Have a Constitution?

| Answer | Ukraine | Kyiv | Crimea |
|---|---|---|---|
| Yes | 16 | 14 | 37 |
| Yes, somewhat | 16 | 19 | 27 |
| No, somewhat | 17 | 15 | 9 |
| No | 25 | 35 | 4 |
| Not enough information | 14 | 13 | 17 |
| Don't know | 12 | 4 | 6 |

Source: Elihie N. Skoczylas, *Ukraine 1996. Public Opinion on Key Issues* (Washington, DC: International Foundation Electoral Systems, 1997), p.104.

On 31 May 1995, the Crimean parliament adopted the draft of a new constitution. In contrast to the May 1992 constitution, which described the Crimean Republic and Ukraine as two separate sovereign states, the new draft described the Crimea as a component of Ukraine. Its powers would be

---

368    'Russkiye na Ukraine', a poll by the Kyiv-based Ukrainian Centre for Political and Conflict Studies. Copy in the possession of the author. A summary was reported in ITAR-TASS, 10 November 1996.

outlined according to the 17 March 1995 Ukrainian legislation 'On the Crimean Autonomous Republic' and 'On the Division of Power Between the Ukrainian State Organs of Power and the Crimean Republic'. The Crimean presidency and 1992 constitution were henceforth well and truly buried.[369]

Socialist Party leader Oleksandr Moroz was chairman of the Ukrainian parliament in 1994-1998 during the height of the Crimean separatist threat. Abolishing the presidency was seen across the entire political spectrum in Kyiv as facilitating compromise with the Crimea. 'No one doubts now that the adoption of this decision was timely and purposeful', Moroz told the Ukrainian parliament.[370] Moroz believed that 'quelling the separatist tendencies' was made easier once the Crimean presidency was abolished.[371] Attitudes towards Meshkov in Ukraine had always been more negative than positive which meant there were few protests in Ukraine at abolishing the Crimean presidency. In a Democratic Initiatives April 1994 poll only 14 per cent of Ukrainians held a positive opinion of Meshkov.[372] Abolishing the Crimean presidency was supported by 56 per cent of respondents in a Sotsis Gallup poll held in April 1995. Only 16 per cent opposed this move. Not surprisingly, the highest support for this step was in Western and South Western Ukraine where support ranged between 74-76 percent. Even in North Eastern, Eastern and Southern Ukraine those supporting the abolishing of the Crimean presidency varied between 47-51 per cent. Only in the Crimea did a majority (56 per cent) oppose the move. More ethnic Ukrainians (60 per cent) than ethnic Russians (42 per cent) backed the step, as seen in Tables 6.7 and 6.8.[373]

---

369   ITAR-TASS, 31 May 1995. Of the two previous constitutions (6 May and 25 September 1992) Kyiv preferred to use as the basis for the 1996-1998 constitution the latter because it was perceived as not 'pro- separatist' (in comparison to the 6 May 1992 version). On this question see the interview with A. Danelian, chairman of the Crimean Constitutional Commission and Deputy Chairman of the Crimean Supreme Council, in *Krymskiye izvestiya*, 25 October 1995.

370   *Holos Ukrayiny*, 15 April 1998.

371   *Silski Visti*, 7 May 1998.

372   'The Results of Four polls Conducted During the 1994 Election Campaign in Ukraine', *Political Portrait of Ukraine*, no.4, 1994. 40 per cent were indifferent, 22 were negative and the remainder could not give an answer.

373   *Demokratychna Ukrayina*, 27 April 1995.

Table 6.7 Regional Attitudes to Abolishing the Crimean Presidency

| Attitude | Lviv | Kyiv | Donetsk | Simferopol |
|---|---|---|---|---|
| Yes | 56.5 | 53.3 | 34.3 | 18.1 |
| No | 14.3 | 8.6 | 22.4 | 46.0 |
| Don't Know | 24.1 | 22.9 | 31.6 | 27.6 |
| What Decision? | 5.0 | 15.2 | 11.7 | 8.3 |

Source: 'Sotsialno-Politychnyi Portret Chotyriokh Mist Ukrayiny', *Politychnyi Portret Ukrayiny*, no.13, 1995.

Table 6.8 Do You Agree With Placing the Crimean Government Under the Ukrainian Government?

| Attitude | Lviv | Kyiv | Donetsk | Simferopol |
|---|---|---|---|---|
| Yes | 66.6 | 55.6 | 44.1 | 16.0 |
| No | 9.3 | 7.7 | 20.0 | 51.1 |
| Don't Know | 20.1 | 21.3 | 27.9 | 26.8 |
| What Decision? | 4.0 | 15.4 | 8.0 | 6.0 |

Source: 'Sotsialno-Politychnykh Portret Chotyriokh Mist Ukrayiny', *Politychnyi Portret Ukrayiny*, no.13, 1995.

The August 1995 Ukrainian presidential decree 'On the Bodies of State Executive Power of the Autonomous Republic of the Crimea' included 2 important provisions:

- Crimean prime minister to be appointed and dismissed by the Crimean Supreme Soviet with the agreement of the Ukrainian president;
- State administrations from the *rayon* level upwards were subordinated to the Crimean government and Ukrainian president.

Ukrainian objections had been against the Crimean demand for 'statehood', separate citizenship, ownership over all natural resources in the Crimea,[374] control over appointments within the security forces and the re-

---

374    Kyiv was undoubtedly concerned that the Crimea would attempt to control oil and gas deposits on the peninsula and those lying off the Black Sea coast.

institution of the presidency.[375] On 1 November 1995 the Crimean parliament approved the new post-Meshkov draft constitution. The final draft included the following important provisions:[376]

- The Republic of Crimea was an autonomous component of Ukraine;
- The Crimea does not possess separate citizenship to that in the remainder of Ukraine;
- Sevastopol is a part of the Crimea;
- Russian, Ukrainian and Tatar are official languages, while Russian is the official language of government and business;
- The head of the Crimean Security Service and Ministry of Internal Affairs will be appointed by the Ukrainian authorities in coordination with the Crimean parliament;
- The Crimean parliament retains the right to appoint its own Prime Minister.

Ukraine did not want to see the new Crimean constitution adopted by referendum which may have led to additional questions being added by separatists. In addition, the new Crimean constitution created a parliamentary autonomous republic that, if it had been adopted before the Ukrainian constitution, may have given support to the radical left within the Ukrainian parliament. The Ukrainian left were opposed to *both* a Crimean and a Ukrainian presidency and, as seen in proposals for deepening Ukraine's move to a parliamentary republic by the Anti-Crisis coalition headed by Prime Minister Yanukovych, continue to support deepening of the 2004-2006 constitutional reforms that would transform Ukraine into a parliamentary republic. The Anti-Crisis coalition, established in July 2006, consists of the Party of Regions, Communist and Socialist Parties.

On 4 April 1996 the Ukrainian parliament adopted a law 'On the Autonomous Republic of Crimea', approving 116 out of 136 articles of the Crimean constitution. This did not include the 'separatist' clauses that had re-

---

375    *Demokratychna Ukrayina*, 28 September 1995.
376    UNIAN, 1 November and *The Ukrainian Weekly*, 5 November 1995.

ferred to separate citizenship, state symbols, the 'Crimean people' and Russian as the state language.[377] National democrats disliked provisions referring to the 'mythical people of the Crimea'.[378] It had also refused to allow the Crimean Supreme Soviet to enact legislation, removed any references to the head of executive authority in the Crimea and the Crimean status of Sevastopol.

The ability to reach a compromise on a non-separatist constitution in 1996-1998 was due to the marginalisation of Russian nationalists after 1995 and the rise of dual Communist-centrist control over Crimean politics. In the first half of the 1990s the PEVK claimed to have 30,000 members. The PEVK claimed as one of its successes, 'throwing Meshkov out of the Crimea...'[379] The election of Grach as chairman of the Crimean Supreme Soviet after the March 1998 elections was particularly important in ensuring a compromise could be reached with Kyiv. As Stewart argues, 'The result was a constitution which differed significantly from those of 1992 and 1995 and bore the distinct seal of Grach's attempts to consolidate his power in Crimea and raise his profile in Kyiv and Ukraine as a whole.'[380]

On the eve of the adoption of the Crimean constitution in 1998, Grach warned that 'anti-constitutional bedlam' could lead to another 'Kosovo'. The Crimea, he insisted, had no choice but to act within Ukraine's legal and constitutional field.[381] Grach appealed to President Kuchma to 'restore constitutional order in the Crimea'.[382]

The Crimean constitution recognising the Crimea as within a 'unitary' Ukraine was adopted by the Crimean Supreme Soviet on 21 October 1998 by a vote of 82 out of 100 deputies. It was then ratified by the Ukrainian parliament on 23 December by 230 votes; the ratification just scraped through as a minimum of 226 votes is required. The new constitution did not mention the

---

377   See Olha Chorna, 'To chy maie Krym svoiu Konstytutsiu?', *Kyivski vidomosti*, 10 April 1996.
378   *Pravda Ukrayiny*, 8 July 1997.
379   Cited by Volodymyr Yavorivsky, then head of the Democratic Party, the 1998 election ally of the re-named Party of Economic Revival (*Ukrayina moloda*, 15 April 1998).
380   Susan Stewart, 'Autonomy as a Mechanism for Conflict Regulation: The Case of Crimea', *Nationalism and Ethnic Politics*, vol.7, no.4 (Winter 2001), p.124.
381   *Krymskiye Izvestiya*, 23-24 October 1998.
382   ITAR-TASS, 16 December 1999.

Crimea as a 'state' with separate citizenship.[383] Henceforth Crimea's 'Constitution Day' was 21 October (not 6 May which would have been based on the 1992 draft constitution[384]).

Continued opposition to the Crimean constitution came from both national democrats in Ukraine and Russian nationalists in the Crimea. The former claimed the 1998 constitution gave the Crimea too many powers while the latter believed it gave the Crimea too few. Russian nationalists accused Grach of being a 'Banderite'[385] and of being hostile to the Russian language (Ukrainian is referred to as the state language of Ukraine).[386] Article 2 of the Crimean constitution gives a higher status to Ukrainian legislation over Crimean legislation. To then Crimean Supreme Soviet chairman Grach the constitution is a, 'special law, second in importance after the constitution of Ukraine itself'.[387]

### Elections Since 1998

Since 1998-1999 the Crimea has been ruled by two political forces. Under Kuchma's presidency the Communists controlled the leadership of the Supreme Soviet while the Crimean government was controlled by the NDP whose Crimean leader, Serhiy Kunitsyn, was also Prime Minister. The NDP was a failed 'party of power' in Ukraine under the Pustovoitenko government (1997-1999). In the 2002 Ukrainian parliamentary elections the NDP was one of five political parties that made up the pro-Kuchma For a United Ukraine (ZYU) bloc. The NDP's influence waned in the Crimea after Yushchenko was elected president in 2005. In 2006 it was eclipsed by the ascendancy of the Party of regions, the only former pro-Kuchma centrist party to enter the 2006 parliament.

Prior to the 1998 elections (see tables 6.9 and 6.10) open conflict between the pro-presidential Crimean government and the pro-Communist Su-

---

383   Interfax, 22 October 1998.
384   ITAR-TASS, 7 September 1999.
385   Slang word meaning having sympathy for the Organisation of Ukrainian Nationalists – Stepan Bandera faction.
386   Intelnews, 22 October 1998.
387   *Nezavisimaya Gazeta*, 6 February 1999.

preme Soviet had led to a vote of no confidence in the government. Kunitsyn's dismissal set the stage for further personalised conflict between Kunitsyn and Grach during the elections to the Crimean Supreme Soviet. In June 2001 the Crimean Supreme Soviet voted 55 out of 100 deputies to dismiss the government (in 2000 it voted by 68 to also dismiss the government). These votes were largely symbolic as the approval or dismissal of the Crimean government by the Supreme Soviet has to be approved by the Ukrainian president.[388]

Table 6.9 The 1998 Ukrainian Parliamentary Elections in the Crimea (Proportional Party Lists)

| Bloc or Party | Per Cent |
|---|---|
| Communists | 39.34 |
| Soiuz | 10.68 |
| Rukh | 6.76 |
| Green Party Ukraine | 5.70 |
| NDP | 4.41 |

Source: Central Election Commission, www.cvk.gov.ua

Table 6.10 The 2002 Ukrainian Parliamentary Elections in the Crimea (Proportional Party Lists)

| Bloc or Party | Per Cent |
|---|---|
| KPU | 33.91 |
| Social Democratic Party united | 12.47 |
| Our Ukraine | 9.77 |
| For a United Ukraine | 5.92 |
| Russian Bloc | 4.76 |

Source: Central Election Commission, www.cvk.gov.ua

After the 2002 elections the NDP expanded its control from the Crimean government to the Crimean Supreme Soviet because Grach had been disal-

---

388   See Mykyta Kasianenko, 'Kolaps "pravovoho polia" v Krymu', *Den*, 6 March 2001 and 'Crimean Crosswords. Autonomy's Parliament and Government Back on Settling Scores', *Research Update* (Ukrainian Centre Independent Political Research), vol.7, no.26 (25 June 2001).

lowed from standing in Crimean local elections. Grach was elected to the Ukrainian parliament from the Communist Party. In the 2002 elections in the Crimea the main contest was between the pro-presidential ZYU and the Communist Party. ZYU backed the Kunitsyn Bloc in the Crimean elections and it obtained the largest number of seats in the Crimean Supreme Soviet. This assisted the NDP in removing the Communists from control over the Crimean Supreme Soviet, thereby giving control over the local parliament *and* government to the pro-Kuchma 'party of power', the NDP. This move to assert total control by the 'party of power' repeated similar steps taken in the Ukrainisan parliament by pro-Kuchma forces.

The Crimean results of the 2002 elections to the Ukrainian parliament showed that the region did not fundamentally differ from other Eastern Ukrainian regions in the political attitudes of its population. According to proportional voting for the 33 registered parties and blocs the Communists obtained the largest number of votes with 33.91 per cent. This figure resembles the highest recorded votes for the Communists in Ukraine which were to be found in the two Donbas *oblasts* of Donetsk and Luhansk.

The Communists have     been a stabilising force in the Crimea because the largest local party in the peninsula supported Ukraine's territorial integrity. The Communists were also important in assisting in the marginalisation of Russian nationalists in the Crimea. The former Russian bloc, now called Union (*Soiuz*), failed to generate any support in the 1998, 2002 or 2006 elections. In the 1998 elections *Soiuz* fought the elections alone and came 21st out of 30 parties and blocs who competed with only 0.70 per cent. In the Crimea though, it came second after the Communists with the more respectable 10.68 per cent. In the city of Sevastopol the *Soiuz* Party came 5th with only 2.25 per cent, only slightly more than support for Rukh at 1.77 per cent. In the 2002 elections the Russian Party (which included *Soiuz*) and the Union of Ukraine, Belarus and Russia bloc (known by its abbreviation ZUBR) only obtained 0.73 and 0.43 per cent respectively, coming 16th and 17th in Ukraine out the 33 registered parties and blocs. In the Crimea itself both blocs (Russia Party and ZUBR) fared better than in Ukraine as a whole. In the Crimea the Russian Party and ZUBR came 5th and 14th with 4.76 and 0.93 per cent respectively. In Sevastopol the Russia Bloc and ZUBR did better. There the Russia bloc came 3rd (after the Communists and ZYU) with 8.83 per cent and

ZUBR came 11th with 2.14 per cent. Clearly, Crimean voters, like elsewhere in Ukraine, prefer the pro-Soviet and pro-Russian Communists to pure ethnic Russian nationalist political parties.

In the 1998 elections, two pro-presidential parties (ZYU, SDPUo) obtained higher votes than the two Russian nationalist parties in the Crimea. In the Crimea the SDPUo obtained one of its highest votes in Ukraine with 12.47 per cent, far higher than that for ZYU at 5.92. Pro-presidential Crimean businessmen and state officials may have defected to the SDPUo from the NDP who, together with the Agrarians, dominated the ZYU bloc in the Crimea.

Both Russian nationalist groups fared worse than the pro-reform Our Ukraine which came third in the Crimean elections to the Ukrainian parliament with 9.77 per cent, giving it third place. This was the most surprising result of the Crimean elections to the Ukrainian parliament. This relatively high vote for our Ukraine (especially in comparison to the Donbas where it failed to even cross the four per cent threshold) was mainly obtained from Crimean Tatar voters who make up 15 per cent of the local population. The two leaders of the Crimean *Mejlis*, Chubarov and Dzhemilev, were on the Our Ukraine party list. Tatars were able to vote in larger numbers in the 2002 elections because 90 per cent of them had become Ukrainian citizens, unlike in the 1998 elections when they were still mainly Uzbek citizens.

As in the remainder of Ukraine, pro-presidential centrist parties did best in elections to the Ukrainian parliament in the 10 Crimean majoritarian districts (whereas the Communists and Our Ukraine did better in the proportional lists). Pro-presidential candidates masqueraded as 'independents', or in the case of the 2002 elections, described themselves as 'self-nominated'.

Of the ten majoritarian deputies elected only three declared their party allegiances, one from the Communists and two from the SDPUo. The remaining seven 'self-nominees' joined pro-presidential centrist factions in the Ukrainian parliament which emerged after ZYU disintegrated. Two of the ten deputies were former Crimean Prime Minister Anatoliy Franchuk and his son, Ihor, both of whom had personal ties to President Kuchma. Elections to the Crimean Supreme Soviet were undertaken on the basis of a different law whereby all 100 deputies were elected by majority voting in 100 separate constituencies. A fully majoritarian law favoured the pro-presidential centrist NDP.

The Crimean Election Commission de-registered Grach on 25 February 2002 because he allegedly filled out his income declaration incorrectly. Suspicion that this was politically motivated could be seen when the Central Election Commission did not question his income declaration and maintained him on the Communist Party of Ukraine list in the elections to the Ukrainian parliament. On 29 March 2002 the Crimean Appeals Court rejected a complaint by Grach. After he was de-registrated Grach threatened to organise a referendum on Crimea's status and called for a boycott of elections to the Ukrainian parliament, but these came to nothing. This was especially after the idea of a referendum received no official support from Russia (the exception was from maverick Moscow Mayor Yuriy Luzhkov). Grach's de-registration aimed to remove him from Crimean politics in which he had played a cenral role in the 1990s. A smaller Communist presence in the Crimean Supreme Soviet without its charismatic leader meant that Crimea's Communists suffered further setbacks in the peninsula. Removing Grach from the Crimea also increased his profile in Kyivan politics. In Kyiv, Grach has personal ambitions to lead the Communist Party of Ukraine by replacing the un-charismatic Communist leader Petro Symonenko.

The results of the elections to the Crimean Supreme Soviet markedly differed from elections to the Ukrainian parliament, itself an indication that Crimean's vote differently in Crimean and Ukrainian elections. In the Crimea the largest number of seats went to the pro-presidential Kunitsyn bloc that won 39 seats and the Grach (Communist Party) list obtained only 28 seats. This was the reverse of the Crimean vote to the Ukrainian parliament where the Communist Party of Ukraine easily beat ZYU and the SDPUo in the proportional half of elections. Poor Communist results in elections to the Crimean Supreme Soviet reflected a pattern in national elections to the Ukrainian parliament. The Communist faction was reduced by nearly half in the 2002-2006 Ukrainian parliament and again to only 21 deputies elected to the 2006 parliament. In the Crimea the Communists also fared badly in their traditional stronghold of Sevastopol where their presence on the city council decreased nearly ten fold. The Communists also lost control of most Crimean mayorships; the only one they were able to maintain control of was in Kerch.

Seven Tatars were elected to the Crimean Supreme Soviet, an increase of only one on the 1998-2002 Crimean Supreme Soviet. This is still less than the 14 seats the Tatars were proportionately allocated in the 1994-1998 Cri-mean Supreme Soviet.

As in the national elections to the Ukrainian parliament, Russian nation-alists fared badly in the Crimea. The Russian Bloc only obtained four seats. The Communists were reduced from forty to twenty five per cent of seats in the Crimean Supreme Soviet. Pro-Ukrainian centrist forces took back control of the Crimean Supreme Soviet, after two periods when the peninsula was controlled first by Russian separatists (1994-1995) and then by Communists who are in favour of a revived USSR (1998-2002).

Ukraine's drive against the NDP's control over the Crimea began in spring 2005 when Ukrainian Republican Party 'Sobor' leader Anatoliy Matvi-enko removed Kunitsyn as Crimean Prime Minister.[389] Crimean Prime Minis-ter Kunitsyn initially refused to resign but was in the end forced to go and was given the ceremonial position of presidential adviser. NDP leader Pusto-voitenko, who coordinated parties backing the Yanukovych 2004 campaign, complained that NDP member Kunitsyn's resignation was 'political repres-sion'. Kunitsyn was, in effect, made an offer he could not refuse. Kunitsyn complained that, 'Every week 100 inspectors arrive from Kyiv. They said to me either you leave or we'll lock you up...'[390] Kunitsyn believed that, 'Yu-shchenko is a person of morals' but that this did not apply, 'to those coming down to Crimea' and claiming to act on his behalf. Files on Kunitsyn's corrupt background, which are more than likely available, were used to force him to resign. Kunitsyn's replacement, Matvienko, was a surprising choice as he heads a national democratic party. The Ukrainian Republican Party 'Sobor' was a member of Prime Minister Tymoshenko's bloc in the 2002 elections but split in the 2006 elections between the Tymoshenko bloc and Our Ukraine.

Southern Ukraine is less industrial than Eastern Ukraine and therefore less russified; the exception to this being the Crimea. A Ukrainian Barometer poll gave Yanukovych 30.8 percent support in Southern Ukraine and the Cri-mea, only slightly less than Yushchenko's 27.4 support.[391] In the largely agri-cultural Kherson *oblast*, Yushchenko and Yanukovych came neck to neck in all three rounds of the 2004 elections. In Odesa and Mykolaiv *oblasts*, which

389    *Ukrayinska Pravda*, 20 April 2005.
390    *Kyiv Weekly*, 15-22 April 2005.
391    *Ukrayinska Pravda*, 26 March, 2005.

are more industrial, Yushchenko obtained approximately one third to Yanukovych's two thirds of the votes in all three rounds of the 2004 elections. This support dissipated throughout the course of 2005 and by the March 2006 elections Yushchenko's support had declined to such an extent that the Party of Regions had become the dominant political force in Southern Ukraine and the Crimea.

In the Crimean autonomous republic, Yushchenko's 12-16 percent votes were far lower than Yanukovych's 69-82 percent in the 26 December 2004 repeat of the second round of the elections. Nevertheless, these were far better than Yushchenko's vote in Yanukovych's home base of Donetsk where he obtained results that ranged between 2-5 percent in all three rounds.[392]

The election of Yushchenko led to the disintegration of the pro-Kuchma Stability faction in the Crimean parliament which grouped 85 out of 100 deputies. Stability faction leader Borys Deych explained that, 'the Crimea cannot live as a separate part of the state. Everything that is happening in Ukraine spreads to the Crimea'.[393] Deych confided that, 'we are not in opposition to the new authorities' and we 'declare our support for the president's course'. The former pro-Kuchma People's Union 'Stability' (38 deputies) and the newly created pro-Yushchenko Power in Unity (15 deputies) give Yushchenko a slim majority of 53 out of 100 Crimean deputies in 2005-2006. 61 deputies actually voted for the Crimea's first national democratic Prime Minister Matvienko. The Power in Unity faction was headed by the National Bank Crimean departmental head, Anatoliy Burdyuhov.

This slim pro-Yushchenko majority in the Crimean Supreme Soviet only lasted until the March 2006 elections when the Party of Regions won a majority of the seats. In the 2006 Crimean elections to the Ukrainian parliament the top five parties and blocs that made it through the low 3 percent threshold were the same as those who won the majority of votes in the Crimean Supreme Soviet. The Party of Regions obtained on average 50-60 percent of the vote, giving it a massive lead over the other four political forces. The Communists and the Natalia Vitrenko bloc trailed the bottom of the five with

---

392    www.cvk.gov.ua.
393    *Dzerkalo tyzhnya*, 19-25 March 2005.

between 5 and 4 percent respectively. In between these three political forces, sharing second and third place, were Our Ukraine and the Yulia Tyoshenko bloc with a combined total of 14-20 percent.

## Conclusions

This chapter surveys nearly a decade of Crimean politics from 1994 to the present that begins with Russian nationalists taking power in the Crimea. Permitting the Crimean presidential elections to take place was a major strategic mistake on the part of Kyiv. After only fifteen months the Crimean presidency was abolished in March 1995. The downfall of Meshkov and Russian nationalism in the Crimea led to their marginalisation. This allowed the Crimean 'party of power' and Communists, both of whom have always supported Ukraine's sovereignty over the Crimea, to adopt a Crimean constitution in 1998 that recognised Ukrainian sovereignty. Since the 1998, 2002 and 2006 elections two political forces, centrists (NDP, the Party of Regions) and the Communists, have dominated Crimean politics. National democrats and Russian nationalists are marginalised in the Crimea with the former receiving the bulk of their support from Crimean Tatars.

# 7    Security Forces in the Crimea

One of the first areas that the independent Ukrainian state prioritised was developing security forces and steps were made in this area even before Ukraine became independent in 1991. President Leonid Kravchuk replaced the commanders of Ukraine's two military districts (Trans-Carpathia and Odesa, which also included Moldova and the Crimea).[394] This eliminated any ambiguous chain of command and removed pro-Soviet *hardliners*. Newly appointed district commanders were members of the Union of Ukrainian Officers. Ukraine took over Soviet military equipment located within the two former Soviet districts. By February 1992, 80 per cent of former USSR security forces in Ukraine had taken the oath of loyalty to Ukraine. The former Soviet security forces had been therefore psychologically broken. This has since been described as the worst single defeat of the Soviet Army since World War II. The Soviet armed forces no longer constituted a security threat to the Ukrainian state. The exception was the Black Sea Fleet, although even here it did not completely back Russia. This was important in creating a new chain of command based upon the former Soviet security forces located in Ukraine.

This chapter is divided into four sections. The first outlines the manner in which Ukraine took control of the security forces in the Crimea. The second describes how the Ukrainian authorities applied military pressure against Russian nationalists in the Crimea. The third surveys the conflict over control over the security forces in the Crimea. The final section provides an overview of the conflict over the Black Sea Fleet and over military bases in the Crimea.

---

394    These two districts became the Western and southern 'Operational Commands' respectively in the mid 1990s and a third was added based in Dnipropetrovsk entitled Northern for Ukraine's Eastern border.

### Ukraine Takes Control and Builds Security Forces in the Crimea

In the former USSR the Crimea had 25,000 security forces and the Black Sea Fleet. By the mid 1990s the number had doubled and included 15,000 Ministry Internal Affairs (MVS) personnel.[395] By 1994 Sevastopol had a sizeable Ukrainian military presence – marines (Ukrainian navy), a mechanised infantry brigade, a command battalion and a patrol service regiment.[396] Nearby at Bolgrad in Odesa *oblast* the Ukrainian 1st Airborne division was stationed. In June 1994, these airborne units were dispatched to the Belbek airfield near Sevastopol so that Ukraine could, if a conflict began, bring in additional forces.

The 32nd Army Corps is based in Simferopol and came under Ukrainian control from April 1992 when its pro-Russian commander was removed and replaced by Major-General Viktor Paliy, who was appointed on 28 July 1992. The 32nd Army Corps controlled all security forces based in the Crimea (except the MVS, National Guard and Border Troops). Kyiv therefore quickly asserted control over the armed forces stationed in the Crimea after Ukraine became an independent state.

Numerous rallies by Russian nationalists in the first half of the 1990s called for the removal of 'Ukrainian' security forces in the Crimea. This demand was opposed by pro-Ukrainian loyalists from the 'party of power', and by national democrats and Tatars. In June 1995 a Union of Soviet Security Officers was established in Sevastopol. It pledged, 'to have the force which would be able counteract armed groups of Tatar and Ukrainian nationalists'.[397] Russian nationalist leader Yury Meshkov was a former counterintelligence officer in Soviet military intelligence (GRU) and the core of the Republican Movement of the Crimea (RDK), established on 24 August 1991, were former KGB officers and Afghan veterans.

After Russian nationalists were removed from the Crimean presidential and parliamentary leadership in spring 1995 the local authorities again reverted to supporting the presence of Ukrainian security forces in the Crimea (as they had under Crimean Supreme Soviet chairman Nikolai Bagrov). A

---

395    ITAR-TASS, 8 April 1994
396    *Krasnaya Zvezda*, 1 March 1994.
397    ITAR-TASS, 23 June 1995.

Crimean Supreme Soviet resolution 'extended patronage' to the armed forces, navy, border troops and national guard in the region (i.e. the local authorities committed themselves to supporting them socio-economically in such areas as food and housing).[398] Only Russian nationalists have therefore unsuccessfully attempted to gain control over the security forces or have them removed from the Crimea.

*Internal Troops*

When Ukraine declared independence it had no security force units of its own. It distrusted the MVS Internal Troops as these were regarded as loyal to Moscow. The MVS Internal Troops were nationalised and given to the newly created National Guard and to the Border Troops in a 30 August 1991 decree of the parliamentary presidium. The MVS Internal Troops began creating their own *spetsnaz* (special forces) units in March 1994 based in three locations in Ukraine, Kyiv (Bars), Zaporizhzhia (Jaguar), and Vinnytsia (Hepard). Each of these three *spetsnaz* units had responsibility for different regions of Ukraine - Bars (central), Hepard (Western) and Jaguar (Eastern). Interestingly, the region with the greatest degree of potential threat from separatists, Southern Ukraine and the Crimea, was jointly covered by *all* three units. These units have a similar function to the Dzerzhinsky division in the Russian Federation which was used to attack the Russian parliament in October 1993. All three *spetsnaz* units and their air transport are maintained on alert 24-hours a day in the event of their requirement for security operations. In addition to these *spetsnaz* units, two MVS Special Motorised Militia Units were based in the Crimea from the mid 1990s. These units are meant to be used for public disorder and were taken from the Internal Troops of the MVS in late 1991 and then given back to them in 1995.

*Border Troops*

On the second anniversary of Ukraine's independence (24 August 1993) the Ukrainian flag was hoisted on 19 Border Troop vessels. Flags were also simultaneously raised on ships in Kerch, Feodosiya and other Crimean ports. These became the coast guard of the Southern district of Ukraine's

---

398    UNIAN, 26 January 1996.

Border Troops. The coast guard of the Border Troops possesses a brigade of ships in Kerch, a special division in Yalta, a separate brigade of river cutters and a centre for the preparation of marine experts in Ismail. The Border Troops main Crimean bases are in Simferopol, capitol city of the Crimea, Yalta, Yevpatoria, Kerch and Feodosiya. The Border Troops have expanded their specialist units to deal with the growing contingencies they are faced with.[399]

### National Guard

The National Guard were officially established on 4 November 1991 when Ukraine did not have a president and they came under parliament's control. Until they were returned to MVS Internal Troops in January 2000 they were the only security force unit that had always been under dual parliamentary-executive control. The National Guard took the bulk of the MVS Internal Troops functions, except guarding prisons, and increased their numbers from 30,000 troops to a peak of 50,000. They were modelled on the elite of the armed forces, such as airborne units, and one of their main functions was the defence of constitutional order and Ukraine's territorial integrity. The National Guards first military action was the sealing of the Moldovan-Ukrainian border in March 1992.

The responsibilities of the National Guard would be to repel external and internal 'enemy attacks' as well as, 'Participate in the liquidation of subversive-reconnaissance and terrorist groups and illegally formed armed military units'. This was clearly a reference to separatists. The largest workloads of the National Guard were in the Crimea and Donetsk. The National Guard in the Crimea was based on its 7th division and included a Simferopol brigade, Simferopol regiment, Sevastopol battalion, Kerch, Dzhankoy and Yevpatoria companies and Cobra special forces.

In the Crimea the National Guard backed Border Troops, 'defended constitutional order' and, if required, helped install a 'state of emergency regime'. In May 1996 a brigade of Crimean marines and a motor rifle battalion were transferred from the armed forces to the National Guard on the peninsula, giving them their own marines. Nearly all of the units in the Crimean Na-

---

399   UNIAR, 24 August 1993.

tional Guard were designated as '*spetsnaz*' (2 mountain units, Cobra and Levanda, a special forces battalion in Simferopol), signifying the degree to which Kyiv thought the region required highly specialised security forces. The Crimean division was one of the best equipped and trained within the National Guard or armed forces. It incorporated special forces trained especially for mountainous operations, marines and air mobile units.

The only region of Ukraine where the National Guard was permanently stationed was in the Crimea from early 1993 as Russian nationalist agitation began to escalate for the Crimea's separation from Ukraine. The occupation of the Crimean Supreme Soviet and mass demonstrations by Crimean Tatars in November 1992 had reduced the hostility of the Crimean leadership towards the stationing of the National Guard on their territory and it was therefore deployed with the consent of the autonomous republic's leaders.In the Crimea the National Guard backed Border Troops to counter threats which could conceivably come from outside the Crimea (e.,g. Russian or Muslim volunteers rushing to defend their brethren in a conflict), which the Border Troops would be the first units to block. But, the real threat in the Crimea, as recognised by the National Guard, was from domestic separatism, the Black Sea Fleet or Tatar fundamentalism. Hence, why the National Guard was unpopular with pro-Russian separatists on the peninsula who accused them 'of all sorts of sins'.[400]

### Military Pressure on the Crimea

The third plank (after legal and economic pressure) in Kyiv's policy towards the Crimea was that of ensuring and bolstering a security force presence on the ground. The Ukrainian authorities were unlikely to allow the resolution attached to the reintroduced May 1992 constitution that forbids the sending of Crimean draftees to serve outside the peninsula (it was proposed that they would serve either in military units based only in the Crimea or in the Black Sea Fleet). The chief of the Crimean military commissariat, Aleksandr

---

[400]   *Narodna Armiya*, 28 March 1995.

Volkov, rejected such a demand.[401] But the deputy commander of the Black Sea Fleet stated his readiness to take all Crimean conscripts and ensure Crimean security after a Ukrainian withdrawal.[402] The chairman of the Crimean Supreme Soviet commission on military and security issues also called for the withdrawal of the National Guard and its replacement by a 'Crimean Republican Guard'. President Meshkov established a presidential service for security and interstate affairs headed by Colonel Vladimir Bortnikov from the former Russian KGB which had an initial staff of 39.

The tug of war over control of the security forces based in the Crimea was potentially the most dangerous aspect of the crisis between the Crimea and Kyiv. President Meshkov's appointment of Kuznetsov to head the Ministry of Internal Affairs meant that he, 'is now in charge of a massive arsenal of weapons found on Crimean territory', according to the MVS. On 18 May 1994, Ukrainian First Deputy Interior Minister, Colonel-General Valentyn Nedryhailo, attempted to take control of the MVS headquarters in Simferopol with 20 *Spetsnaz* police officers from Kyiv in order to place it directly under Kyiv's jurisdiction.[403]

The unresolved question of control over the Crimean MVS had led to an upsurge in organised crime on the peninsula which, 'is overrun by racketeering', according to Kuznetsov.[404] President Kuchma's proclaimed campaign against corruption and organised crime faced tough and armed resistance in the Crimea where it antagonised local politicians, many of whom were tied to organised crime.

The bulk of the rumours that were given wide circulation in the Russian media regarding Ukrainian military movements at the time proved to be false. According to Russian military sources the combined Ukrainian security presence in the Crimea increased from 18,000-51,000 in the first half of the

---

401    On the war of decrees over the basing of Crimean conscripts in the Crimea see *Narodna Armiya*, 5 April, UNIAR, 12 and 14 April and *Holos Ukrayiny,* 16 April 1994.

402    Taras Kuzio, 'Crimean Crisis Deepens', *Jane's Intelligence Review Pointer*, no.8 (June 1994).

403    See ITAR-TASS, 19 and 23 May and UNIAN, 25 and 28 May 1994. Changes to Ukrainian legislation on the Militia made in an attempt to bring the Crimean MVS back under Kyiv's control was published in *Holos Ukrayiny*, 8 July 1994.

404    *Krasnaya Zvezda*, 16 August 1994.

1990s. Of these upwards of 15,000 were in the MVS and the remainder included Naval, Air Force, Air Defence, the 32nd Army Corps, 2 *Spetsnaz* brigades, Border Troops and National Guard.[405] The capitol of the Crimea, Simferopol, included the headquarters of a mechanised division, the military construction academy and Border Troops.[406] Ukraine's elite first airborne division based at Bolgrad in Odesa *oblast*, which was used in the Odesa incident with the Black Sea Fleet in April 1994, was also in close proximity to the Crimea.

The existence of the 32 Army Corps HQ in Simferopol provided Ukraine with command, control, communications, intelligence and logistical capability for its armed forces in the Crimea. This allowed it to rapidly build up their size. Ukrainian security planning in the Crimea also possessed the advantage of controlling Northern Crimea. This is where the bulk of the ethnic Ukrainian population is concentrated and it could be detached from the coastline south of the peninsula cutting across the Crimea in the event of separatist strife. Kyiv also continued to control the Eastern approaches of the Crimea at Kerch from where Russian reinforcements and Cossacks could possibly have arrived in the event of a conflict. The island of Tuzla is crucial to Ukrainian strategic planning in defending the Eastern approaches to the Crimea.

A tank and anti-aircraft unit attached to the Black Sea Fleet were transferred to the Fleet's headquarters in Sevastopol in May 1994 at the height of the Crimean constitutional conflict. A marine brigade was also brought to the 'military danger' state of increased readiness where personnel are issued with weapons, first aid kits and bullet proof vests while being combined to barracks. The Black Sea Fleet's press office warned that, 'It is clear that whatever the development of the situation, the Black Sea Fleet cannot remain outside events unfolding around it'.[407] Black Sea Fleet exercises were held in May 1994 during which 'unidentified armed soldiers' were repulsed after attempting to take over a unit of the Ukrainian Air Defence in Sevastopol.

Kyiv was unlikely to have used force to bring to heel the Crimea except as a final last resort, although it was prepared for every contingency. With the MVS in the Crimea divided in its loyalties any conflict on the peninsula would have been left to the National Guard and Border Troops to deal with, backed

---

405    *Krasnaya Zvezda*, 1 March and *The New York Times*, 30 May 1994.
406    *Post Postup,* no.11 (15-21 April 1994).
407    AFP, 20 May 1994.

by the military and the Security Service (SBU). If these forces had proved to be insufficient to deal with the conflict, specialist units of the Ukrainian armed forces (airborne, marines and *Spetsnaz*) would have additionally intervened. Although domestic affairs are beyond the prerogative of the Ukrainian military, Crimean separatism is both an object of domestic politics and of external relations with Russia. The Ukrainian military are closely tied to the *raison d'etre* of the Ukrainian state and its territorial integrity. Widespread public support for acting against a Crimean separatist drive to independence would have existed. A typically strong response was given by then Defence Minister Vitaliy Radetsky: 'The toughest and most extreme measures will be taken against the violators of the state borders and Ukraine's territorial integrity. We are not going to bargain with anyone.'[408]

The Ukrainian National Guard, which was deployed in the Crimea from 1992 and normally had a compliment of 1,000 men, was increased to 3,000 in the first half of the 1990s with an additional 29 armoured personnel carriers (APC's) in their two main bases in Simferopol and Sevastopol. Assault rifles, light machine guns, grenade launchers and other military equipment were transferred to the National Guard in the Crimea. Additional APC's were removed from storage near Yalta. National Guard units were also moved to new bases in Kerch and Yevpatoriya.[409] A field hospital was prepared to take casualties in the event of conflict.

### Subversion

A group of commanding officers of the SBU, led by the first deputy head, arrived in Simferopol in May 1994. Oleksander Skipalsky, chief of Military Counter Intelligence and a national-democrat parliamentary deputy, accused the Russian intelligence services of interference in the Crimea. 'Such actions are a gross violation of the agreement concluded by the special services of Ukraine and Russia which specifies that subversive work against each other is inadmissible.'[410]

A Russian FSB (Federal Security Service) officer was arrested in Simferopol in June 1995 after he was found in possession of technical specifica-

---

408    Ostankino Television, 20 May 1994.
409    ITAR-TASS, 19 and 22 May, Reuters, 22 May 1994.
410    *Ukrainian News*, no.20 (23 May 1994).

tions of an amphibious warfare ship.[411] Russia denied he was a spy.[412] Russian prisoners-of-war in Chechnya admitted that the FSB was training five-man subversive groups for covert operations in the Crimea.[413] The intelligence and counter-intelligence department of the Black Sea Fleet regularly wrote inflammatory articles for the fleet's newspaper *Flag Rodiny*. The Black Sea Fleet backs, 'the most ardent supporters of anti-Ukrainian activities by the Russian Communities (of the Crimea)'.[414] The Congress of Russian Communities of the Crimea, an offshoot of Meshkov's Republican Movement and Party, were provided with free premises by the Black Sea Fleet to hold meetings. The head of the Congress of Russian Communities of the Crimea, R. Telyatnikova, was awarded a Black Sea Fleet banner and '300-years of the Russian navy' medal for organising rallies in support of the Black Sea Fleet. Similar accusations were made in summer 2005 when the Crimea was the scene of anti-NATO and anti-American demonstrations.[415]

The SBU undertook measures to stabilise the situation and prevent ethnic conflict.[416] Deputy Prime Minister Vasyl Durdynets took charge of all security forces in the Crimea.[417] These measures suggested that Kyiv was ready as a *final resort*, if subversive measures failed, to use force in the Crimea in 1994-1995. Acting head of the Crimean MVS warned, 'We will act decisively and consistently in the defence of the territorial integrity of Ukraine'.[418]

Moscow understood from Ukraine's actions that it could not act in the same manner as it had in Georgia and Moldova because Ukraine would act decisively and had sufficient forces on the ground to deal with Crimean separatism. Russia also could not condemn Ukraine's tough response when it was militarily intervening in Chechnya against separatism. Then Foreign Minister Anatoly Zlenko said force would not be used, 'unless, of course, the other side provokes it'. Kravchuk warned that any actions aimed at changing

---

411   NTV, 5 June 1995.
412   Interfax, 6 June 1995.
413   UNIAN, 17 April 1995.
414   *Vseukrainskiye Vedomosti*, 12 April 1997.
415   'Russian Subversion in the Crimea', *Jane's Intelligence Digest*, 3 November 2006.
416   UNIAN, 1 July 1995.
417   UNIAR, 31 July 1995.
418   UPI, 19 May 1994.

Ukraine's borders would be deemed a violation of Ukraine's constitution and the Helsinki accords, 'and will cause the Ukrainian authorities to react in kind'.[419]

Prior to using the final option of force, Ukraine used covert actions to subvert Russian nationalists. Yevhen Marchuk, then head of the SBU, said they were countering the propaganda of separatist political parties: 'We are doing what the special services should do and this is under relevant control. We have been doing something. I cannot dwell on this in public but this is within the framework of Ukrainian laws.'[420]

Marchuk, 'favoured the neutralisation of such phenomenon by political methods, involving special services in this work within the framework of the law'. The SBU was successfully implementing the presidential decree of 18 May 1994 which had foiled Meshkov's attempts to place the Crimean MVS under his control. Instead they had been transferred directly under Kyiv's control.[421] Marchuk claimed the SBU had 4 priorities: corruption, organised crime, the economy and 'protection of civil peace'. The SBU opposed the 'miliarisation' of the power ministries in the Crimea.[422] Marchuk's priority in the Crimea was to block attempts at infringing Ukraine's territorial integrity and he admitted that, 'The situation in the Crimea is being successfully controlled by them' (i.e. the SBU).[423] Marchuk continued to subvert the separatist movement from within when he was Deputy Prime Minister with responsibility for national security in 1994-1995. His policies, based on tried and tested KGB methods, overcame the challenge to Ukraine's territorial integrity without the use of violence.

### Paramilitaries

If a Crimean conflict began to develop Russian Cossack, Ukrainian Cossack and Russian and Ukrainian nationalist paramilitaries expressed their willingness to join the fray on either side. The paramilitary arm of the Ukrainian National assembly, the Ukrainian People's Self Defence Forces (UNSO),

419   *Postfactum Daily News*, 21 April 1992.
420   Marchuk on Radio Ukraine World Service, 16 March 1994.
421   *Uriadovyi Kurier*, 21 May 1994.
422   Marchuk on Radio Ukraine World Service, 26 May 1994.
423   *Kyivski vidomosti*, 6 May 1994.

had already sent volunteers to the Crimea as 'active holiday-makers'.[424] Russia's Don Cossacks (who had already begun delivering weapons to the Crimea as early as October 1993) signed an agreement with the Crimean leadership to provide volunteers. Russian Cossacks obtain volunteers from Russian skinhead groups which have multiplied in Russia and have been accused by Amnesty International of racist attacks. Russian Cossacks are allied with two local structures: the Russian Orthodox Church (officially registered as the 'Ukrainian Orthodox Church' under the Russian Orthodox Patriarch) and extreme Russian nationalist groups. One of the most active Russian nationalists is Tsekov, leader of the Russian Community of Crimean and head of the Russian Bloc political association. Russian Cossacks swear an oath of allegiance to the Russian Orthodox Church. The Church aggressively supports its dominance by seeking to block the construction of mosques and churches with allegiance to rival Ukrainian autocephalous denominations that are traditionally allied to national democrats. The Russian Orthodox Church and its Cossack allies have come into conflict with Tatars when placing crosses and monuments at sites that are sacred or sensitive to their history.

Airfields were placed on high alert to prevent them from bringing in Russian forces in the event that Russia intervened on Meshkov's side. There was also a threat from Russian nationalist paramilitaries to seize airfields, such as the important Belbek airfield outside Simferopol, in order to control the skies over the Crimea. Airfields received reinforcements and portable air defence units were brought into the Crimea. Then Minister of Defence Radetsky admitted that force would be used against any planes or helicopters trying to land at these airfields.[425]

The Confederation of Caucasian Mountain Peoples, which has close ties to the Tatars, would have also intervened against Russia in the event of a Crimean conflict that would have inflamed Muslim-Russian relations through-

---

424    UNIAN, 2 June 1994. See T.Kuzio, 'Ukrainian Paramilitaries', *Jane's Intelligence Review*, December 1992 and 'Paramilitary Groups in Ukraine', *Jane's Intelligence Review* , March 1994.

425    *Kyivski vidomosti*, 20 April 1994.

out the CIS. Cooperation was already well established between Ukrainian paramilitaries and the Chechen leadership in the Chechen conflict where
Ukrainian paramilitaries had by then participated on the Chechen side. At
least 100 Tatars fought in Chechnya from the Adalet Party led by former airbourne officer Fevzi Kubedinov. Adalet had 1,500 paramilitaries who were
from former airbourne forces who were used by the Tatar *Mejlis* for security
and bodyguard operations.[426] Aidar Ismailov, head of the Crimean Islamic
Party, said: 'Russia will now have to deal with the entire Muslim world as
each Muslim under Sharia law is obliged to help another Muslim in dis-
tress.'[427] The Crimean Islamic Party would support Chechen Muslims, 'in their
struggle for independence'.

Russian Cossacks and nationalists stoke up fear of Islamic fundamentalism among Crimean Tatars. Russian Cossacks and nationalist groups
praise the 15 November 1944 deportation of 380,000 Tatars and 50,000 demobilised Tatar Soviet troops to Central Asia. Russian Cossacks and nationalists also raise exaggerated fears of Russophones losing their land and
property and of being themselves deported after the Tatars create a separate
Islamic Crimean republic. Fears of Islamic fundamentalism are exaggerated
as traditionally Tatars have practiced a moderate form of Islam. Nevertheless,
the example of Chechnya is instructive. Chechen nationalists, who also traditionally practiced a moderate form of Islam, became progressively Islamicised
during the second conflict with Russia after 1999. Saudi missionaries with
large financial resources are seeking converts among younger, disgruntled
Tatars for the stricter Wahabbi form of Islam. Crimea's senior Muslim clergy-
man, Mufti Emirali Adzi Ablaev, remains confident that Wahabbism will not
take root among Crimean Tatars. 'Our nation, our ancestors, never had those
trends, those sects, and they won't have them now', he said. He continued,

---

426    *Obshchaya Gazeta*, 18 November 1999.
427    ITAR-TASS, 6 October 1999.

'among our people, such ideologies and ideas have never been present and never will be'.[428]

### Reluctance to Use Force

While the Ukrainian authorities increased their security presence on the Crimean peninsula they nevertheless, were reluctant to utilise force to bring the Crimea to heel. A number of reasons existed for this reluctance to use force. Attempts at suppressing secessionist rebellions in other post Soviet states have ended disastrously. In Moldova it led to the creation of the secessionist Trans-Dniestr enclave backed by the Russian army. In Azerbaijan the conflict over Nagorno Karabakh led to constant *coup d'etats* and changes in the presidential leadership of that country. Most dramatically, in Georgia its military defeat in Abkhazia led to a *coup d'etat*, civil war and the removal from power of nationalist President Zviad Gamsakurdia. After President Edward Shevardnadze came to power in 1992 he was forced to take Georgia into the CIS and allow Russia to maintain its three military bases. Georgia continues to have two frozen conflicts in Abkhazia and South Ossetia.

The Ukrainian leadership believed that the 'Abkhazian' syndrome was perhaps a dry run for the Crimea.[429] If the Ukrainian authorities stormed into the Crimean Supreme Soviet, in the manner of the Georgian National Guard in Sukhumi, Russia would have inevitably been drawn into the conflict either officially or through the use of surrogate forces drawing on Cossacks and the Black Sea Fleet.

The Russian authorities have often decreed their right to intervene in the 'Near Abroad' in defence of Russians or 'Russian speakers' (compatriots) and they would not therefore have remained passive towards a conflict in the Crimea. It is no coincidence that Ukraine has always been a strong opponent of Russia acquiring a UN or OSCE mandate to undertake 'peacekeeping' missions throughout the CIS. Russian mandates, along the lines of those they have pursued in Moldova and Georgia, would legitimise Russian 'peacekeeping' which has merely served to freeze conflicts on the ground.

---

428   Askold Krushelnycky, 'Ukraine: Crimea's Tatars - Clearing The Way For Islamic Extremism? (Part 4)', *RFERL Features*, 26 August 2004.

429   See Igor Rotar, 'Crimea-Abkhazia-PriDniestr. Similarities and Differences', *Nezavisimaya Gazeta*, 2 March 1994.

A second factor which discouraged the Ukrainian authorities from utilising military force against the Crimea was the impact it would potentially have had upon the regional balance in southern and Eastern Ukraine. Eastern-southern Ukraine voted against Kravchuk in the 1994 presidential elections in favour of the more 'pro-Russian' Kuchma. Russians do not constitute a majority in any Ukrainian administrative region other than the Crimea. Nevertheless, Russians and Russian-speaking Ukrainians form large constituencies in regions such as Odesa and the Donbas which at that time had latent autonomous tendencies. These would have been accentuated in the event of a Crimean violent conflict that would have been inevitably exploited by Russia.[430] In Ukraine there is a pro-Russian lobby in Eastern and Southern Ukraine that has given its support to the Communists and to pro-Russian centrists in each election.[431]

### Tug of War over the Crimean Security Forces

Ukrainian-Crimean relations went into deeper crisis in May 1994. The Crimean Supreme Soviet approved a law by 69 votes (with 2 Communists voting against, 2 abstentions and the 14 Tatars refusing to vote) restoring the 6 May 1992 Crimean constitution. Kyiv regarded this as tantamount to renewing the May 1992 declaration of independence. A rather dangerous demand, in Kyiv's eyes, was the resolution attached to the new law, which forbid the sending of Crimean draftees to serve outside the peninsula. They were to serve either in military units based in the Crimea or in the Black Sea Fleet.

---

430   On regionalism in Ukraine see R. Solchanyk, 'The Politics of State Building: Centre-Periphery Relations in Post-Soviet Ukraine', *Europe-Asia Studies*, vol.46, no.1 (January-February 1994), pp.47-68, Ian Bremmer, 'The Politics of Ethnicity: Russians in the New Ukraine', *Europe-Asia Studies*, vol.46, no.2 (March-April 1994), pp.261-283; Andrew Wilson, 'The Growing Challenge to Kyiv from Donbas', *RFE/RL Research Report*, vol.2, no. 33 (20 August 1993).

431   The poll was conducted by the Kyiv International Institute of Sociology in April 1994. Its results are reflected in other polls in Ukraine. See the poll by the same institute and the Peter Mohyla Academy which gave only 33 percent and 50 percent support for Ukrainian independence in Eastern and Southern Ukraine respectively. Support for unification with Russia in these regions was also as high as 65 percent and 49 percent respectively (*Ukrayinske Slovo*, 20 February 1994).

Meshkov attempted to change the leadership of the local MVS, SBU and Ministry of Justice. Meshkov's actions were illegal and they were vetoed by a Ukrainian presidential decree.

The Ukrainian parliament responded to the Crimean new law and resolution with its own demand that they be both reversed within ten days (a similar response in May 1992 defused the crisis by assisting both sides to reach a compromise). The Ukrainian resolution pointed out that, 'The Crimea has no right to handle issues which are considered to be the prerogative of Ukrainian bodies of power' (i.e. foreign and security policies). Lawyers and deputie's from Kyiv and the Crimea were to use these ten days to attempt to reach a peaceful compromise acceptable to both sides.

The Ukrainian reaction was predictably sharp across the entire political spectrum. President Kravchuk stated that he would ask parliament to grant him sweeping powers if Crimea did not back down over this question. The SBU refused to obey Meshkov's changes in its local leadership and pledged their continued loyalty to Kyiv and Marchuk. The law on the SBU defined the Crimean SBU as a regional, not a separate component of the SBU. Meshkov also attempted to replace the Crimean SBU head with the former Chief of Staff of the $32^{nd}$ Corps under Kuznetsov, but this also failed. An 18 May 1994 presidential decree brought the Crimean SBU directly under Kyiv's control. Major-General Ivan Kolomytsev became head of the Crimean directorate within the SBU with the additional rank of deputy chairman of the SBU.

When he became President in January 1994, Meshkov subordinated a third of the Crimean *Berkut* (the Soviet era OMON riot police) to himself as his personal bodyguard. The ninth directorate of the KGB guarded high ranking officials and was therefore analogous to the US Secret Service. After the KGB became the SBU in 1992 the ninth directorate was separated and became the Directorate on State Protection. Meshkov did not trust this unit and issued a decree on 11 March 1994 creating his own Presidential Security Service with a compliment of 100 Berkut officers. The unit was led by a Russian citizen, Colonel Viktor Bortnikov. Meshkov rejected the refusal of the Crimean Supreme Soviet, which feared it could be used against itself, to give the unit legal status. The Supreme Soviet argued that the creation of the unit had contradicted the Crimean constitution. On 29 August 1994 the head of the Crimean Supreme Soviet stated that Meshkov's decrees on this question had no legal force and they therefore demanded that the unit be disarmed. [432]

Meshkov did not attempt to take control of the Border Troops or the National Guard. The former were unimportant to his designs while the latter were totally loyal to Kyiv. Potentially the most explosive situation surrounded the armed forces. On 15 March 1994 Meshkov issued a decree that all conscripts would only serve in the Crimea. Oleksandr Volkov, the head of the Crimean military commissariat, was not consulted on this question and he, like the Sevastopol military commissariat and commander of the 32$^{nd}$ Corps, refused to implement these 'unlawful decrees'.[433] They pledged their continued loyalty to Kyiv.

On 2 April 1994 a presidential decree revoked Meshkov's decree.[434] Defeated Crimean presidential, pro-Ukrainian candidate Bagrov also backed Ukrainian legislation. The Crimean 'party of power' opposed Meshkov's attempt at gaining control over the security forces, knowing that this might lead to violent conflict with Kyiv. Deputy Defence Minister Ivan Bizhan visited the Crimea at this time. This was a deliberately timed visit to show that Ukraine controlled the armed forces in the Crimea. He visited the head quarters of the 32nd Corps mechanised division, the military construction academy and Border Troops head quarters in Simferopol. At the end of Bizhan's visit he reported that he was confidant Ukraine could deal with 'any eventuality'.[435] Ukrainian legislation ruled out the use of the armed forces in domestic questions but, Bizhan argued that the Crimea was an exception. He did not elaborate but presumably he believed that separatism was foreign inspired and a threat to the country's territorial integrity, the ultimate guarantors of which were the President (also Commander-in-Chief) and the armed forces.

Besides the military the other main struggle between Meshkov and Kyiv was over the MVS which, at the lower rank level, was locally recruited. Deputy Head of the Ukrainian MVS, Valentyn Nedryhailo, took control of the MVS chief office in Simferopol with the help of Berkut riot police in May 1994. They claimed that the rightful head of the Crimean MVS, Oleksandr Plyuta, was il-

---

432    UNIAN, 29 August 1994.
433    Ukrainian Television-1, 28 March 1994.
434    *Narodna Armiya*, 5 April 1994.
435    *Post Postup*, 15-21 April 1994.

legally removed by Meshkov on 11 April and replaced by retired General Valery Kuznetsov. Kuznetsov was the former commander of the 32nd Army Corps in Simferopol who had been removed from this position in April 1992 for refusing to institute the Ukrainian oath of loyalty. Kyiv was also afraid that Kuznetsov and Meshkov would have access to the MVS weapons arsenal. Hence, under the 18 May 1994 decree, Kyiv nationalised all buildings, weapons and vehicles from the Crimean MVS to prevent them falling into Meshkov's and Kuznetsov's hands.

Colonel Valeriy Chernyshov was appointed the head of the Crimean directorate within the Ukrainian MVS with the double rank of deputy head of the Ukrainian MVS. Kyiv sent telegrams to all councils in the Crimea ordering them to only obey the Ukrainian head of the Crimean directorate of the MVS and not Meshkov. Kyiv's attempt to remove Kuznetsov was described by Meshkov as a 'coup' attempt. Kuznetsov ordered the Crimean MVS 'to obey only me'. Meshkov argued that, 'If need be, we have enough forces and equipment to not allow the situation to get out of control'.[436] The Crimean MVS did not back Meshkov. His appointed commander, Kuznetsov, admitted that he had only minority support within the Crimean MVS.[437]

Kravchuk's 18 May decree led to changes in the law on the MVS by the Ukrainian parliament. This showed again that despite left-wing control over parliament there was near unanimity in defence of Ukraine's territorial integrity. The MVS and SBU came under direct Kyiv control after the 18 May 1994 presidential decree.

Kyiv was not initially willing to force the issue and enforce the 18 May decree. A compromise ensured for a few months whereby both Meshkov's appointee, Kuznetsov, and the head of the Crimean directorate of the MVS, Chernyshov, jointly ran the MVS. During this period the MVS compromised and it reverted to Ukrainian control. The compromise meant that Kuznetsov and Meshkov had lost less face, according to Valeriy Pietukhov, head of the Crimean MVS criminal department. Pietukhiv claimed Kuznetsov had no support base within the MVS which indicated that the MVS was not willing to be dragged into a potential conflict between Kyiv and the Crimea. In such a con-

---

436    ITAR-TASS, 19 May 1994.
437    UNIAN, 29 June 1994.

flict the lightly armed MVS would have been pitted against the armed forces, MVS Internal Troops and the National Guard. The Crimean MVS clearly understood the dangers of Meshkov's recklessness.[438]

1,000 National Guard were already stationed in the Crimea from 1992 and in 1994, when tension escalated, another 2,000 were deployed in the peninsula. In the event that direct presidential rule would have been established in the Crimea the National Guard would have been used to enforce it. The Ukrainian marines, based especially around Sevastopol, were also issued with full military kit and placed on the highest alert of 'military danger' when tensions rose. In spring 1994 then Minister of Defence, Radetskyi, admitted that he had been given orders to defend Ukraine's territorial integrity at all costs.[439] Although the armed forces were not to be used in domestic questions the Crimea has always been a special case. Indeed, NATO Partnership for Peace exercises in the Crimea and Odesa often used scenarios where the armed forces dealt with externally supported separatism.[440]

### Trans-Dniestr and the Crimea

The Trans-Dniestr Republican leadership in Moldova never hid its strategic objective of uniting with pro-Russian regions of Southern-Eastern Ukraine (so-called *Novorossia* [New Russia] the Tsarist term for the region) into a new state. This would then link up with Russia and the Crimea through Eastern Ukraine, thereby cutting the truncated Ukraine off from the Black sea. The Chairman of the Trans-Dniestr Republican Supreme Soviet, Grigorii Marakutsa, described his region as 'an inalienable part of the Russian state's Southern region, which also includes Crimea, Odesa *oblast* and a number of other (Ukrainian) *oblasts* and is known as *Novorossia*.'[441]

Trans-Dniestr Republican officers, trainers and weapons used in Abkhazia in 1992-1993 made their way to the Crimea. Weapons and ammunition from the Russian 14th Army were covertly supplied to Kuznetsov's

---

438    *Kyivski vidomosti*, 11 August 1994.
439    *Kyivski vidomosti*, 20 April 1994.
440    *Kyivski vidomosti*, 20 April 1994.
441    *Patriot*, no.20, 1994.

MVS and Meshkov's presidential republican guard.[442] If Kravchuk had won the 1994 elections this might have inflamed the situation as he obtained very few votes in the Crimea.[443] He may have adopted a hard line with Meshkov who defeated 'his' preferred candidate (Bagrov). This, in turn, may have encouraged Russia to intervene along the lines of its surrogate support for separatists in Georgia and Moldova. Black Sea Fleet personnel could have melted into the local population and re-emerged as 'Crimeans' (just as the 14th Army became Trans-Dniestrians in Moldova). Russian Black Sea Fleet personnel were evident in summer 2006 anti-NATO demonstrations in the Crimea.

In April 1994 the Minister of Defence (Radetskyi), the Air Force commander (Major-General Antonets), the Chief of Staff (Anatoliy Lopata), chief of the second directorate of military counter intelligence (Major-General Kravchenko), head of intelligence of the armed forces (Major-General Vegunnikov), and chief of staff of the National Guard (Mokhov) visited the Crimea when Meshkov was on a visit to the offshore zone of Cyprus. This was a very high powered team and the timing of the visit was not coincidental as it was intended to check on the combat readiness of local security forces in the event of conflict at a time when Meshkov was away from the Crimea. The Ukrainian armed forces and National Guard mountain trained in the Carpathians between 1993-1994. The only other mountainous region in Ukraine is in the Crimea.[444] This indicates that the training was in the event of conflict in the Crimea.

Some Russian nationalists sought to repeat the Trans-Dniestr and Abkhaz scenarios in the Crimea in the first half of the 1990s. Attempts at smuggling weapons into the Crimea were undertaken from the Trans-Dniestr through Odesa (the city was plagued by violence from organised crime until 1997-1998 when Mayor Eduard Gurfits was removed by Kyiv). Weapons

---

442    Deliveries of 28 officer-instructors of the Trans-Dniestr Republican 'Ministry of State Security' as well as weapons and ammunition from Colonel Mikhail Bergman, military commander of the Tiraspol garrison of Russia's 14th Army, to the Crimea began in June (UNIAN, 25 June 1994).

443    If Kravchuk had won we would 'have to deal with a civil war in the Crimea, similar to the Tyraspil conflict'. See Maryna Chorna, 'The Crimean Labyrinth: All Paths Lead to the MIC', *Demos*, vol.1, no.4 (November 1994), p.13.

444    *Segodnya*, 25 May 1994.

were very easy to purchase in the Crimea, according to the local head of the MVS, Hennadiy Moskal.[445] Russian Cossacks from the Union of Cossack Troops of Russia and Near Abroad who were active in the Trans-Dniestr came in small numbers to the Crimea to support Meshkov. They were allegedly on hire as hit men by various parties, such as the Crimean Christian Liberal Party (hit men from the Trans-Dniestr were used in Odesa frequently, such as in the murder of the editor of *Vechirnyi Odesa*). The National Guard backed up the Border Troops in sealing the Crimea to try and prevent weapons from being smuggled in, particularly by checking the Kerch-Caucasus ferry.

Colonel Mikhail Bergman, commander of the Tiraspol garrison, admitting supplying military supplies from the Trans-Dniestr to the Crimea. 28 officer-instructors were sent to Meshkov from the Trans-Dniestr Ministry of State Security in June 1994 led by its deputy head, Oleh Hudymo.[446] The situation only stabilised from mid 1995 after Russian nationalists were removed from power in the Crimea. Deputy Commander of MVS Internal Troops, Volodymyr Povazhniuk, claimed 'Today the situation in the Crimea is stabilising and is controlled'.[447] The local authorities were again cooperating closely with Ukraine's special MVS units and National Guard.

### Conflict Over the Black Sea Fleet

Between September-December 1991 the commander of the Black Sea Fleet was theoretically willing to transfer the fleet to Ukrainian control. It is not clear if Moscow would have agreed to this (as it possessed nuclear weapons and was therefore classified as 'strategic'). Then parliamentary speaker Kravchuk was over-cautious about taking over the Black Sea Fleet until the December 1991 referendum on independence.

This caution had positive and negative aspects. On the positive side it led to 70 per cent of the Black Sea Fleet personnel voting for Ukrainian independence in the referendum because there was no atmosphere of conflict.

---

445   *Ukrayina moloda*, 13 February 1998.
446   UNIAN, 25 June 1994.
447   *Holos Ukrayiny*, 18 July 1995.

On the negative side Ukraine lost its chance (which it might have had prior to December 1991) to gain 100 per cent control over the Black Sea Fleet. This might have been theoretically possible as the Soviet centre was then *de facto* paralysed and the chain of command was in a state of confusion in Moscow. Russia initially therefore claimed that the Black Sea Fleet was not hers, but part of the CIS 'strategic force'. This was because individual states, such as Ukraine, could not allegedly afford to run their own navies. Russia also initially backed off claiming Sevastopol as Russian but suggested that it should come under both republican and union authority.

The Black Sea Fleet commander blocked the introduction of the Ukrainian oath of loyalty and instead began introducing a CIS (but not Russian) loyalty oath in January 1992. A free for all took place as different units took either the CIS or Ukrainian oaths. A major victory for Ukraine was the oath taken by the Sevastopol garrison in July 1992 with its vessels defecting to Odesa to join the Ukrainian navy. If naval commanders decided to side with Ukraine they moved their vessels to Odesa, where the military district commander is based in the Ukrainian chain of command.

The Black Sea Fleet commander also prevented the replacement of pro-Soviet *hardliners* with Union of Ukrainian Officers (UUO) officers, which had taken place else where in Ukraine. It is still unclear how three quarters of Black Sea Fleet personnel could vote for Ukrainian independence in December 1991 and then not take the Ukrainian oath of loyalty in January-February 1992 unless there was pressure by high ranking officers on the lower ranks. The Black Sea Fleet may have also included a higher than average proportion of *hardliners* because of the symbolic nature of Sevastopol and the Black Sea Fleet to Russian historical myths and nationalism.[448]

These hardliners stayed in place, although cut off from Moscow, and become a Russian military enclave. During this period (1991-1993) the Black Sea Fleet could have theoretically also gone the same way in the Crimea as the 14th Army in Moldova. That it did not do so is due to two former Soviet functionaries continuing in power in Kyiv (Kravchuk) and Simferopol (Bagrov). The situation in the Crimea and Ukraine was different to that in Moldova and

---

448    See Serhiy Plokhy, 'The City of Glory: Sevastopol in Russian Historical Mythology', *Journal of Contemporary History*, vol.35, no.3 (July 2000), pp.369-384.

Georgia where anti-Russian nationalists came to power who sought a decisive break with the Soviet past and were antagonistic to local national minorities.

In April 1992 both Kravchuk and Russian President Borys Yeltsin signed decrees nationalising the Black Sea Fleet and then both withdrew them after tension rose between Russia and Ukraine. Kravchuk pushed as far as he could and then back tracked when meeting serious opposition, just like Bagrov had undertaken when negotiating a sovereignty deal with Kyiv. The compromise accepted by both sides concluded that the Black Sea Fleet was inherited by *both* Ukraine and Russia. This step meant Russia acknowledged that Ukraine had a right to create its own navy (which it had refused to accept until then) based on a portion of the Black Sea Fleet vessels.

### 1992-1993

Attempts either unilaterally to take over, or jointly divide, the Black Sea Fleet during 1992-1993 failed and the situation was not resolved until 1997. In contrast to the relatively trouble free nationalisation of Soviet armed forces in Ukraine the Black Sea Fleet was problematical precisely because of its indirect link to the status of the Crimea and Sevastopol. Attempts by Ukraine to nationalise those portions of the Black Sea Fleet based in Ukraine in April 1992 were thwarted by the pro-Russian and pro-CIS Black Sea Fleet command.

In June 1992 a summit was held between President's Kravchuk and Yeltsin in Dagomys. The 18-point agreement reached at the summit resolved to divide the Black Sea Fleet into two equal proportions by 1995, an aim which would defuse the political situation in the Crimea which had declared independence the month before. But, before the ink was even dry on the agreement it collapsed and both Presidents had to travel two months later to Yalta to sign a second agreement. The Yalta agreement clearly spelled out (which the Dagomys agreement had not) how the Black Sea Fleet would be staffed and supplied as well as the mechanics of how it would be divided by 1995.

By spring 1993 both sides were trading charges about the lack of progress on the Black Sea Fleet Fleet agreement and the continued unilateral takeover of facilities by both sides. Ukrainian deputies and the Ministry of Defence campaigned for the annulment of the Yalta agreement believing that Russia was gaining the most from it. They were opposed to the fact that Black Sea Fleet ships were being used in the Abkhaz conflict without consultation with Kyiv.[449]

Both sides regarded the agreement in different ways. Ukraine perceived it as launching the division of the Black Sea Fleet, the Russian portion of which after 1995 would leave Ukrainian territory. The Russian side had less inclination to divide the Black Sea Fleet, arguing that it could not physically be removed as no new base had been built to accommodate it. Russian negotiators argued that a united Black Sea Fleet should remain in Sevastopol after 1995. During the course of 1992-1993 senior Russian officials repeatedly stated that the Russian portion of the Black Sea Fleet would continue to be based in Sevastopol after its division.

The Russian and Ukrainian sides interpreted the Dagomys-Yalta agreements differently over the question of whether the land-based facilities should be divided as well as the ships. The number of incidents where Russian and Ukrainian naval units came into conflict was gradually increasing which threatened to ignite a larger conflict in the Crimea. By April-May 1993 the situation had severely deteriorated in the Black Sea Fleet.[450] Over 80 per cent of the vessels raised the Tsarist St.Andrew flag showing their allegiance to Russia. The Ukrainian Defence Ministry demanded that those ships which had raised the Russian flag should be withdrawn from Ukrainian territory.

President Kravchuk then proposed further talks to settle the lingering dispute and counter claims made by each side. Russian State Duma resolutions claiming sovereignty over Sevastopol merely inflamed the situation. The local situation continued to deteriorate; in October 1996 when a column of Russian sailors passed two Ukrainian navy officers the first saluted while the second spat at them.[451]

The summit between Russian and Ukrainian presidents in Moscow in June 1993 again reiterated that the practical formation of the Russian and

---

449   *Holos Ukrayiny*, 2 and 13 April 1993. See also Roman Solchanyk, 'Ukrainian-Russian Summit at Dagomys', *RFE/RL Research Report*, vol.1, no.30 (24 July 1992).
450   *Moscow News*, no.23, 1993.
451   AP, 25 October 1996.

Ukrainian navies would begin in September 1993 and be completed by the end of 1995. The conditions under which the Russian navy would be stationed in Ukraine would be stipulated at a later date.[452]

The agreement was met with hostility in both Kyiv and Moscow, albeit for different reasons. The Ukrainian parliament refused to ratify the agreement because of the two clauses dealing with dual citizenship and lease of Sevastopol to the Russian Black Sea Fleet after 1995. The Russian parliament called the agreement a 'tragedy', demanded that the Black Sea Fleet remain united and refused to accept the concept of leasing Sevastopol (as this would be tantamount to a recognition of Ukrainian sovereignty).

On 3 September 1993 both Presidents met again at Massandra to resolve the Black Sea Fleet and other outstanding questions, although in a more heated atmosphere.[453] President Yeltsin wanted to trumpet a victory for his nationalist credentials on the eve of disbanding the Russian parliament. The Russian side refused to discuss the proposals put forward by their opposite Ukrainian numbers on the division of the Black Sea Fleet. Instead, they used Ukraine's economic crisis and the threat of halting energy supplies to pressure it to agree to Russia's demands. The agreement drew up a committee to report back within one month as to whether, as Moscow had demanded, the Black Sea Fleet should be taken over by Russia completely in return for the cancellation of Ukrainian debts. In addition, Russia was to lease Sevastopol as the base for the Russian Black Sea Fleet.

By the end of September 1993 Russia had annulled the accords because of different interpretations of any nuclear agreement. A major unresolved question rested over whether it should include all nuclear weapons in Ukraine or only Russian-built SS-19 missiles, which Kyiv insisted were the only ones covered by START 1?[454] The nuclear agreement was dependent upon the Ukrainian parliament ratifying the START 1 treaty, a step it had been reluctant to undertake until then.

---

452   See Roman Solchanyk, 'The Ukrainian-Russian Summit: Problems and Prospects', *RFE/RL Research Report*, vol.2, no.27 (2 July 1993).
453   See Bohdan Nahaylo, 'The Massandra Summit and Ukraine', *RFE/RL Research Report*, vol.2, no.37 (17 September 1993).
454   *Narodna Armiya*, 24 September 1993.

Then Prime Minister Kuchma resigned on 10 September 1993, partly in response to accusations of incompetence and amid accusations of being too pro-Russian. Defence Minister Konstantin Morozov also resigned the following month in protest at the Massandra accords. Morozov wrote in an open letter to President Kravchuk that he would disclaim all responsibility for the defence of Southern Ukraine. The Massandra accords were condemned by nearly all Ukrainian political parties who formed a congress in 'total opposition' to President Kravchuk and whom they demanded should be be impeached for 'national treason'.[455]

## 1994

The attempts to reach a compromise on the Crimea within the 10-13 days deadline in May-June 1994 led to the sixth round of negotiations over the Black Sea Fleet. Failure to reach a negotiated settlement during 1992-1994 rested not over the division of the Black Sea Fleet but the status of its on-shore infra structure and bases. This was directly linked to Russian claims of sovereignty over the Crimea.

Russia continued to insist that Sevastopol be leased or given to the Russian Black Sea Fleet for a 99-year term lease with the Ukrainian Navy either vacating the Crimea completely or moving to Balaklava. Sergey Lavrov, Russian Deputy Foreign Minister, insisted that the Black Sea Fleet, 'with all the infrastructures in Crimea, is used by Russia and receives Russian markings'.[456] Meanwhile, President Yeltsin refused to consider signing an interstate treaty with Ukraine recognising current borders until the Black Sea Fleet question was resolved.

If the question of the Black Sea Fleet were resolved, according to then Defence Minister Radetskyi, the Crimean crisis would have been defused. Ukraine's successful nationalisation of the former Soviet conventional and nuclear armed forces on its territory was thwarted by then commander Kasatanov in the Black Sea Fleet. For his actions in blocking Ukraine's takeover, Kasatanov was rewarded with the post of first deputy commander of the Russian navy.

---

455    *Demokratychna Ukrayina*, 7 September 1993.
456    See the telegram by Lavrov to the Sevastopol city council in *Slava Sevastopolya*, 2 February 1994.

The Ukrainian position constantly shifted from initially demanding the right to all vessels on Ukrainian territory or seeking a compromise 50:50 division. As the Crimean crisis escalated the support for Crimean separatism grew which made finding a resolution to the Black Sea Fleet more difficult. President Yeltsin's spokesman, Viacheslav Kostikov, pointed out that, 'The Ukrainian side refuses to deal with realities and is becoming more and more inconsistent and unpredictable in its actions and announcements'.[457] The dominating presence of Russian nationalism in Crimean institutions until 1995 gave Russia an added lever.

At issue was less a claim towards possession of the vessels as the real issues were bases, such as Sevastopol, and ownership over, and influence in, the Crimea. Between 1992-1994 the Black Sea Fleet was the subject of five failed attempts to reach a compromise, one of which brought down former Defence Minister Morozov who accused President Kravchuk and former Prime Minister Kuchma of a 'sell-out' to Moscow at the Massandra summit in September 1993. The fifth round of talks in April 1994 collapsed over Defence Minister Pavel Grachev's demands for the withdrawal of Ukraine's navy from the Crimea.[458] Incredibly, Grachev openly demanded that:

> Sevastopol should be the main base of Russia's Black Sea Fleet. We consider that as well as Sevastopol, the fleet should also be based in Balaklava, Feodosiya, Kerch and Donuzalev where the main forces of Russia's Black Sea Fleet are deployed and also where units and formations are stationed. It is clear that we have the right to, and we will not, undermine the combat readiness of the Black Sea Fleet, a battle worthy and full-blooded formation of the armed forces of the Russian Federation...[459]

Although the Ukrainian authorities agreed to sell or transfer 30 per cent

---

457    The 'realities' referred to are an obvious reference to Ukraine's weak economic position and the pro-Russian lobby in the Crimea (UPI, 23 April 1994).

458    On the collapse of these talks, where Grachev stormed out after not being granted what he had demanded, see *Narodna Armiya*, 26 April 1994. See also, 'The Black Sea Fleet - A Deadly Game of Chess', *Jane's Intelligence Review Pointer*, no.7 (April 1994).

459    Radio Moscow International, 10 May 1994.

of their 50 per cent share to Russia to pay energy debts, Russia continued to adopt a more strident position. This included a 99-year lease of the city of Sevastopol (and not just the port), a division of the coastal infrastructure (as well as vessels) and removal of all Ukrainian naval forces from the Crimea (a demand backed by then Crimean President Meshkov).[460] Russian naval plans included basing 70 per cent of the Russian Fleet in Sevastopol, 10 per cent in Donuzlav, 5 per cent in Balaklava and 7 per cent each in Feodosiya and Kerch.

Russia had local support in the Crimea for its insistence that the city and port of Sevastopol be leased to Russia indefinitely. On the same day as presidential elections on 26 June 1994, Sevastopol held an opinion poll 'On the status of Sevastopol as a Russian town'. The question asked, 'Are you in favour of the status of Sevastopol city as the main base of the Russian Federation's Black Sea Fleet, in accordance with the Russian-Ukrainian protocol of 3 September 1993?'[461] With 89 per cent endorsement in the referendum the Sevastopol city council backed Russian demands that the Ukrainian navy and the National Guard completely vacate the city's naval base.[462]

### Kravchuk, Kuchma and the Crimea

The election of President Kuchma in July 1994 was supported by nearly 90 per cent of the Crimean electorate. In the words of President Meshkov, Kuchma's lack of 'nationalist hang-ups' and support for economic reform meant that relations between Kyiv and Simferopol would improve. President Meshkov regarded the election of Kuchma as leading to the renewal of closer ties with the CIS. In particular he saw the event as leading to, 'as strong a union with Russia as possible'.[463]

Both President Kuchma and the Crimean leadership regarded the high vote for Kuchma in different ways. President Kuchma regarded it as a vote for the Crimea to remain within Ukraine. The Crimean leadership, on the other hand, regarded it as the first step of the Crimea's and Ukraine's unification

---

460    On the tense negotiations of the sixth round of talks see *Uriadovyj Kurier*, nos. 80-81 and 82 (26 and 28 May 1992).
461    *Krasnaya Zvezda*, 2 June 1994.
462    UNIAN, 25 June 1994.
463    *Holos Ukrayiny*, 14 July 1994.

with Russia. The deputy chairman of the Crimean Supreme Soviet, Aleksey Melnikov, predicted that the Crimea would be independent by the end of 1994 after the moratorium on a referendum for independence would be lifted in October-November when local elections were held.[464] President Meshkov warned that Kuchma was failing to pay off the political support made by the Crimean electorate which would lead to unspecified measures being taken in the future.

Conflict between Kyiv and the Crimea therefore continued, although without the threat of military sanctions used by former President Kravchuk. The visit to the Crimea on 29 July 1994 by Sergei Baburin, a Russian nationalist deputy, inflamed the situation further. Baburin stated that the peninsula is viewed as part of 'Russia', a statement that was followed by a vote by 36 out of 42 deputies in Sevastopol city council to confirm the city as the main base of the Russian Black Sea Fleet and that the city legally belonged to Russia. On 8 September the Crimean Supreme Soviet voted to support the decision of the Sevastopol council on providing it with Russian legal status.[465]

A polite condemnation came immediately from President Kuchma, whose reaction was described as 'the most acceptable one' by the chairman of Sevastopol city council, as well as more strongly worded statements from the Sevastopol Prosecutor's office and the Ministry of Justice. The latter accused the Sevastopol council of violating the Ukrainian constitution because the city is under republican jurisdiction which can be altered only by the Ukrainian parliament.[466] The Ukrainian parliament re-convened from its Summer recess on 15 September 1994 and one of the first items on the agenda was the Sevastopol city council vote. The Crimean leadership again miscalculated the mood of the newly elected Ukrainian parliament which voted 303:5 in favour of rescinding the Sevastopol vote; that is, a constitutional majority. The overwhelming vote by the Ukrainian parliament, coupled with the emotions stirred up by the Crimean threat to Ukraine's territorial integrity, were factors that President Kuchma, on the one hand, and the Rus-

---

464    UNIAR, 2 August 1994.
465    *Holos Ukrayiny*, 10 September 1994.
466    UNIAR, 25 August and *Holos Ukrayiny*, 30 August and 7 September 1994.

sian leadership, on the other, had to take into account.[467] Both sides did so but in different ways.

The Union of Ukrainian Officers, Rukh and Congress of Ukrainian Nationalists, all of whom were represented in the Ukrainian parliament, issued radical appeals to dissolve the Sevastopol city council. The Union of Ukrainian Officers added that the Ukrainian parliament should also vote in favour of a nuclear status for Ukraine as a way of defending the country against Russian support for Crimean separatism. The military council of the Ukrainian Navy also lodged a strong protest at the Sevastopol city council's vote.[468]

The political temperature between Kyiv and the Crimea continued to deteriorate after numerous complaints from Ukrainian organisations in the Crimea and Sevastopol received widespread prominence in the Ukrainian central media. These included continued, 'attacks by extremists upon representatives of civic organisations who defend Ukrainian interests, citizens who speak the Ukrainian mother tongue or are loyal to the Ukrainian state'.[469] The establishment of new branches of Rukh in the Crimea was also described as, 'a path towards kindling nationalism, confrontation and antagonism'.[470] The Procurator-General, MVS and SBU warned in a joint statement that confrontation between the Crimean parliament and President in September 1994 could lead to civil disorder,.[471]

After the April 1994 Odesa incident[472], former President Kravchuk ac-

---

467   The debate included calls for abolishing Crimean autonomy and a scuffle between Pavlo Movchan, head of the Ukrainian Language Society, with a Crimean deputy.

468   *Holos Ukrayiny,* 30 August, 2 September and ITAR-TASS, 27 August 1994.

469   See the appeal of the second Congress of Ukrainian Citizens of Sevastopol in *Vechirnij Kyiv,* 26 July 1994.

470   *Krasnaya Zvezda,* 18 August 1994.

471   See the statements by the President and law enforcement bodies respectively in *Holos Ukrayiny,* 10 and 13 September 1994.

472   This refers to the act of piracy undertaken by pro-Russian Black Sea Fleet officers who unilaterally transferred the Cheleken fleet survey ship from Odesa to Sevastopol. Nearly 200 paratroopers of the first aeromobile division at Bolgrad stormed the base and arrested Russian officers while Ukrainian fighter planes threatened to attack the Cheleken vessel. The base was then nationalised by the Ukrainians and transferred to the Ukrainian navy. Black Sea Fleet ships sent to defend the base were turned back by strong statements made by Defence Minister Radetsky. The incident showed how quickly a small conflict could escalate in the Black Sea Fleet and Crimea. One high ranking Russian diplomat was quoted as saying, 'the incident in Odesa is the most large-scale and brazen anti-Russian action of all taken by the

cepted that locating both Russian and Ukrainian navies in Sevastopol after the division of the Black Sea Fleet would be to invite future conflict. Former President Kravchuk therefore agreed to relocate the Ukrainian navy to other Crimean ports, such as Balaklava and Donuzalev. The sticking points remained President Kravchuk's insistence that, 'the base for the Russian fleet will not be leased in perpetuity, but for a specified period'. Then Defence Minister Radetsky talked of only a five year lease while Volodymyr Bezkorovaynyy, Ukraine's naval commander, discussed 15-20 years 'until Russia sets up a base on its own territory on the Krasnodar coast'.[473]

Sevastopol would continue to be a base for the Ukrainian military and National Guard units to ensure Ukrainian sovereignty. Only some of the Sevastopol bays would be leased to Russia, but not the city itself.[474] Both former President Kravchuk and then Defence Minister Radetskyi bitterly complained that although the Ukrainian side took into account Russian interests the opposite was not the case with Moscow.[475] 'We take into consideration Russia's interests, but Russia does not admit ours and exercises unilateral pressure', Radetsky complained.[476] Former President Kravchuk acknowledged the strength of feeling when he said: 'It is a very sensitive subject for Russia. Especially the question of Sevastopol. It is painful for historical reasons for the Russian mentality, for the Russian government.'[477]

The Russian side also purposefully dragged out the negotiations over the Black Sea Fleet to await the outcome of the Ukrainian presidential elections in 1994 where the two leading candidates were Kravchuk and Kuchma.

---

Ukrainian side' (*The Washington Post*, 11 April 1994). See also *Narodna Armiya*, 12 and 15 April as well as the sharp statement by the Ukrainian Congress of National Democratic Forces, *Narodna Hazeta*, no.16 (April 1994).

473   UNIAN, 21 June 1994.

474   Radio Ukraine, 20 April 1994. The Ukrainian Civic Congress, Cossacks and Ukrainian naval personnel in Sevastopol demanded that the city remain a Ukrainian naval base (*Kyivskiye Vedomosti*, 21 April 1994).

475   See Kravchuk's speech to the Bolgrad first aeromobile division where he stated that, 'Ukraine cannot accept the formulation which Russia wants to force upon it, namely that Sevastopol is a base of the Russian navy' (ITAR-TASS, 16 June 1994). Kravchuk told servicemen that, 'The Ukrainian armed forces are prepared to defend their land, sovereignty and the inviolability of state borders' (Reuters, 17 June 1994).

476   *Holos Ukrayiny*, 3 June 1994.

477   *The Independent on Sunday*, 17 April 1994.

Moscow did not hide its preference for Kuchma in Ukraine to win the presidential elections because they believed he would support a close alliance with Russia that would, in their view, *de facto* resolve the Crimean and Black Sea Fleet questions.[478] The head of the Russian Duma's committee on the CIS, Konstantin Zatulin, openly supported Kuchma because with Kravchuk, 'in the past there has been outright anti-Russian hysteria, bordering on an outright clash'.[479] Ostankino television, which broadcast throughout the former USSR and had a greater number of viewers in Eastern-Southern Ukraine than Ukrainian television, also backed Kuchma.[480]

After the 1994 presidential elections the Black Sea Fleet negotiations continued but the Ukrainian position, although devoid of the ideological baggage of the Kravchuk era, nevertheless maintained the same position as that outlined by Radetsky in April 1994 in his meeting with Grachev. The negotiations were not helped by Russian heavy handedness and un-diplomatic behaviour. Defence Minister Grachev recommended that the new Ukrainian Minister of Defence undertake a reshuffle in his Ministry which would lead to a breakthrough in the Black Sea Fleet negotiations. The Ukrainian Ministry of Defence issued a sharply worded response that condemned Grachev's interference into the personnel matters of a neighbouring country.[481] In Ukrainian eyes this was another example how Russia was unable to treat Ukraine as an independent, 'foreign' country. In a similar vein, Admiral Baltin, commander of the Black Sea Fleet, continued to argue that the Fleet question could only be resolved, 'by means of unity and convergence between the two Slavonic nations in the economic, political and military spheres'.[482] In other words, joint bases in Sevastopol and a joint Fleet would be used as tools to reintegrate Ukraine and Russia.

The Black Sea Fleet negotiations therefore continued to remain tense.

---

478   See comments by deputy editor of *Moscow News*, Alexei Pushkov, a foreign policy specialist, in *The Christian Science Monitor*, 22 June 1994. Ukrainian accusations of Russian staling over negotiations on the Fleet and an inter-state treaty are made in *Vechirnij Kyiv*, 24 May 1994.

479   Interview on Russian television, 17 June 1994. See also interviews with President Kuchma in *Trud*, 21 June and *Komsomskaya Pravda*, 27 June 1994.

480   On the ratings of Ukrainian and Russian television in Ukraine see *Politychnyj Portret Ukrayiny*, no.3 (Kyiv: Academic Research Institute Democratic Initiative, 1993).

481   *Narodna Armiya*, 8 September 1994.

482   *Slava Sevastopolya*, 17 September 1994.

Ukraine's position remained essentially the same since April 1994 and the failure to reach an agreement floundered on the question of Crimean bases and the division of the Fleet's infrastructure. The division of Black Sea Fleet vessels 669:164 in Russia's favour had long ago been agreed by both sides, although the nature of the compensation to Ukraine for its share transferred to Russia was still unresolved.[483] Ukraine would only agree to leasing for a maximum of 25-year term, not 99 years as Russia insisted upon, and only for some bays in Sevastopol, but not the entire city. Ukraine would continue to also use Sevastopol, a demand strongly backed by the Ukrainian Defence Ministry, but its navy would be mainly based in Balaklava, Kerch, Feodosiya and Donuzlav.

Russia misjudged the 1994 Ukrainian election results working in their favour over the question of bases in the Crimea (see Table 7.1). 'The point is undoubtedly about Russia not encroaching on Ukraine's territorial integrity...' Ukrainian parliamentary chairman and Socialist Party leader Oleksandr Moroz,told Ukrainian naval personnel. In addition, in the words of Socialist Volodymyr Mukhin, chairman of the parliamentary committee on Defence and State Security,

> The stance of the Russian delegation at the talks has re-mained, as before, brutal and unchanged. The representa-tives of the Russian delegation did not display any compro-mises or concessions.

Deputy Defence Minister Bizhan noted that the Russian position had remained the same for two years; in other words, Russia had not altered its negotiating position in the light of Kuchma's electoral victory in 1994.[484] The Ukrainian leadership also continued to oppose dual citizenship for Russian naval officers living in Ukraine.

Ukrainian frustration at the unreasonable demands made by the Rus-sian side led to many hints that they would change tactics and demand that the Russian portion of the Black Sea Fleet vacate the Crimea and other

---

483   See the comments on the lack of any changes to Ukraine's position on the Black Sea Fleet question by Defence Minister Valeriy Shmarov (ITAR-TASS, 26 August) and the division of the Black Sea Fleet vessels (*Holos Ukrayiny*, 18 August 1994).

484   UNIAN, 13 September 1994.

Ukrainian ports. Russian naval units in Ukraine therefore would be little different to foreign forces based without the host's consent in Moldova and Georgia. If Ukraine were to adopt this position it would have appealed to the UN Security Council to treat Russian naval forces in Sevastopol and elsewhere in Ukraine on the same level as unwelcome Russian armed forces in other CIS states. The West would, Kyiv hoped, be then forced to act as an intermediary to negotiate the withdrawal of Russian naval forces within a deadline.[485] Such a theory rested on the premise that the West was willing to confront Russia. In the case of Moldova and Georgia the Russian bases continue to remain in place, despite Moscow's agreement to withdraw them by 2002 at the 1999 OSCE summit in Istanbul.

The agreement on the Black Sea Fleet was to be an appendix to the Russian-Ukrainian Treaty then also under negotiation. Then newly appointed Foreign Minister Hennadiy Udovenko called for the 'normalisation' of Ukrainian-Russian relations. But this could only be undertaken, he added, on the basis of partnership, 'rather than the relations of a senior with a junior' (a reoccurring Ukrainian demand for equal relations in the 1990s). It could also not be undertaken at the expense of Ukrainian statehood and sovereignty (a reference to the Crimea). Zatulin, head of the Russian Duma's committee on the CIS, called for a 'strategic partnership' and 'special relations' between Russia and Ukraine that would take into account a recognition of the two countries interdependence.[486] This was too far for Ukrainian officials to go.

The 'normalisation' of relations referred primarily, in Udovenko's view, to the removal of ideological tension and the resumption of bilateral economic ties. Normalisation of relations between Russia and Ukraine included instituting an active political dialogue and developing foreign policy cooperation in a more dynamic manner, especially within the CIS and OSCE and in peacekeeping operations.

The normalisation of Russian-Ukrainian relations primarily rested on finalising a treaty between both states that was in limbo from winter 1992.

---

485    Reuters, 27 May 1994. Of course, this is not necessarily incompatible with a lease where the fixed time period of the lease would be used to scale down Russian naval forces so that they could completely withdrew from Ukrainian territory when the lease expired. The author elaborated such a series of proposals as 'Eight Steps to Solving the Black Sea Fleet Question' in *Narodna Armiya*, 17 May 1994.
486    ITAR-TASS, 29 July 1994.

The negotiations were kept secret even though 80 per cent of the treaty was prepared by the end of 1994. The difficulties in the remaining 20 per cent of the treaty rested over sensitive issues, such as dual citizenship. According to Oleksandr Chalyy, head of the Contractual and Legal department of the Ministry of Foreign Affairs, agreement was reached on articles dealing with the legal status of national minorities. Russia no longer insisted on the inviolability of Ukraine's territorial integrity being no longer applicable if Ukraine withdrew from the CIS.[487]

President Kuchma was careful to rule out any confederation with Russia or other CIS states which would have been strongly opposed domestically by a wide array of political forces.[488] The Ukrainian leadership also had to take into account the protests and warnings that flowed from a large number of political parties, nationalist groups and the Writers Union about various articles of the Russian-Ukrainian treaty.[489]

At the CIS summit in Moscow on 9 September 1994 the cautious Kuchma line was again in evidence. Ukraine opposed any return to supranational structures, which it defined as the stepping stone to a revived USSR, Kyiv rejected CIS political-military integration, especially a military union, joint military forces or peacekeeping activities.[490]

---

487    *Uriadovyj Kurier*, nos.128-129 and 137 (8 August and 6 September 1994).

488    *Holos Ukrayiny*, 26 August 1994.

489    See the statements by the Democratic Coalition 'Ukraine' (*Visti z Ukrayiny*, 8-14 September), Peasant Democratic Party (*Vechirnij Kyiv*, 30 August) and the Congress of Ukrainian Nationalists (*Visti z Ukrayiny*, 1-7 September 1994).

490    *Holos Ukrayiny*, 13 September and Reuters, 9 September 1994.

Table 7.1 What should Ukraine do in answer to Russian demands that Sevastopol become an exclusively Russian base?

| Answer | Per Cent |
|---|---|
| Demand the Withdrawal of Russian forces from the Crimea and Sevastopol | 28 |
| Divide Sevastopol 50:50 | 27 |
| Difficult to Answer | 22 |
| Give the Ukrainian Navy the Bulk of Sevastopol | 12 |
| Give the Russian Navy the Bulk of Sevastopol | 6 |
| Agree that the Ukrainian Navy Vacates Sevastopol | 5 |

Source: *Den*, 17 January 1997.

### *1995-1997: Towards an Agreement*

In an address to the head's of district state administration's, President Kuchma said that there could not be any question of any Ukrainian-Russian 'strategic partnership' if both countries could not even live in peace in one city (Sevastopol). Ukraine would never give up Sevastopol, Kuchma cautioned, and would only agree to the basing of *both* navies in this city. Kuchma added that Ukraine would never agree to its navy leaving the city of Sevastopol and permit only the Black Sea Fleet to remain in the port.

The Fleet was seventy per cent in disrepair and its military worthiness would continue to decline over time. Ukrainian experts predicted that within a short period of time the Fleet would be only suitable for metal scrap yards. Over seventy per cent of Black Sea Fleet vessels were in disrepair because there was no procedure to pay for maintenance work and no contracts had been signed to undertake repairs. The Black Sea Fleet was 462.77 billion *karbovantsi* ($2.64 million) in debt for past repairs, according to Russian sources.

Russia and Ukraine finally took the initial steps to resolve the Black Sea Fleet question after the November 1995 Sochi summit. In 1993-1994, Ukraine took over the Mykolaiv, Saki, Ochakov and Danubian flotilla bases outside the Crimea. But the question of Sevastopol, which had sentimental value to Russia, was still to be resolved. Ukraine offerred two bays to Russia (Sevastopolskaya and Yuzhnaya) while insisting that three would be maintained by itself (Streletskaya, Karantinnaya and Kazachya).

Between December 1995-March 1996 Ukraine received 150 naval installations from the Black Sea Fleet and twenty ships from the Donuzlav base (including a division of missile patrol boats, large amphibious warfare ships, and three *Zubr* modern hover crafts). The deadlines were originally unrealistic as there were reportedly more stocks of ammunition in Donuzlav than with the former Russian 14th Army in Moldova. These naval bases and coastal installations included Donuzlav (the most modern base and Black Sea Fleet reserve headquarters) and arsenal, the Novoozernaya port, the Mirnyi airport and some aircraft, the Kerch naval and military base (including its arsenal), and the Yevpatoriya military base whose marine regiment was disbanded. Russia was tasked to re-locate any units not disbanded to Sevastopol, the Feodosiya testing ground, weapons range and ship repair plant, and the military airports of Gvardeiskaya and Kacha (near Simferopol).

After further negotiations the Black Sea Fleet question was only finally resolved in May 1997 during President Borys Yeltsin's visit to Kyiv. Russia obtained three bays leased over twenty years and Ukraine took two of the Sevastopol bays. A portion of Ukraine's share of the Black Sea Fleet was transferred to Russia in payment for accumulated energy debts.

The agreement on the Black Sea Fleet was only reached because an interstate treaty was signed at the same time. The Black Sea Fleet agreement and treaty meant Russia recognised Ukraine's sovereignty over Sevastopol and the Crimea. It took another two years for Russia to ratify the treaty in order that Ukraine would moderate its stance on adopting the Crimean constitution in October-December 1998. The Ukrainian parliament had ratified the treaty with Russia in January of that year.

## Conclusions

The security forces could have been dragged into an ethnic conflict in the Crimea during Meshkov's presidency in 1994-1995. Between 1991-1993, and since 1996, pro-Ukrainian loyalists running the Crimea from 'parties of power' and the Communist Party have never attempted to take control away from Kyiv over security forces stationed in the Crimea or to demand their removal. Meshkov attempted to take over the SBU, MVS and, half heartedly, the armed forces. He failed to place the SBU and armed forces under his control after they categorically refused to follow his orders. The main struggle between Meshkov and Kyiv was therefore over the MVS because Internal Troops always remained under Kyiv's control whilst the loyalty of *Berkut* riot police divided. Within the MVS, Meshkov's commander Kuznetsov only had limited support.

Meshkov never attempted to gain control over Border Troops in the Crimea. Such a step would have been seen as an attempt at Crimea's secession from Ukraine by attempting to gain control over the Crimea's borders. Meshkov also never made a play at controlling the National Guard as they were the staunchest pro-Ukrainian security force in the Crimea.

In May 1997 after seven years of tough negotiations and Russian threats, the Black Sea Fleet's presence in Sevastopol was legalised for 20 years. The agreement was synchronised with the signing of the inter-state treaty the same month. Similarly, in 1998 the adoption of the first non-separatist constitution and Russian parliamentary ratification of the 1997 treaty were also synchronised by both sides. By 1998 the question of who had jurisdiction over security forces in the Crimea had been resolved in Ukraine's favour. The following year the National Guard was disbanded in Ukraine and its units returned to the MVS. In the Crimea the National Guard had been the main security force ensuring that conflict in the region had not escalated into violence.

# Bibliography on Nation Building and Inter-Ethnic Relations in Ukraine and the Crimea

## National Integration

Arel, Dominique, 'Ukraine - The Temptation of the Nationalising State' in Vladimir Tismaneanu (ed.), *Political Culture and Civil Society in Russia and the New States of Eurasia* (Armonk, NY: M.E. Sharpe, 1995), pp.157-188.

Barrington, Lowell, 'The Domestic and International Consequences of Citizenship in the Soviet Successor States', *Europe-Asia Studies*, vol.47, no.5 (July 1995), pp.731-763.

Bilinsky, Yaroslaw, 'Are the Ukrainians a State Nation?', *Problems of Communism*, vol.61, nos.1-2 (January-April 1992), pp.134-135.

Birch, Julian, 'Ukraine - A Nation-State or a State of Nations?', *Journal of Ukrainian Studies*, vol.21, nos.1-2 (Summer-Winter 1996), pp. 109-124.

Casanova, Jose, 'Ethno-linguistic and religious pluralism and democratic construction in Ukraine' in Barnett R. Rubin and Jack Snyder (eds.), *Post-Soviet Political Order. Conflict and State Building* (London and New York: Routledge, 1998), pp.81-103.

Furtado Charles F. and Hechter Michael, 'The Emergence of Nationalist Politics in the USSR: A Comparison of Estonia and the Ukraine' in Alexander J. Motyl (ed.), *Thinking Theoretically About Soviet Nationalities. History and Comparison in the Study of the USSR* (New York: Columbia University Press, 1992), pp.169-204.

Kennedy, Michael, 'The Spatial Articulation of Identity and Social Problems: Estonia, Ukraine and Uzbekistan Through Focus Groups', in Kimitaka Matsuzato (ed.), *Regions: A Prism to View the Slavic-Eurasian World. Towards a Discipline of "Regionology"* (Sapporo: Slavic Research Center, Hokkaido University, 2000), pp. 208-44.

Kolsto, Pal, 'Ukraine: Building a Nation on Marginal Differences' in his *Political Construction Sites. Nation-Building and the Post-Soviet States* (Boulder, CO: Westview, 2000), pp.168-193.

Kuzio, Taras, 'Can Western Multiculturalism be Applied to the Post-Soviet States: A Critical Response to Kymlicka', *Journal of Contemporary European Politics*, vol.13, no.2 (August 2005), pp.217-232.

Kuzio, Taras, 'The Nation-Building Project in Ukraine and Identity: Toward a Consensus' in Taras Kuzio and Paul D'Anieri (eds.), *Dilemmas of State-Led Nation Building in Ukraine* (Westport, CT: Praeger, 2002), pp.9-28.

Kuzio, Taras, 'The Myth of the Civic State: A Critical Survey of Hans Kohn's Framework for Understanding Nationalism', *Ethnic and Racial Studies*, vol.25, no.1 (January 2002), pp.20-39.

Kuzio, Taras, 'Nationalising States or Nation Building: A Review of the Theoretical Literature and Empirical Evidence', *Nations and Nationalism*, vol.7, part 2 (April 2001), pp.135-154.

Kuzio, Taras and Nordberg, Marc, 'Nation and State Building, Historical Legacies and National Identities in Belarus and Ukraine: A Comparative Analysis', *Canadian Review of Studies in Nationalism*, vol.26, nos.1-2 (1999), pp.69-90.

Kuzio, Taras, 'Defining the Political Community in Ukraine: State, Nation, and the Transition to Modernity' in Taras Kuzio, Robert S. Kravchuk and Paul D'Anieri (eds.), *State and Institution Building in Ukraine* (New York: St. Martin's Press, 1999), pp. 213-244.

Kuzio, Taras, 'The Perils of Multiculturalism: A Theoretical and Area Studies Approach to the Former USSR', *Contemporary Political Studies*, vol.1, 1998, pp.108-123.

Kuzio, Taras, *Ukraine. State and Nation Building. Routledge Studies of Societies in Transition 9* (London and New York: Routledge, 1998).

Maryniak, Iryna, 'Belarus and Ukraine. Nation Building in Babel', *Index on Censorship*, vol.22, no.2 (March 1993), pp.20-33.

Olszanski, Tadeusz O., 'Ukrainian People or Ukrainian Nation?', *Canadian Review of Studies in Nationalism*, vol.27, nos.1-2 (2000), p.45-48.

Ponarin, Edward, 'The Prospects of Assimilation of the Russophone Populations in Estonia and Ukraine: A Reaction to David Laitin's Research', *Europe-Asia Studies*, vol.52, no.8 (December 2000), pp.1535-1541.

Riabchouk, Mykola, 'Civil Society and National Emancipation: The Ukrainian Case' in Zbigniew Rau (ed.), *The Reemergence of Civil Society in Eastern Europe and the Soviet Union* (Boulder, CO: Westview, 1991), pp.95-112.

Riabchouk, M., 'Civil Society and Nation Building in Ukraine' in Taras Kuzio (ed.), *Contemporary Ukraine. Dynamics of Post-Soviet Transformation* (Armonk, NY: M.E. Sharpe,, 1998), pp.81-98.

Ryabchuk, Mykola, 'Ukrainian Case to Ukrainian Cause', *The Harriman Review*, vol.12, no.2 (Fall 1999), pp.19-25.

Shevchuk, I. Yuri, 'Citzenship in Ukraine: A Western Perspective' in S.J. Micgiel (ed.), *State and Nation Building in East Central Europe. Contemporary Perspectives* (New York: Institute on East Central Europe, Columbia University, 1996), pp. 351-369.

Shved, V'iacheslav, 'The Conceptual Approaches of Ukrainian Political Parties to Ethno-Political Problems in Independent Ukraine', *Journal of Ukrainian Studies*, vol.19, no.2 (Winter 1994), pp.69-84.

Shular, Leonid, 'Ethnonational Aspects of National state Development in Ukraine', *International Journal of Sociology*, vol.29, no.3 (Fall 1999), pp.49-65.

Shulman, Stephen, 'Sources of Civic and Ethnic Nationalism in Ukraine', *Journal of Communist Studies and Transition Politics*, vol.18, no.4 (December 2002), pp.1-30.

Slezkine, Yuri, 'Can We Have Our Nation State and Eat It Too?', *Slavic Review*, vol.54, no.3 (Fall 1995), pp. 717-719.

Sochor, Z., '"No Middle Ground." On the Difficulties of Crafting a Political Consensus in Ukraine', *The Harriman Review*, vol.9, nos.1-2 (Spring 1996), pp.57-61.

Solchanyk, R., 'Ukraine, Belorussia, and Moldova: Imperial Integration, Russification and the Struggle for National Survival' in Lubomyr Hajda and

Mark Beissinger (eds.), *The Nationalities Factor in Soviet Politics and Society*. The John M. Olin Critical Series (Boulder, CO: Westview, 1990), pp. 175-203.

Stepanenko, Viktor, 'A State to Build, A Nation to Form. Ethno-Policy in the Ukraine', in Anna-Maria Biro and Petra Kovacs (eds.), *Diversity in Action. Local Public Management of Multi-Ethnic Communities In Central and Eastern Europe* (Budapest: LGI Managing Multiethnic Communities Project, 2001).

Subtelny, O., 'Imperial Disintegration and Nation-State Formation: The Case of Ukraine' in J.W. Blaney (ed.), *The Successor States to the USSR* (Washington, DC: Congressional Quarterly, 1995), pp.184-195.

Szporluk, R., 'Nation-Building in Ukraine: Problems and Prospects' in J.W. Blaney (ed.), *The Successor States to the USSR* (Washington, DC: Congressional Quarterly, 1995), pp.173-183.

Szporluk, R., 'Ukraine: From an Imperial Periphery to a Sovereign State', *Daedalus*, vol.126, no.3 (Summer 1997), pp.85-120.

Uehling, Greta, 'The first independent Ukrainian census in Crimea: Myths, miscoding and missed opportunities', *Ethnic and Racial Studies*, vol.27, no.1 (January 2004), pp.149-170.

Vishnevsky, Yuri & Rosenblum, Dan, 'Ukraine: The Birth of a Nation', *Forum*, vol.9, no.2 (Winter-Spring 1995), pp.25-29.

Yakovenko, Nataliya, 'Early Modern Ukraine Between East and West: Projectories of an Idea', in Kimitaka Matsuzato (ed.), *Regions: A Prism to View the Slavic-Eurasian World. Towards a Discipline of "Regionology" (*Sapporo: Slavic Research Center, Hokkaido University, 2000), pp. 50-69.

Zimmerman, William, 'Is Ukraine a Political Community?', *Communist and Post-Communist Studies*, vol.31, no.1 (1998), pp.43-55.

**National Identity**

Basiuk, Victor, 'Ukraine: Toward a Viable National Ethos' in Sharon L. Wolchik and Volodymyr Zviglyanich (eds.), *Ukraine. The Search for a National Identity* (Lanham, MD: Rowman & Littlefield, 2000), pp.31-48.

Barrington, Lowell, 'Views of the Ethnic "Other" in Ukraine', *Nationalism and Ethnic Politics*, vol.8, no.2 (Summer 2002), pp. 83-96.

Dawson, Jane I., *Eco-Nationalism. Anti-Nuclear Activism and National Identity in Russia, Lithuania and Ukraine* (Durham, NC: Duke University Press, 1996).

Guboglo, M.N., 'The Disintegration and Synthesis of Identity in Post-Soviet Space and Time (The Case of Ukraine)', *The Harriman Review*, vol.9, nos.1-2 (Spring 1996), pp.92-102.

Hrytsak, Yaroslav, 'National Identities in Post-Soviet Ukraine: The Case of Lviv and Donesk' in Zvi Gitelman *et al.* (eds.), *Cultures and Nations of Central and Eastern Europe. Essays in Honor of Roman Szporluk* (Cambridge, MA: Harvard University Press, 2000), pp.263-282.

Kulyk, Volodymyr, 'The Search for Post-Soviet Identities in Ukraine and Russia and Its Impact on Relations between the Two States', *The Harriman Review*, vol.9, nos.1-2 (Spring 1996), pp.16-27.

Kuzio, Taras, 'National Identity in Independent Ukraine: An Identity in Transition', *Nationalism and Ethnic politics*, vol.2, no.4 (Winter 1996), pp.582-608.

Pirie, Paul S., 'National Identity and Politics in Southern and Eastern Ukraine', *Europe-Asia Studies*, vol.48, no.7 (November 1996), pp.1076-1104.

Shulman, Stephen, 'The Cultural Foundations of Ukrainian National Identity', *Ethnic and Racial Studies*, vol.22, no.6 (November 1999), pp.1011-1036.

Shulan, Stephn, 'Sources of Civic and Ethnic Nationalism in Ukraine', *Journal of Communist Studies and Transition Politics*, vol.18, no.4 (December 2002), pp.1-30.

Shulman, Stephen, 'The Contours of Civic and Ethnic National Identification in Ukraine', *Europe-Asia Studies*, vol.56, no.1 (January 2004), pp.35-56.

Stepanenko, Victor and Sorokopud, Sergei, 'The Construction of National Identity: A Case Study of the Ukraine' in Christopher Williams and Thanasis D.Sfikas (eds.), *Ethnicity and Nationalism in Russia, the CIS and the Baltic States* (Aldershot: Ashgate, 1999), pp.184-210.

Subtelny, Orest, 'The Ambiguities of National Identity: The Case of Ukraine' in Sharon L. Wolchik and Volodymyr Zviglyanich (eds.), *Ukraine. The Search for a National Identity* (Lanham, MD: Rowman & Littlefield, 2000), pp.1-10.

Takach, Arthur, 'In Search of Ukrainian National Identity: 1840-1921', *Ethnic and Racial Studies*, vol.19, no.3 (July 1996), pp.640-659.

Wilson, Andrew, 'Redefining ethnic and linguistic boundaries in Ukraine: indigenes, settlers and Russophone Ukrainians' in Graham Smith *et al.*, *Nation-building in the Post-Soviet Borderlands. The Politics of National Identities* (Cambridge: Cambridge University Press, 1998), pp.119-138.

Wolczuk, Kataryna, 'History, Europe and the 'National Idea': the Official Narrative of National Identity in Ukraine', *Nationalities Papers*, vol 28, no 4 (December 2000), pp 671-94.

**National Identity and Foreign Policy**

Bilinsky, Yaroslav, 'Basic Factors in the Foreign Policy of Ukraine: The Impact of the Soviet Experience' in F.S. Starr (ed.), *The Legacy of History in Russia and the New States of Eurasia*, (Armonk, NY: M.E. Sharpe, 1994), pp.171-192.

Bojcun, Marko, 'Where is Ukraine? Civilization and Ukraine's Identity' *Problems of Post-Communism*, Vol. 48, No. 5 (September-October 2001), pp. 42-51.

Burant, Stephen R., 'Foreign Policy and National Identity: A Comparison of Ukraine and Belarus', *Europe-Asia Studies*, vol.47, no.7 (November 1995), pp.1125-1144./

D'Anieri, Paul, 'Nationalism and International Politics: Identity and Sovereignty in the Russian-Ukrainian Conflict', *Nationalism and Ethnic Politics*, vol.3, no.2 (Summer 1997), pp.1-28.

Furtado, C. F., 'Nationalism and Foreign Policy in Ukraine', *Political Science Quarterly*, vol.109, no.1 (Spring 1994), pp.81-104.

Karaganov, Sergei, 'Russia and the Slav Vicinity' in Vladimir Baranovsky (ed.), *Russia and Europe. The Emerging Security Agenda* (Oxford: Oxford University Press, 1997), pp.289-300.

Kremen, Vasily, 'The East Slav Triangle' in Vladimir Baranovsky (ed.), *Russia and Europe. The Emerging Security Agenda* (Oxford: Oxford University Press, 1997), pp.271-288.

Kuzio, Taras, 'National Identity and Foreign Policy: The East Slavic Conundrum' in Taras Kuzio (ed.), *Contemporary Ukraine. Dynamics of Post-Soviet Transformation*, (Armonk, NY: M.E. Sharpe, 1998), pp.221-244.

Kuzio, Taras, 'Identity and Nation Building in Ukraine. Defining the 'Other'', *Ethnicities*, vol.1, no.3 (December 2001), pp.343-366.

Kuzio, Taras, 'European, Eastern Slavic, and Eurasian: National Identity, Transformation, and Ukrainian Foreign Policy' in Jennifer D.P. Moroney, Taras Kuzio and Mikhail Molchanov (eds.), *Ukrainian Foreign and Se-*

*curity Policy. Theoretical and Comparative Perspectives* (Westport, CT: Praeger, 2002), pp.197-226.

Kuzio, Taras, 'National Identities and Virtual Foreign policies Among the Eastern Slavs', *Nationalities Papers*, vol.31, no.4 (December 2003), pp.431-452.

Laba, Roman, 'The Russian-Ukrainian Conflict: State Nation and Identity', *European Security*, vol.4, no.3 (Autumn 1995), pp.457-487.

Lapychak, C., 'The Quest for a Common Destiny', *Transition*, vol.2, no.18 (6 September 1996).

Molchanov, Mikhail A., 'Borders of Identity: Ukraine's Political and Cultural Significance for Russia', *Canadian Slavonic Papers*, vol.38, nos.1-2 (March-June 1996), pp. 177-193.

Molchanov, M., 'National Identity and Foreign Policy Orientation in Ukraine', in Jennifer D.P. Moroney, Taras Kuzio and Mikhail Molchanov (eds.), *Ukrainian Foreign and Security Policy. Theoretical and Comparative Perspectives* (Westport, CT: Praeger, 2002), pp.227-262.

Nordberg, M., 'Interdependence and National Identity in Ukraine and Belarus', *South Eastern Political Review*, vol.25, no.4 (December 1997), pp.611-640.

Petrochenkov, Valery, 'Common Cultural Heritage: A Basis for Establishing New Relations between Ukraine and Russia', *The Harriman Review*, vol.9, nos.1-2 (Spring 1996), pp.28-31.

Prizel, Ilya, 'The Influence of Ethnicity on Foreign Policy: The Case of Ukraine' in Roman Szporluk (ed.), *National Identity and Ethnicity in Russia and the New States of Eurasia* (Armonk, NY: M.E. Sharpe, 1994), pp.103-128.

Prizel, I., 'Ukraine's Foreign Policy as an Instrument of Nation Building' in John W. Blaney (ed.), *The Successor States to the USSR* (Washington, DC: Congressional Quarterly, 1995), pp.196-207.

Prizel, I., 'Ukraine's Lagging Efforts in Building National Institutions and the Potential Impact on National Security', *The Harriman Review*, vol.10, no.1 (Winter 1997), pp.24-34.

Prizel, I., *National Identity and Foreign Policy. Nationalism and Leadership in Poland, Russia, and Ukraine* (Cambridge: Cambridge University Press, 1998), pp.300-371.

Prizel, I., 'Nation-Building and Foreign Policy' in Sharon L. Wolchik and Volodymyr Zviglyanich (eds.), *Ukraine. The Search for a National Identity* (Lanham, MD: Rowman & Littlefield, 2000), pp.11-30.

Shulman, Stephen, 'Cultures in Competition: Ukrainian Foreign Policy and the "Cultural Threat" from Abroad', *Europe-Asia Studies*, vol.50, no.2 (March 1998), pp. 287-303.

Shulman, Stephen, 'Competing versus Complimentary Identities. Ukrainian-Russian Relations and the Loyalty of Russians in Ukraine', *Nationalities Papers*, vol.26, no.4 (December 1998), pp.599-614.

Shulman, Stephen, 'The Internal-External Nexus in the Formation of Ukrainian National Identity: The Case for Slavic Integration' in Taras Kuzio and Paul D'Anieri (eds.), *Dilemmas of State-Led Nation Building in Ukraine* (Westport, CT: Praeger, 2002), pp.103-130.

Taras, Ray, Filipova, Olga, Pobeda, Nelly, 'Ukraine's Transnationals, Far-Away Locals and Xenophobes: The Prospect for Europeanness', *Europe-Asia Studies*, vol.56, no.6 (July 2004), pp.835-856.

White, Stephen, McAllister, Ian M., Light, Margo, Lowenhardt, John, 'A European or a Slavic Choice? Foreign Policy and Public Attitudes in Post-Soviet Europe', *Europe-Asia Studies*, vol.54, no.2 (March 2002), pp.181-202.

Zimmerman, W., 'The Diminishing Burden of the Soviet Past: Russian Assessments of Russian-Ukrainian Linkages' in Z.Gitelman *et al.* (eds.)., *Cultures and Nations of Central and Eastern Europe. Essays in Honor of Roman Szporluk* (Cambridge, MA: Harvard University Press, 2000), pp.633-646.

**Regionalism and Separatism**

Aberg, Martin, 'Putnam's Social Capital Theory Goes East: A Case Study of Western Ukraine and L'viv', *Europe-Asia Studies*, vol.52, no.2 (March 2000), pp.295-317.

Barrington, L., 'Region, Language and Nationality: Rethinking Support in Ukraine for Maintaining Dtstance from Russia' in Taras Kuzio and Paul D'Anieri (eds.), *Dilemmas of State-Led Nation Building in Ukraine* (Westport, CT: Praeger, 2002), pp.131-146.

Barrington, Lowell, 'Examining rival theories of demographic influence on political support: the power of regional, ethnic and linguistic divisions in Ukraine', *European Journal of Political Research*, vol.41, no.4 (June 2002), pp.455-491.

Barrington, Lowell and Herron, Eric, 'One Ukraine or Many?: Regionalism in Ukraine and Its Political Consequences', *Nationalities Papers*, vol.32, no.1 (March 2004), pp.53-86.

Barrington, Lowell, 'Region, Language and Nationality: Rethinking Support in Ukraine for Maintaining Distance from Russia' in Taras Kuzio and Paul D'Anieri (eds.), *Dilemmas of State-Led Nation Building in Ukraine* (Westport, CT: Praeger, 2002), pp. 131-146.

Belitser, Natalia and Bodruk, Oleg, 'Conflicting Loyaltes in the Crimea' in Michael Waller, Bruno Coppieters and Alexei Malashenko (eds.)., *Conflicting Loyalties and the State in Post-Soviet Russia and Eurasia* (London: Frank Cass, 1998), pp.53-79.

Birch, S., and Zinko, Ihor, 'The Dilemma of Regionalism', *Transition*, vol.2, no.22 (1 November 1996).

Birch, S., 'Interpreting the Regional Effect in Ukrainian Politics', *Europe-Asia Studies*, vol.52, no.6 (September 2000), pp.1017-1042.

Bremmer, I., 'Ethnic Issues in Crimea', *RFE/RL Research Report*, vol.2, no.18 (30 April 1993),

Bukkvoll, Tor, 'A Fall From Grace for Crimean Separatists', *Transition*, vol.1, no.21 (17 November 1995).

Chiper Ioan, 'Bessarabia and Northern Bukovina' in Tuomas Forsberg (ed.), *Contested Territory. Border Disputes at the Edge of the Former Soviet Empire* (Aldershot: Edward Elgar, 1995), pp. 107-127.

Dawson, Jane I., 'Ethnicity, Ideology and Geopolitics in Crimea', *Communist and Post-Communist Studies*, vol.30, no.4 (1998), pp.427-444.

*Development's in Crimea: Challenges for Ukraine and Implications for Regional Security. Proceedngs from an International Conference, October 23-25 1994, Kyiv, Ukraine* (Washington, DC: The American Association for the Advancement of Science, the Ukrainian Center for Independent Political Research, Kyiv and The Harriman Institute, Columbia University, 1994).

Drohobycky, Maria (ed.), *Crimea. Dynamics, Challenges, and Prospects* (Lanham, MD: Rowman & Littlefield Publishers and the American Association for the Advancement of Science, 1995).

Friedgut, Ted, 'Pluralism and Politics in an Urban Soviet: Donets'k' in Carol Saivetz and Anthony Jones (eds.), *In Search of Pluralism: Society and Post-Soviet Politics* (Boulder, CO: Westview, 1994), pp.45-61,

Friedgut, T., 'Perestroika in the Provinces: The Politics of Transition in Donets'k' in T.H. Friedgut and Jeffrey W. Hahn (eds.), *Local Power and Post-Soviet Policies* (Armonk, NY: M.E. Sharpe, 1994), pp.162-184.

Hesli, V., 'Public Support for the Devolution of Power in Ukraine: Regional Patterns', *Europe-Asia Studies*, vol.47, no.1 (January-February 1995), pp.91-121.

Holdar, Sven, 'Torn Between East and West: The Regional Factor in Ukrainian Politics', *Post-Soviet Geography*, vol.36, no.2 (February 1996), pp.112-132.

Hughes, James, and Sasse, Gwendolyn, 'Comparing Regional and Ethnic Conflicts in Post-Soviet Transition States' in James Hughes and Gwendolyn Sasse (eds.), *Ethnicity and Territory in the Former Soviet Union: Regions in Conflict* (London: Frank Cass, 2002), pp.1-35.

Hughes, James, and Sasse, Gwendolyn, 'Conflict and Accommodation in the FSU: The Role of Institutions and Regimes' in J. Hughes and G. Sasse (eds.), *Ethnicity and Territory in the Former Soviet Union: Regions in Conflict* (London: Frank Cass, 2002), pp.220-240.

Jackson, Louise, 'Identity, Language and Transformation in Eastern Ukraine: A Case Study of Zaporizhzhia' in Taras Kuzio (ed.), *Contemporary Ukraine. Dynamics of Post-Soviet Transformation* (Armonk, NY: M.E. Sharpe, 1998), pp.99-114.

Jung, Monika, 'The Donbas Factor in the Ukrainian Elections', *RFE/RL Research Report*, vol.3, no.12 (25 March 1994).

Katchanovski, Ivan, *Cleft Countries. Regional Political Divisions and Cultures in Post-Soviet Ukraine and Moldova*. Soviet and Post-Soviet Politics and Society (Stuttgart: ibidem-Verlag, 2006).

Korostelina, Carina, 'The Socio-Psychological Roots of the Ethnic Problems in Crimea', *Demokratizatsiya*, vol.8, no.2 (Spring 2000), pp.219-231.

Kubicek, P., 'Regional Polarisation in Ukraine: Public Opinion, Voting and Legislative Behaviour', *Europe-Asia Studies*, vol.52, no.2 (March 2000), pp.273-294.

Kushnirsky, F.I., 'Free Economic Zones in Ukraine: The Case of Odesa', *Ukrainian Economic Review*, vol.11, no.3 (1996), pp.117-124.

Kuzio, T. and Meyer, David, J., 'The Donbas and Crimea: An Institutional and Demographic Approach to Ethnic Mobilisation in Two Ukrainian Regions' in Taras Kuzio, Robert S. Kravchuk and Paul D'Anieri (eds.), *State and Institution Building in Ukraine* (New York: St. Martin's Press, 1999), pp.297-324.

Markus, U., 'Crimea Restores 1992 Constitution', *RFE/RL Research Report*, vol.3, no.23 (10 June 1994).

Marples, D.R., and Duke, David F., 'Ukraine, Russia and the Question of Crimea', *Nationalities Papers*, vol.23, no.2 (June 1995), pp.261-289.

Martyniuk, J., 'Roundup: Attitudes toward Ukraine's Borders', *RFE/RL Research Report*, vol.1, no.35 (4 September 1992).

Materski, Wojciech, 'Eastern Poland' in T. Forsberg (ed.), *Contested Territory. Border Disputes at the Edge of the Former Soviet Empire* (Aldershot: Edward Elgar, 1995), pp.143-155.

Meyer, D. J., 'Why Have Donbas Russians Not Ethnically Mobilized Like Crimean Russians Have? An Institutional/Demographic Approach' in John S. Micgiel (ed.), *State and Nation Building in East Central Europe. Contemporary Perspectives* (New York: Institute on East Central Europe, Columbia University, 1996), pp. 317-330.

Mihalisko, Kathleen, 'The Other Side of Separatism: Crimea Votes for Autonomy', RL 60/91, *Report on the USSR*, vol.3, no.3 (1 February 1991).

Nemiria, Grigory, 'Regionalism: An Underestimated Dimension of State-Building' in Sharon L. Wolchik and Volodymyr Zviglyanich (eds.), *Ukraine. The Search for a National Identity* (Lanham, MD: Rowman & Littlefield, 2000), pp.183-198.

O'Loughlin, John, O., 'The Regional Factor in Contemporary Ukrainian Politics: Scale, Place, Space, or Bogus Effect?', *Post-Soviet Geography and Economics*, vol.42, no.1 (2001), pp.1-33.

Oltay, Edith, 'Minorities as Stumbling Block in Relations with Neighbours', *RFE/RL Research Report*, vol.1, no.19 (8 May 1992).

Ozhiganov, Edward, 'The Crimean Republic: Rivalries for Control' in Arbatov, Alexei *et al.* (ed.), *Managing Conflict in the Former Soviet Union: Russian and American Perspectives* (Cambridge, MA: The MIT Press, 1997), pp.83-135.

Packer, John, 'Autonomy within the OSCE: The Case of Crimea' in Markku Suksi (ed.), *Autonomy: Applications and Implications* (The Hague: Kluwer Law International, 1998), pp.295-316.

Petersenm Philip, 'Crimea - Triumph of Moderation or Eye of the Storm?' *Jane's Intelligence Review*, vol.7, no.4 (April 1995).

Ryabchuk, M., 'Two Ukraines?' *East European Reporter*, vol.5, no.4 (July-August 1992).

Rubchak, Marian, 'Ethnonationalist Construction of Identity: The Lviv Paradigm', *National Identities*, vol.2, no.1 (March 2000), pp.21-34.

Sasse, G., 'The Crimean Issue', *Journal of Communist Studies and Transition Politics*, vol.12, no.1 (March 1996), pp.83-100.

Sasse, Gwendolyn, 'The 'New' Ukraine: A State of Regions' in James Hughes and Gwendolyn Sasse (eds.)., *Ethnicity and Territory in the Former Soviet Union: Regions in Conflict* (London: Frank Cass, 2002), pp.69-100.

Stewart, Susan 'Autonomy as a Mechanism for Conflict Regulation: The Case of Crimea', *Nationalism and Ethnic Politics*, vol.7, no.4 (Winter 2001), pp.113-141.

Socor, Vladimir, 'Five Countries Look at Ethnic Problems in Southern Moldova', *RFE/RL Resarch Report*, vol.3, no.32 (19 August 1994).

Solchanyk, Roman, 'Ukrainian-Russian Confrontation Over the Crimea',*RFE/RL Research Report*, vol.1, no.7 (21 February 1992).

Solchanyk, R., 'The Crimean Imbroglio: Kiev and Simferopol', *RFE/RL Research Report*, vol.1, no.33 (21 August 1992).

Solchanyk, R., 'Centrifugal Movements in Ukraine on the Eve of the Independence Referendum', RL 408/91, *Report on the USSR*, vol.3, no.48 (29 November 1991).

Solchanyk, R., 'The politics of state building: centre-periphery relations in post-Soviet Ukraine', *Europe-Asia Studies*, vol.46, no.1 (January-February 1994), pp.47-68.

Subtelny, O., 'Russocentrism, Regionalism, and the Political Culture of Ukraine' in V.Tismaneanu (ed.), *Political Culture and Civil Society in Russia and the New States of Eurasia. The International Politics of Eurasia*. Vol.7 (Armonk, NY: M.E. Sharpe, 1995), pp.189-207.

Svetova, Svetlana, 'Chronology of Events in Crimea', *RFE/RL Research Report*, vol.3, no.19 (13 May 1994).

Szporluk, R., 'The Strange Politics of L'viv: An Essay in Search of An Explanation', in Zvi Gitelman (ed.), *The Politics of Nationality and the Erosion of the USSR* (London: Macmillan, 1992), pp.215-31.

Tulko, Alex, 'Conflicting Reports Fuel Crimean Tension', *Transition*, vol.1, no.6 (28 April 1995).

Umbach, Frank, 'The Crimean Question', *Jane's Intelligence Review*, vol.6, no.5 (May 1994).

Walkowitz, Daniel (eds.), *Workers of the Donbass Speak: Survival and Identity in the New Ukraine* (New York: State University of New York Press, 1995).

Wilson, Andrew, 'The Growing Challenge to Kiev from the Donbas', *RFE/RL Resarch Report*, vol.2, no.33 (20 August 1993).

Wilson, Andrew, 'Crimea's Political Cauldron', *RFE/RL Research Report*, vol.2, no.45 (12 November 1993).

Wilson, Andrew and Khmelko, Valerii, 'Regionalism and Ethnic and Linguistic Cleavages in Ukraine' in Taras Kuzio (ed.), *Contemporary Ukraine. Dynamics of Post-Soviet Transformation* (Armonk, NY: M.E. Sharpe, 1998), pp.60-80.

Zon, Hans van, Batako, Andre, Kreslavska, Anna, *Social and Economic Change in Eastern Ukraine: The Example of Zaporizhzhya* (Brookfield, VT: Ashgate, 1998).

**Inter-Ethnic Relations and Nationality Policies**

Bugajski, Janusz, 'Ethnic Relations and Regional Problems in Independent Ukraine' in Sharon L. Wolchik and Volodymyr Zviglyanich (eds.), *Ukraine. The Search for a National Identity* (Lanham, MD: Rowman & Littlefield, 2000), pp.165-182.

Deychakiwsky, Orest, 'National Minorities in Ukraine', *The Ukrainian Quarterly*, vol.50, no.4 (Winter 1994), pp.371-389.

Jaworsky, John, 'Nationalities Policy and Potential for Inter-Ethnic Conflict in Ukraine' in Magda Opalski (ed.), *Managing Diversity in Plural Societies. Minorities, Migration and Nation-Building in Post-Communist Europe* (Nepean, Ontario: Forum Eastern Europe, 1998), pp.104-127.

Lakiza-Sachuk, Natalia, 'Ethnic Conflicts in Ukraine' in Michael Waller, Bruno Coppieters and Alexei Malashenko (eds.)., *Conflicting Loyalties and the State in Post-Soviet Russia and Eurasia* (London: Frank Cass, 1998), pp.33-52.

Little, David, *Ukraine: The Legacy of Intolerance* (Washington, DC: US Institute for Peace, 1991).

Naboka, Serhiy, 'Nationalities Issues in Ukraine', *Uncaptive Minds*, vol.5, no.1 (Spring 1992), pp.75-80.

Paniotto, Vladimir, 'The Levels of Anti-Semitism in Ukraine', *International Journal of Sociology*, vol.29, no.3 (Fall 1999), pp.66-75.

Resler, Tamara J., 'Dilemmas of Democratisation: Safeguarding Minorities in Russia, Ukraine and Lithuania', *Europe-Asia Studies*, vol.49, no.1 (January 1997), pp. 89-106,

Siegelbaum, Lewis H., and Walkowitz, Danieil J., *Workers of the Donbass Speak: Survival and Identity in the New Ukraine, 1989-1992* (Albany, NY: SUNY Press, 1992),

Shevtsova, Lilia, 'Ukraine in the Context of New European Migrations', *International Migration Review*, vol.26, no.2 (Summer 1992), pp.258-268.

Sochor, Zenia A.,'Ethnic Politics in Ukraine' in Andreas Klinke, Ortwin Renn, and Jean-Paul Lehners (eds.)., *Ethnic Conflict and Civil Society: Proposals for a New Era in Eastern Europe* (Aldershot: Ashgate, 1997), pp. 127-150.

Stewart, Susan, 'Ukraine's Policy toward Its Ethnic Minorities', *RFE/RL Research Report*, vol.2, no.36 (10 September 1993).

Stroschein, Sherrill, 'Measuring Ethnic Party Success in Romania, Slovakia, and Ukraine. Ethnic conflict need not mean war; it can take place peacefully in the political arena', *Problems of Post-Communism* vol. 48, no. 4 (July-August 2001), pp. 59-69.

*Ukraine: The Situation of Ethnic Minorities* (Ottawa: Research Directorate, Immigration and Refugee Board, September 1993).

Weller, Craig, 'Mass Attitudes and Ethnic Conflict in Ukraine' in Taras Kuzio and Paul D'Anieri (eds.), *Nation Building, Regionalism and Identity in Ukraine* (Westport, CT: Praeger, 2002), pp.71-102.

Yevtukh, Volodymyr, 'Ukraine's Ethnic Minorities: Between Politics and Reality', Deychakiwsky, Orest, 'National Minorities in Ukraine', *The Harriman Review*, vol.9, nos.1-2 (Spring 1996), pp.62-64.

**National Minorities**

*Russians*

Arel, D. and Khmelko, V., 'The Russian Factor and Territorial Polarization in Ukraine', *The Harriman Review*, vol.9, nos.1-2 (Spring 1996), pp. 81-91.

Barrington, Lowell. 'Russian-speakers in Ukraine and Kazakhstan: 'Nationality,' 'Population,' or Neither?' *Post-Soviet Affairs*, vol. 17, no. 2 (April-June 2001), pp. 129-158.

Bremmer, I., 'The politics of ethnicity: Russians in the new Ukraine', *Europe-Asia Studies*, vol.46, no.2 (March-April 1994), pp.261-283.

Bremmer, I., 'How Russian the Russians? New Minorities in the Post-Soviet Regions', *The Harriman Review*, vol.9, nos.1-2 (Spring 1996), pp.65-69.

Cipko, 'The Second Revival: Russia's Ukrainian Minority as an Emerging Factor in Eurasian Politics', *The Harriman Review*, vol.9, nos.1-2 (Spring 1996), pp.70-80.

Golovakha, Evgenii, Panina, Natalia and Nikolai, Churilov, 'Russians in Ukraine' in Vladimir Shlapentokh *et al.* (eds.), *The New Russian Diaspora. Russian Minorities in the Former Soviet Repubics* (Armonk, NY: M.E. Sharpe, 1994), pp.59-71.

Klatt, Martin, 'Russians in the 'Near Abroad'', *RFE/RL Research Report*, vol.3, no.32 (19 August 1994).

Kolsto, P., 'The Eye of the Whirlwind: Belarus and Ukraine' in his *Russians in the Former Soviet Republics* (London: Hurst & Co, 1995), pp.166-199.

Kolsto, P., 'Ethnicity and Subregional Relations. The Role of the Russian Diasporas' in Dwan Renata *et al.* (eds.), *Building Security in the New States of Eurasia. Subregional Cooperation in the Former Soviet Space* (Armonk, NY: M.E. Sharpe, 2000), pp.201-226.

Kuzio, Taras, 'Russians and Russophones in the Former USSR and Serbs in Yugoslavia: A Comparative Study of Passivity and Mobilisation', *East European Perspectives*, vol.5. nos.13, 14, 15 (25 June, 9 and 23 July 2003).

Laitin, David D., *Identity in Formation. The Russian-Speaking Populations in the Near Abroad* (Ithaca and London: Cornell University Press, 1998).

Melvin, Neil, 'Russians, regionalism and ethnicity in Ukraine' in his *Russians Beyond Russia. The Politics of National Idendity. Chatham House Paper's* (London: Royal Institute International Affairs, 1995), p.78-99.

Poppe, Edwin and Hagendoorn, Louk, 'Types of Identification Among Russians in the "Near Abroad"', *Europe-Asia Studies*, vol.53, no.1 (January 2001), pp.57-71.

Recktenwald, Marion, 'The "Russian Minority" in Ukraine' in Ted Gurr (ed.), *Peoples Versus States: Minorities at Risk in the New Century* (Wahington, DC: U.S. Institute of Peace, 2000), pp.57-64.

Smith, G. and Wilson, A., 'Rethinking Russia's Post-Soviet Diaspora: The Potential for Political Mobilisation in Eastern Ukraine and North-east Estonia', *Europe-Asia Studies*, vol.49, no.5 (July 1997), pp.845-864.

Solchanyk, R., 'Russians in Ukraine: Problems and Prospects' in Zvi Gitelman *et al.* (eds.), *Cultures and Nations of Central and Eastern Europe. Essays in Honor of Roman Szporluk* (Cambridge, MA: Harvard University Press, 2000), pp.539-554.

Teague, Elizabeth, 'Russians Outside Russia and Russian Security Policy' in Leon Aron *et al.* (ed), *The Emergence of Russian Foreign Policy* (Washington, DC: US Institute of Peace Press, 1994), pp.81-105.


*Tatars*

Allworth, E. (ed.), *Tatars of the Crimea: Their Struggle for Survival* (Durham, NC: Duke University Press, 1988).

Allworth, E. ed*., The Tatars of the Crimea: Return to the Homeland: Studies and Documents* (Durham, NC: Duke University Press, 1998).

Budzhurova, Lilya R., 'The Current Sociopolitical Situation of the Crimean Tatars,' *The Harriman Review*, vol. 11, nos. 1-2, (1998), pp. 21-27.

Lazzerini, Edward J, 'Crimean Tatars: The Fate of a Severed Tongue' in Isabelle Kreindler (ed.), *Sociolinguistic Perspectives on Soviet National*

*Languages* (Berlin: Mouton de Gruyter, 1985) pp. 109-124.

Lazzerini, E.J., 'Crimean Tatars' in G. Smith (ed.), *The Nationalities Question in the Post-Soviet States* (London and New York: Longman, 1996), pp.412-435.

Potichnyj, P.J., 'The Struggle of the Crimean Tatars', *Canadian Slavonic Papers*, vol.17, nos.2-3 (Spring-Summer 1975), pp.302-318.

Seytmuratova, Ayshe, *Mustafa Dhemilev and the Crimean Tatars. Story of a Man and His People. Facts, Documents, How to Help* (New York: Center for Democracy, 1986).

Stewart, S., 'The Tatar Dimension', *RFE/RL Research Report*, vol.3, no.19 (13 May 1994).

Uehling, Greta, 'Squatting, Self-Immolation, and the Repatriation of Crimean Tatars', *Nationalities Papers*, vol.28, no.2 (June 2000), pp.317-342.

Williams, Brian G., *The Crimean Tatars. The Diaspora Experience and the Forging of a Nation* (Leiden: Brill, 2001).

Wilson, Andrew, *The Crimean Tatars. A Situation Report on the Crimean Tatars for International Alert* (London: International Alert, 1994).

## Foreign Policy

*Domestic Sources of Security Policy*

Arel, D., 'Kuchmagate and the Demise of Ukraine's "Geopolitical Bluff", *East European Constitutional Review*, vol.10, nos.2/3 (Spring/Summer 2001), pp.54-59.

Bukkvol, Tor, 'Defining a Ukrainian Foreign Policy Identity: Business Interests and Geopolitics in the Formulation of Ukrainian Foreign Policy 1994-1999', in J.D.P. Moroney, T. Kuzio and M. Molchanov (eds.), *Ukrainian Foreign and Security Policy. Theoretical and Comparative Perspectives* (Westport, CT: Praeger, 2002), pp.131-154.

Chudovsky, Victor and Kuzio, Taras, 'Does Public Opinion Matter in Ukraine? The Case of Foreign Policy', Communist and Post-Communist Studies, vol.36, no.3 (September 2003), pp.273-290.

Haran, Olexiy, 'Between Russia and the West: Domestic Factors of Ukraine's Foreign Policy', *The Harriman Review*, vol.9, nos.1-2 (Spring 1996), pp.117-123.

Kuzio, Taras, 'The Domestic Sources of Ukrainian Security Policy', *Journal of Strategic Studies*, vol.21, no.4 (December 1998), pp.18-49.

Nordberg, Marc, 'Domestic Factors Influencing Ukrainian Foreign Policy', *European Security*, vol.7, no.3 (Autumn 1998), pp.63-91.

Shulman, Stephen, 'The Role of Economic Performance in Ukrainian National-ism', *Europe-Asia Studies*, vol.55, no.2 (March 2003), pp.217-239.

Shulman, Stephen, 'Nationalist Sources of International Integration', *International Studies Quarterly*, vol.44, no.3 (September 2000), pp.365-390.

Shulman, Stephen, 'Asymmetrical International Integration and Ukrainian National Disunity', *Political Geography*, vol.18, no.8 (November 1999), pp.913-939.

Shulman, Stephen, 'National Integration and Foreign Policy in Multiethnic States', *Nationalism and Ethnic Politics*, vol.4, no.4 (Winter 1998), pp.110-132.

White, Stephen, McAllister, Ian M., Light, Margo, Lowenhardt, John, 'A European or a Slavic Choice? Foreign Policy and Public Attitudes in Post-Soviet Europe', *Europe-Asia Studies*, vol.54, no.2 (March 2002), pp.181-202.


*Russian-Ukrainian Relations*

Bukkvoll, T., 'Off the Cuff Politics – Explaining Russia's Lack of a Ukraine Strategy', *Europe-Asia Studies*, vol.53, no.8 (December 2001), pp.1141-1157.

Clement, Hermann, 'Ukraine: Causes and Consequences of Economic Ties with Russia and Their Influence on Relations between the Two States', *The Harriman Review*, vol.9, nos.1-2 (Spring 1996), pp.148-159.

Crow, S., 'Russian Parliament Asserts Control Over Sevastopol', *RFE/RL Research Report*, vol.2, no.31 (30 July 1993).

D'Anieri, Paul, 'Interdependence and Sovereignty in the Ukrainian-Russian Relationship', *European Security*, vol.4, no.4 (Winter 1995), pp.603-621.

D'Anieri, Paul, 'Dilemmas of Interdependence. Autonomy, Prosperity, and Sovereignty in Ukraine's Russia Policy', *Problems of Post-Communism*, vol.44, no.1 (January-February 1997) pp. 16-25.

D'Anieri, Paul, *Economic Interdependence in Ukrainian-Russian Relations* (New York: New York State University Press, 1999).

Derlugian, Georgi, M., 'Ukraine and the Fourth Russian Empire', *The Harriman Review*, vol.9, nos.1-2 (Spring 1996), pp.133-137.

Feldhusen, Anka, 'The 'Russian Factor' in Ukrainian Foreign Policy', *Fletcher Forum on International Affairs*, vol. 23, no. 2 (Fall 1999), pp. 119-38.

Goncharenko, Alexander, *Ukrainian-Russian Relations: An Unequal Partnership. RUSI Whitehall Paper 32* (London: Royal United Services Institute, 1995).

Haran, Olexiy, and Pavlenko, Rostyslav, 'Ukraine's Russian Policy under Kuchma: Paradoxes of 'Strategic Partnership' in Nicolas Hayoz and Andrej

N. Lushnycky (eds.) *Ukraine at a Crossroads*. Interdisciplinary Studies on Central and Eastern Europe. Vol. 1 Edited by Rolf Fieguth and Nicolas Hayoz. (Bern: Peter Lang, 2005), pp.167-194.

Holman, G.Paul, 'Russo-Ukrainian Relations: The Containment Legacy' in Raymond Duncan and Paul G. Holman (eds.), *Ethnic Nationalism and Regional Conflict. The Former Soviet Union and Yugoslavia* (Boulder, CO: Westview, 1994), pp.77-100.

Kincade, William H. and Melnyczuk, Natalie, 'Eurasia Letter: Uneighborly Neighbors', *Foreign Policy*, vol.94 (Spring 1994), pp.84-104.

Kulinich, N.A., 'Ukraine's Russian Dilemma and Europe's Evolving Geography' in Sharon L. Wolchik and Volodymyr Zviglyanich (eds.), *Ukraine. The Search for a National Identity* (Lanham, MD: Rowman & Littlefield, 2000), pp.95-106.

Kuzio, Taras, 'Russian Policy to Ukraine During Elections', *Demokratizatsiya*, vol.13, no.4 (Fall 2005), pp.491-517.

Lester, Jeremy, 'Russian Political Attitudes to Ukrainian Independence', *The Journal of Post Communist Studies and Transition Politics*, vol.10, no.2 (June 1994), pp.193-233.

Liesman, Steve, 'Can Ukraine Slip Russia's Grip?', *Central European Economic Review*, April 1995.

Lieven, A., *Ukraine and Russia. A Fraternal Rivalry* (Washington DC: US Institute of Peace, 1999).

Markus, U., 'Shoring up Relations wth Russia', *Transition*, vol.1, no.6 (28 April 1995).

Marples, D., 'Ukraine's Relatuons with Russia in the Contemporary Era', *The Harriman Review*, vol.9, nos.1-2 (Spring 1996), pp.103-112.

Morrison, J., 'Pereyaslav and after: the Russian-Ukrainian relationship', *International Affairs*, vol.69, no.4 (October 1993), pp.677-704.

Moshes, Arkadi, 'Conflict and Co-operation in Russo-Ukrainian Relations' in Bruno Coppieters, Alexei Zverev and Dmitri Trenin (eds.), *Common-*

*wealth and Independence in Post-Soviet Eurasia* (London: Frank Cass, 1998), pp.125-139.

'Peoples, Nations, Identities. The Russian-Ukrainian Encounter', *The Harriman Review*, vol.9, nos.1-2 (Spring 1996).

Rumer, Eugene B., 'Eurasia Letter: Will Ukraine Return to Russia?', *Foreign Policy*, no.96 (Fall 1994), pp.129-144 and no.97 (Winter 1994-1995), pp.178-181.

Sanders, Deborah, *Security Cooperation between Russia and Ukraine in the Post-Soviet Era* (New York: Palgrave, 2002).

Shenfield, Stephen, D., 'Alternative Conceptions of Russian State Identity and Their Implications for Russian Attitudes Towards Ukraine', *The Harriman Review*, vol.9, nos.1-2 (Spring 1996), pp.142-147.

Solchanyk, R., 'The Ukrainian-Russian Summit: Problems and Prospects', *RFE/RL Research Report*, vol.2, no.27 (2 July 1993).

Solchanyk, R., 'Russia, Ukraine and the Imperial Legacy', *Post-Soviet Affairs*, vol.9, no.4 (October-December 1993), pp.337-365.

Solchanyk, R., 'Ukraine, the (Former) Center, Russia and "Russia"', *Studies in Comparative Communism*, vol.25, no.1 (March 1992), pp.31-45.

Solchanyk, R., 'Ukraine and Russia: The Politics of Independence', *RFE/RL Research Report*, vol.1, no.19 (8 May 1992).

Solchanyk, R., 'The Crimean Imbroglio: Kiev and Moscow', *RFE/RL Research Report*, vol.1, no.40 (9 October 1992).

Solchanyk, R., 'The Draft Union Treaty and the 'Big Five', RL 177/91, *Report on the USSR*, vol.3, no.18 (3 May 1991).

Solchanyk, R., 'The Gorbachev-Eltsin Pact and the New Union Treaty', RL 180/91, *Report on the USSR*, vol.3, no.19 (10 May 1991).

Solchanyk, R., 'Ukraine and the Union Treaty', RL 263/91, *Report on the USSR*, vol.3, no.30 (26 July 1991).

Solchanyk, R., 'Ukraine and Russia: Before and After the Coup', RL 346/91, *Report on the USSR*, vol.3, no.39 (27 September 1991).

Solchanyk, R., 'Ukraine, the Kremlin, and the Russian White House', RL

384/91, *Report on the USSR*, vol.3, no.44 (1 November 1991).

Spillman, Kurt *et al.* (eds.), *Between Russia and the West : Foreign and Security Policy of Independent Ukraine* (New York: Peter Lang, 2000).

Tolz, Vera, 'Ukraine in the Russian National Consciousness' in her *Russia. Inventing the Nation* (London: Arnold and New York: Oxford University Press, 2001), pp.209-34.

Tolz, Vera, 'Rethinking Russian-Ukrainian relations: a new trend in nation-building in post-communist Russia', *Nations and Nationalism*, vol.8, part 2 (April 2002), pp.235-253.

Torbakov, Igor, 'A Rebirth of Ukrainian Geopolitics', *The Harriman Review*, vol.9, nos.1-2 (Spring 1996), pp.138-141.

Travkin, Nikolai, 'Rusia, Ukraine, and Eastern Europe' in Stephen Sestanovich (ed.), *Rethinking Russia's National Interests* (Washington, DC: CSIS, 1994), pp.24-41.

Vlasov, Sergei, 'Ukrainian Foreign Policy: Between Russia and the West' in Bruno Coppieters, Alexei Zverev and Dmitri Trenin (eds.), *Commonwealth and Independence in Post-Soviet Eurasia* (London: Frank Cass, 1998), pp.125-155.

Vydrin, Dmytro, 'Ukraine and Russia' in Robert D.Blackwill and Sergei Karaganov (eds.), *Damage Limitation or Crisis? Russia and the Outside World, CSIA Studies in International Security No.5* (Cambridge, MA: Center for Science and International Affairs, John F. Kennedy School of Government and Washington / London: Brassey's, 1994), pp.123-137.

Zhovnirenko, Pavlo, 'The Problem of Security in Ukrainian-Russian Relations: A Search for Common Interests', *The Harriman Review*, vol.9, nos.1-2 (Spring 1996), pp. 129-132.

*Dr. Andreas Umland (Ed.)*

# SOVIET AND POST-SOVIET
# POLITICS AND SOCIETY

ISSN 1614-3515

This book series makes available, to the academic community and general public, affordable English-, German- and Russian-language scholarly studies of various *empirical* aspects of the recent history and current affairs of the former Soviet bloc. The series features narrowly focused research on a variety of phenomena in Central and Eastern Europe as well as Central Asia and the Caucasus. It highlights, in particular, so far understudied aspects of late Tsarist, Soviet, and post-Soviet political, social, economic and cultural history from 1905 until today. Topics covered within this focus are, among others, political extremism, the history of ideas, religious affairs, higher education, and human rights protection. In addition, the series covers selected aspects of post-Soviet transitions such as economic crisis, civil society formation, and constitutional reform.

# SOVIET AND POST-SOVIET POLITICS AND SOCIETY

Edited by Dr. Andreas Umland

ISSN 1614-3515

1   *Андреас Умланд (ред.)*
    Воплощение Европейской конвенции по правам человека в России
    Философские, юридические и эмпирические исследования
    ISBN 3-89821-387-0

2   *Christian Wipperfürth*
    Russland – ein vertrauenswürdiger Partner?
    Grundlagen, Hintergründe und Praxis gegenwärtiger russischer Außenpolitik
    Mit einem Vorwort von Heinz Timmermann
    ISBN 3-89821-401-X

3   *Manja Hussner*
    Die Übernahme internationalen Rechts in die russische und deutsche Rechtsordnung
    Eine vergleichende Analyse zur Völkerrechtsfreundlichkeit der Verfassungen der Russländischen Föderation
    und der Bundesrepublik Deutschland
    Mit einem Vorwort von Rainer Arnold
    ISBN 3-89821-438-9

4   *Matthew Tejada*
    Bulgaria's Democratic Consolidation and the Kozloduy Nuclear Power Plant (KNPP)
    The Unattainability of Closure
    With a foreword by Richard J. Crampton
    ISBN 3-89821-439-7

5   *Марк Григорьевич Меерович*
    Квадратные метры, определяющие сознание
    Государственная жилищная политика в СССР. 1921 – 1941 гг
    ISBN 3-89821-474-5

6   *Andrei P. Tsygankov, Pavel A.Tsygankov (Eds.)*
    New Directions in Russian International Studies
    ISBN 3-89821-422-2

7   *Марк Григорьевич Меерович*
    Как власть народ к труду приучала
    Жилище в СССР – средство управления людьми. 1917 – 1941 гг.
    С предисловием Елены Осокиной
    ISBN 3-89821-495-8

8   *David J. Galbreath*
    Nation-Building and Minority Politics in Post-Socialist States
    Interests, Influence and Identities in Estonia and Latvia
    With a foreword by David J. Smith
    ISBN 3-89821-467-2

9   *Алексей Юрьевич Безугольный*
    Народы Кавказа в Вооруженных силах СССР в годы Великой Отечественной войны
    1941-1945 гг.
    С предисловием Николая Бугая
    ISBN 3-89821-475-3

10  *Вячеслав Лихачев и Владимир Прибыловский (ред.)*
    Русское Национальное Единство, 1990-2000. В 2-х томах
    ISBN 3-89821-523-7

11  *Николай Бугай (ред.)*
    Народы стран Балтии в условиях сталинизма (1940-е – 1950-е годы)
    Документированная история
    ISBN 3-89821-525-3

12  *Ingmar Bredies (Hrsg.)*
    Zur Anatomie der Orange Revolution in der Ukraine
    Wechsel des Elitenregimes oder Triumph des Parlamentarismus?
    ISBN 3-89821-524-5

13  *Anastasia V. Mitrofanova*
    The Politicization of Russian Orthodoxy
    Actors and Ideas
    With a foreword by William C. Gay
    ISBN 3-89821-481-8

14  *Nathan D. Larson*
    Alexander Solzhenitsyn and the Russo-Jewish Question
    ISBN 3-89821-483-4

15  *Guido Houben*
    Kulturpolitik und Ethnizität
    Staatliche Kunstförderung im Russland der neunziger Jahre
    Mit einem Vorwort von Gert Weisskirchen
    ISBN 3-89821-542-3

16  *Leonid Luks*
    Der russische „Sonderweg"?
    Aufsätze zur neuesten Geschichte Russlands im europäischen Kontext
    ISBN 3-89821-496-6

17  *Евгений Мороз*
    История «Мёртвой воды» – от страшной сказки к большой политике
    Политическое неоязычество в постсоветской России
    ISBN 3-89821-551-2

18  *Александр Верховский и Галина Кожевникова (ред.)*
    Этническая и религиозная интолерантность в российских СМИ
    Результаты мониторинга 2001-2004 гг.
    ISBN 3-89821-569-5

19  *Christian Ganzer*
    Sowjetisches Erbe und ukrainische Nation
    Das Museum der Geschichte des Zaporoger Kosakentums auf der Insel Chortycja
    Mit einem Vorwort von Frank Golczewski
    ISBN 3-89821-504-0

20    *Эльза-Баир Гучинова*
Помнить нельзя забыть
Антропология депортационной травмы калмыков
С предисловием Кэролайн Хамфри
ISBN 3-89821-506-7

21    *Юлия Лидерман*
Мотивы «проверки» и «испытания» в постсоветской культуре
Советское прошлое в российском кинематографе 1990-х годов
С предисловием Евгения Марголита
ISBN 3-89821-511-3

22    *Tanya Lokshina, Ray Thomas, Mary Mayer (Eds.)*
The Imposition of a Fake Political Settlement in the Northern Caucasus
The 2003 Chechen Presidential Election
ISBN 3-89821-436-2

23    *Timothy McCajor Hall, Rosie Read (Eds.)*
Changes in the Heart of Europe
Recent Ethnographies of Czechs, Slovaks, Roma, and Sorbs
With an afterword by Zdeněk Salzmann
ISBN 3-89821-606-3

24    *Christian Autengruber*
Die politischen Parteien in Bulgarien und Rumänien
Eine vergleichende Analyse seit Beginn der 90er Jahre
Mit einem Vorwort von Dorothée de Nève
ISBN 3-89821-476-1

25    *Annette Freyberg-Inan with Radu Cristescu*
The Ghosts in Our Classrooms, or: John Dewey Meets Ceauşescu
The Promise and the Failures of Civic Education in Romania
ISBN 3-89821-416-8

26    *John B. Dunlop*
The 2002 Dubrovka and 2004 Beslan Hostage Crises
A Critique of Russian Counter-Terrorism
With a foreword by Donald N. Jensen
ISBN 3-89821-608-X

27    *Peter Koller*
Das touristische Potenzial von Kam''janec'-Podil's'kyj
Eine fremdenverkehrsgeographische Untersuchung der Zukunftsperspektiven und Maßnahmenplanung zur
Destinationsentwicklung des „ukrainischen Rothenburg"
Mit einem Vorwort von Kristiane Klemm
ISBN 3-89821-640-3

28    *Françoise Daucé, Elisabeth Sieca-Kozlowski (Eds.)*
Dedovshchina in the Post-Soviet Military
Hazing of Russian Army Conscripts in a Comparative Perspective
With a foreword by Dale Herspring
ISBN 3-89821-616-0

29    *Florian Strasser*
      Zivilgesellschaftliche Einflüsse auf die Orange Revolution
      Die gewaltlose Massenbewegung und die ukrainische Wahlkrise 2004
      Mit einem Vorwort von Egbert Jahn
      ISBN 3-89821-648-9

30    *Rebecca S. Katz*
      The Georgian Regime Crisis of 2003-2004
      A Case Study in Post-Soviet Media Representation of Politics, Crime and Corruption
      ISBN 3-89821-413-3

31    *Vladimir Kantor*
      Willkür oder Freiheit
      Beiträge zur russischen Geschichtsphilosophie
      Ediert von Dagmar Herrmann sowie mit einem Vorwort versehen von Leonid Luks
      ISBN 3-89821-589-X

32    *Laura A. Victoir*
      The Russian Land Estate Today
      A Case Study of Cultural Politics in Post-Soviet Russia
      With a foreword by Priscilla Roosevelt
      ISBN 3-89821-426-5

33    *Ivan Katchanovski*
      Cleft Countries
      Regional Political Divisions and Cultures in Post-Soviet Ukraine and Moldova
      With a foreword by Francis Fukuyama
      ISBN 3-89821-558-X

34    *Florian Mühlfried*
      Postsowjetische Feiern
      Das Georgische Bankett im Wandel
      Mit einem Vorwort von Kevin Tuite
      ISBN 3-89821-601-2

35    *Roger Griffin, Werner Loh, Andreas Umland (Eds.)*
      Fascism Past and Present, West and East
      An International Debate on Concepts and Cases in the Comparative Study of the Extreme Right
      With an afterword by Walter Laqueur
      ISBN 3-89821-674-8

36    *Sebastian Schlegel*
      Der „Weiße Archipel"
      Sowjetische Atomstädte 1945-1991
      Mit einem Geleitwort von Thomas Bohn
      ISBN 3-89821-679-9

37    *Vyacheslav Likhachev*
      Political Anti-Semitism in Post-Soviet Russia
      Actors and Ideas in 1991-2003
      Edited and translated from Russian by Eugene Veklerov
      ISBN 3-89821-529-6

38    *Josette Baer (Ed.)*
      Preparing Liberty in Central Europe
      Political Texts from the Spring of Nations 1848 to the Spring of Prague 1968
      With a foreword by Zdeněk V. David
      ISBN 3-89821-546-6

39    *Михаил Лукьянов*
      Российский консерватизм и реформа, 1907-1914
      С предисловием Марка Д. Стейнберга
      ISBN 3-89821-503-2

40    *Nicola Melloni*
      Market Without Economy
      The 1998 Russian Financial Crisis
      With a foreword by Eiji Furukawa
      ISBN 3-89821-407-9

41    *Dmitrij Chmelnizki*
      Die Architektur Stalins
      Bd. 1: Studien zu Ideologie und Stil
      Bd. 2: Bilddokumentation
      Mit einem Vorwort von Bruno Flierl
      ISBN 3-89821-515-6

42    *Katja Yafimava*
      Post-Soviet Russian-Belarussian Relationships
      The Role of Gas Transit Pipelines
      With a foreword by Jonathan P. Stern
      ISBN 3-89821-655-1

43    *Boris Chavkin*
      Verflechtungen der deutschen und russischen Zeitgeschichte
      Aufsätze und Archivfunde zu den Beziehungen Deutschlands und der Sowjetunion von 1917 bis 1991
      Ediert von Markus Edlinger sowie mit einem Vorwort versehen von Leonid Luks
      ISBN 3-89821-756-6

44    *Anastasija Grynenko in Zusammenarbeit mit Claudia Dathe*
      Die Terminologie des Gerichtswesens der Ukraine und Deutschlands im Vergleich
      Eine übersetzungswissenschaftliche Analyse juristischer Fachbegriffe im Deutschen, Ukrainischen und
      Russischen
      Mit einem Vorwort von Ulrich Hartmann
      ISBN 3-89821-691-8

45    *Anton Burkov*
      The Impact of the European Convention on Human Rights on Russian Law
      Legislation and Application in 1996-2006
      With a foreword by Françoise Hampson
      ISBN 978-3-89821-639-5

46    *Stina Torjesen, Indra Overland (Eds.)*
      International Election Observers in Post-Soviet Azerbaijan
      Geopolitical Pawns or Agents of Change?
      ISBN 978-3-89821-743-9

47    *Taras Kuzio*
      Ukraine – Crimea – Russia
      Triangle of Conflict
      ISBN 978-3-89821-761-3

## FORTHCOMING (MANUSCRIPT WORKING TITLES)

*Stephanie Solowyda*
Biography of Semen Frank
ISBN 3-89821-457-5

*Margaret Dikovitskaya*
Arguing with the Photographs
Russian Imperial Colonial Attitudes in Visual Culture
ISBN 3-89821-462-1

*Stefan Ihrig*
Welche Nation in welcher Geschichte?
Eigen- und Fremdbilder der nationalen Diskurse in der Historiographie und den Geschichtsbüchern in der Republik
Moldova, 1991-2003
ISBN 3-89821-466-4

*Sergei M. Plekhanov*
Russian Nationalism in the Age of Globalization
ISBN 3-89821-484-2

*Robert Pyrah*
Cultural Memory and Identity
Literature, Criticism and the Theatre in Lviv - Lwow - Lemberg, 1918-1939 and in post-Soviet Ukraine
ISBN 3-89821-505-9

*Andrei Rogatchevski*
The National-Bolshevik Party
ISBN 3-89821-532-6

*Zenon Victor Wasyliw*
Soviet Culture in the Ukrainian Village
The Transformation of Everyday Life and Values, 1921-1928
ISBN 3-89821-536-9

*Nele Sass*
Das gegenkulturelle Milieu im postsowjetischen Russland
ISBN 3-89821-543-1

*Julie Elkner*
Maternalism versus Militarism
The Russian Soldiers' Mothers Committee
ISBN 3-89821-575-X

*Maryna Romanets*
Displaced Subjects, Anamorphosic Texts, Reconfigured Visions
Improvised Traditions in Contemporary Ukrainian and Irish Literature
ISBN 3-89821-576-8

*Alexandra Kamarowsky*
Russia's Post-crisis Growth
ISBN 3-89821-580-6

*Martin Friessnegg*
Das Problem der Medienfreiheit in Russland seit dem Ende der Sowjetunion
ISBN 3-89821-588-1

*Nikolaj Nikiforowitsch Borobow*
Führende Persönlichkeiten in Russland vom 12. bis 20 Jhd.: Ein Lexikon
Aus dem Russischen übersetzt und herausgegeben von Eberhard Schneider
ISBN 3-89821-638-1

*Martin Malek, Anna Schor-Tschudnowskaja*
Tschetschenien und die Gleichgültigkeit Europas
Russlands Kriege und die Agonie der Idee der Menschenrechte
ISBN 3-89821-676-4

*Christopher Ford*
Borotbism A Chapter in the History of the Ukrainian Revolution
ISBN 3-89821-697-7

*Taras Kuzio, Paul D'Anieri (Hrsg.)*
Aspects of the Orange Revolution I: Regime Politics and Democratization in Ukraine
ISBN 3-89821-698-5

*Bohdan Harasymiw, Oleh S. Ilnytzkyj (Hrsg.)*
Aspects of the Orange Revolution II: Analyses of the 2004 Ukrainian Presidential Elections
ISBN 3-89821-699-3

*Togzhan Kassenova*
Cooperative Security in the Post-Cold War International System
The Cooperative Threat Reduction Process
ISBN 3-89821-707-8

*Andreas Langenohl*
Political Culture and Criticism of Society
Intellectual Articulations in Post-Soviet Russia
ISBN 3-89821-709-4

*Marlies Bilz*
Tatarstan in der Transformation, 1988-1994
ISBN 3-89821-722-1

*Thomas Borén*
Meeting Places in Transformation
ISBN 3-89821-739-6

*Lars Löckner*
Sowjetrussland in der Beurteilung der Emigrantenzeitung 'Rul', 1920-1924
ISBN 3-89821-741-8

*Ekaterina Taratuta*
The Red Line of Construction
Semantics and Mythology of a Siberian Heliopolis
ISBN 3-89821-742-6

*Bernd Kappenberg*
Zeichen setzen für Europa
Der Gebrauch europäischer lateinischer Sonderzeichen in der deutschen Öffentlichkeit
ISBN 3-89821-749-3

*Claudia Sabic*
"Ich persönlich erinnere mich nicht, aber L'viv schon!"
Kulturelle Entwicklungschancen und -blockaden einer ukrainischen Region
ISBN 3-89821-752-3

*Sonja Schüler*
Die ethnische Dimension der Armut
Roma im postsozialistischen Rumänien
ISBN 3-89821-776-0

*David Rupp*
Die Rußländische Föderation und die russischsprachigen Minderheiten im "Nahen Ausland"
ISBN 3-89821-778-7

*Tim Bohse*
Die Transformation der postsowjetischen russischen Lokalpolitik am Beispiel der Stadt Kaliningrad
ISBN 3-89821-782-5

# *Series Subscription*

Please enter my subscription to the series *Soviet and Post-Soviet Politics and Society*, ISSN 1614-3515, as follows:

❑ complete series       OR       ❑ English-language titles
                                                    ❑ German-language titles
                                                    ❑ Russian-language titles

starting with
❑ volume # 1
❑ volume # ___
     ❑ please also include the following volumes: #___, ___, ___, ___, ___, ___, ___
❑ the next volume being published
     ❑ please also include the following volumes: #___, ___, ___, ___, ___, ___, ___

❑ 1 copy per volume       OR       ❑ ___ copies per volume

## Subscription within Germany:

You will receive every volume at 1$^{st}$ publication at the regular bookseller's price – incl. s & h and VAT.
Payment:
❑ Please bill me for every volume.
❑ Lastschriftverfahren: Ich/wir ermächtige(n) Sie hiermit widerruflich, den Rechnungsbetrag je Band von meinem/unserem folgendem Konto einzuziehen.

Kontoinhaber: _____Kreditinstitut: _____
Kontonummer: _____Bankleitzahl:_____

## International Subscription:

Payment (incl. s & h and VAT) in advance for
❑ 10 volumes/copies (€ 319.80)    ❑ 20 volumes/copies (€ 599.80)
❑ 40 volumes/copies (€ 1,099.80)
Please send my books to:

NAME_____DEPARTMENT_____
ADDRESS _____
POST/ZIP CODE_____COUNTRY _____
TELEPHONE _____EMAIL_____

date/signature_____

A hint for librarians in the former Soviet Union: Your academic library might be eligible to receive free-of-cost scholarly literature from Germany via the German Research Foundation. For Russian-language information on this program, see
     http://www.dfg.de/forschungsfoerderung/formulare/download/12_54.pdf.

Please fax to: **0511 / 262 2201 (+49 511 262 2201)**
or mail to: *ibidem*-Verlag, Julius-Leber-Weg 11, D-30457 Hannover,Germany
or send an e-mail: ibidem@ibidem-verlag.de

*ibidem*-Verlag
Melchiorstr. 15
D-70439 Stuttgart

info@ibidem-verlag.de

www.ibidem-verlag.de
www.edition-noema.de
www.autorenbetreuung.de